Techniques of Teaching

Techniques of Teaching

H.D. Kamat

A. David

CRESCENT PUBLISHING CORPORATION

[The responsibility for the facts stated, conclusions reached and plagiarism, if any, in this book is entirely that of the Author. And the Publisher bears no responsibility for them, whatsoever.]

Techniques of Teaching

Edition 2026

ISBN 81-8342-039-7

Published by :

CRESCENT PUBLISHING CORPORATION
4806/24, Mathur Lane,
Ansari Road, Darya Ganj,
New Delhi - 110002
Mob. : 9711991838, 9999021668
Phone : 011-23244131
E-mail : crescentbook@gmail.com
Website : www.crescentpublishingcorp.weebly.com

Printed at :
Balaji Digital
Delhi

PREFACE

The ways that teachers organise learning situations to help students to learn can be called teaching techniques. When choosing and planning teaching techniques, one should consider the type of learning involved, the ways that different people like to learn, and the context in which they are learning. It can be useful to group teaching techniques into families that share some features. Good teaching is as much about passion as it is about reason. It's about not only motivating students to learn, but teaching them how to learn, and doing so in a manner that is relevant, meaningful, and memorable. It's about caring for your craft, having a passion for it, and conveying that passion to everyone, most importantly to your students, students as consumers of knowledge. It's about doing your best to keep on top of your field, reading sources, inside and outside of your areas of expertise. Good teaching is also about bridging the gap between theory and practice. Be honest about your feelings, opinions, and attitudes toward students and toward the subject matter. Don't be afraid to admit that you don't know all the answers. If a student tells you something in confidence, respect that confidence. Being responsive to listening, questioning, and remembering that each student and class is different. It's about eliciting responses and developing the oral communication skills of the quiet students. It's about pushing students to excel. Teaching is also about style it should be entertaining. Techniques of instruction often reflect the attitudes of society, *i.e.*, authoritarian groups typically sponsor dogmatic methods, while democratic systems may emphasize freedom of thought.

At last we can only say that, good teaching techniques are about having fun, experiencing pleasure and intrinsic rewards ... like locking eyes with a student in the back row and seeing the synapses and neurons connecting, thoughts being formed, the person becoming better, and a smile cracking across a face as learning all of a sudden happens. Good teachers practice their craft not for the money or because they have to, but because they truly enjoy it and because they want to.

H.D. Kamat
A. David

CONTENTS

1

Concepts of Techniques of Teaching

Deciding which Concepts to Teach

If we decide that trying to get students to understand a wide range of concepts is going to be one of our fundamental aims, we then have to decide which specific concepts will be taught. There are three ways in which concepts may crop up:

(1) If, as often happens, somebody prescribes for us the historical topics which we are to cover and even the books we are to use, we must be able to work out in advance which main concepts are inevitably going to be encountered by pupils in their reading or in any simple exposition we might give ourselves, or in any work they might do on that topic.

(2) Given a topic to cover, we need to be able to designate a few concepts which would not necessarily arise in working on the topic, but which we could conveniently and appropriately introduce ourselves, if we chose.

(3) If we were given a free hand to plan the work of a class in history, we ought to be able to construct a syllabus partly in terms of those important concepts which we want students to learn.

Let us take the problems one by one. First—if we were given a prescribed topic to cover, there is one crude but effective way to proceed. Write a very short, very plain account of the topic in about thirty to fifty words. Then go through your account underlining terms denoting concepts which you think could be imperfectly understood by any student in the class you are preparing to teach—erring on the side of pessimism at this point.

Supposing that the English Civil War was our topic and we had a class of thirteen-year-olds, the end result of our preliminary exercise might look like this: 'In 1642, *civil war* broke out between the King and *Parliament.* Many battles were fought, though at first they were not *decisive.* The main weapons used were *pikes* and *muskets.* In the end, Parliament *won.'* If a student had no idea, or a very wrong idea, about the meaning of the underlined words, he would pretty clearly be unable to understand the passage, and so, after a short time, would not be able even to recall the gist of it and would, therefore, be poorly placed for learning, understanding and recalling things about the Civil War.

Next, we can usefully break the problem into three parts. Of all the terms emphasised, the easiest to explain are 'pike' and 'musket', because these terms have what we call concrete referents, i.e., you could in principle show a person a pike and say 'This is a pike'. In practice, you could draw a picture, show a picture, show a model, etc.

The other terms are all *abstractions.* Some of them are of obvious difficulty, e.g., Parliament, Civil War. These are the kind of semi-technical terms characteristic of writing or speech about history which are fairly easy to spot with a little practice.

That leaves two terms, 'decisive' and 'won'. These words are not easy to spot as difficult abstractions which might cause pupils trouble. They are not particularly 'history' words and could well occur in almost any context, especially 'won'. And, most tricky of all, as in the case of 'won', they often don't even sound difficult. However, a pupil's ready acceptance and apparent understanding of an apparently simple term like 'won' could conceal any or all of the following misunderstandings of the idea of 'winning'; in this instance:

(1) 'All the King's army was killed.'

(2) 'The King was killed.'

(3) 'All the King's followers changed their minds and supported Parliament.'

We might call words like 'won' and 'decisive' 'weasel words'. A few further examples are given below in italics:

(1) The Bolsheviks gained *control* of Russia.

(2) The Church *controlled* education.

(3) *Unrest* spread through the country.

(4) There was *discontent* with the republic.

(5) Murad Agha established his *rule* over the oasis.

(6) The UN General Assembly *attacked* the National Assembly as undemocratic.

'Weasel words' have two important characteristics. They do not always leap to the eye as difficult, especially if there are other, more obviously hard words, near them (for example, notice how, in the example above, if we are seeking possible sources of difficulty we tend to notice terms like Bolshevik, Church, republic, oasis, General Assembly, National Assembly, undemocratic). Second, when we think about it, our *own* understanding of them is often a bit vague. We have been content, sometimes, in our reading and thinking, to slur over them, content with a hazy, partial understanding; for example, how clear a picture is brought to your mind by the sentence 'The Church controlled education'?

The second problem, that of adding on concepts which do not unavoidably have to be dealt with, but which you positively want to deal with, may not come up at all. It may be that you have found so many concepts to deal with which are unavoidable that you don't want to add to the list. However, if we go back to our original English Civil War case, you might think you could deal with 'pike' and 'Parliament' and the rest of them, and still have time for more.

It is important to decide exactly which concepts you want to add. It is easy to say at this stage:

> This stuff about pikes and Parliaments is just the surface of things—I want students to see that this Civil War in England was a tragic event, that families were divided among themselves; I want them to get the feel of what this war meant for British history--that is the concept I want to add.

Actually, this statement contains a *judgement* (that the Civil War was tragic), a *fact* (that families were split) and an idea of doubtful meaning ('the feel of what this war meant'). A cooler way of thinking might produce a clearer outcome.

The first move is to think out what area or aspect we want our 'extra' concept to be in. The imaginary teacher quoted above is plainly interested in the fact that the issues of the war were deeply felt, so deeply as to divide families. So he might try writing a short, plain sentence or so on that theme: 'Many people choose sides in this war from strong *convictions*. So sometimes, even if a father choose one side, his son would choose the other. The *issues* went on *dividing people* long after the war itself was over'. So our extra commitment clarifies itself; we have three additional concepts that we want students to grasp: 'convictions', 'issues' and 'dividing people'. Try this technique now to work out what additional concepts you yourself might want to bring in to this Civil War topic.

Our next case presents a different sort of problem—someone has said to you, 'Cover some twentieth-century history with this class of fourteen-year-olds this year—write your own syllabus, you have a free hand'. Let us leave aside for now the constraints imposed by time available, books available and so on and think about this question: would a syllabus made up with concept development clearly in mind look any different from a conventionally planned syllabus?

We have to make a small apparent digression here. Our main problem as history teachers is not going to be with explaining pikes and Zeppelins, but with abstractions. In the first place, it is only a shorthand to speak of people 'knowing' abstractions, or 'learning' them. The following passages all attempted to define the English seventeenth-century Parliament:

(1) 'Parliament was the King's friends, they went about with him.'

(2) 'People used to choose men to speak for them about what they wanted doing. The chosen men were called Parliament.'

(3) 'Parliament was mostly rich men, chosen by other fairly rich men, to makes laws, and run the country.'

(4) 'Parliament was a constantly shifting set of interest groups, in a constantly shifting relationship with the Crown.'

Writer (4), we might guess, has a very firm grasp of the concept of Parliament. But plainly we cannot say that (3) and (2) have *no* understanding of the concept. Even (1) understands that Parliament was a body of people in some sort of relationship to the King, so we cannot even say that (1) has no understanding of the concept. We talk, therefore, of people having *an* understanding of a concept, and of *improving* their understanding. If we have to teach the seventeenth century to a given class, we ask not 'Do they understand what "Parliament" means?' but 'What understanding of the concept of Parliament do they have?'

A second characteristic really follows from the first: a once-for-all explanation of an abstract concept is not sufficient. People extend and improve their understanding of concepts by using them, in speech and writing, in a great variety of ways. We might want to speak of 'teaching' the concept of Parliament, because it is cumbersome to always say, 'I am procuring an extension of the understanding of . . .' That is quite acceptable so long as we remember that 'teaching a concept' extends over months rather than minutes and involves pupils engaging in all manner of activities, using the concept, not simply being told what it means, however carefully. We shall return soon to this question of how to 'teach concepts' in the chapter on 'Intellectual Skills'.

For the moment, however, the main point is that if concepts are not best dealt with by a once-for-all attack, this gives us an important guiding idea for building a syllabus for a year. We could say that we will plan for a given set of concepts to be attacked, using different illustrative historical material of course, more than once in the course of the year.

This could be an insanely complicated method, if we try to plan for work on, say, the concept of 'conscription' to occur in late October, early March, third week of June and so on. So we will plan simply to divide the year into two halves and plan to have the same main concepts dealt with in the second half as in the first, using a different set of illustrative material.

When it comes to designating the actual concepts to be dealt with, the teacher is ultimately alone with his own idea of what is important. The idea of 'over-arching' concepts, ideas at a very high level of generality, like' conflict' or 'communication', as guiding principles really does not give a lot of help when we are required to particularise a syllabus on the twentieth century. We might proceed, as we did before, by making 'brief statements' to ourselves as it were, in answer to the question: 'What are the three or four most important circumstances, events or ideas that an educated person ought to know of, and understand, as a result of learning about twentieth-century history?'

For convenience, we could divide the area into three parts, on traditional lines, political, economic and social. Here is the kind of result we might get, by way of illustration.

> *Political*—Main ideas (1) socialism and nationalism in their various forms. How socialism and nationalism seem to run together in Third World 'liberation movements' after 1945. (2) War. Many wars, on a great scale, great effects. World War I, World War II, Vietnam.
>
> *Economic*—(3) Prosperity, and (4) the argument over state intervention in the economy.
>
> *Social*—(5) Idea of many rapid changes of attitude to women, black people, children, sex, the arts, etc.

If we now try to write short statements about each of our five main ideas, emphasising the abstractions, including 'weasel words', we will get a set of concept lists, concepts which are particular to our concerns, in this particular area of history.

One example might be helpful:

> *'Socialism'* is an *economic* idea and a *political* idea. On economics socialists generally agree that *wealth* ought not to be *distributed* as it is under *capitalist* arrangements, but should be *owned* and *controlled* by the *working class* or *proletariat* or *peasants*. On politics, some believe in *revolution* followed by *dictatorship*, at least for a time, others in *democratic procedures*.

This statement is 59 words long, which is forgiveable in a statement on a very complex idea, but try to make none of your 'statements' any longer than that *Twentieth-century war*, for instance, we might do as briefly as this.

> First we had *mass conscript* armies, fighting huge *mechanised* wars, with a huge *industrial base*. *Total* war, for example, bombing of *civilians*. After 1945, more *guerrilla* wars, *terrorism* and great use of *publicity* and *propaganda*. [34 words].

We have now five general areas, five 'brief statements' and five lists of fairly specific concepts. Now we have to choose what material to use to illustrate them and make a vehicle for developing understanding of them, not once but twice over, in the two halves of the year.

We have to weigh up several factors:

(a) Which material will give the most clear and convenient basis for understanding the given concepts? For instance, the National Socialist movement seems a good example of the twentieth-century phenomenon of the 'running together' of the themes of nationalism and socialism; but is it too confusing an example, since the 'socialism' was so nominal? Would African nationalism in the 1960s be better?

(b) Which material are the students likely to find most stimulating and interesting?

(c) Suppose we could deal with all the concepts quite well using only the history of western Europe and the USA. Should we nevertheless try to use African, Asian, Latin American material on general grounds?

(d) Should we try to keep to chronological order, or use themes? Will the students be confused by a non-chronological approach?

(e) With our main idea number 5, change of attitudes in the course of the twentieth century, we probably cannot successfully deal in the time with attitudes to women, black people, children, sex and the arts—if we have to choose just two, which two will it be?

All these questions call for you to make evaluations of a personal kind, so for the next stage, we will simply assume that the following choices were made.

First Half-year

Broadly chronological approach

World War I ('war' group of concepts)

Russian Revolution and Stalin ('socialism' concepts)

America and the Great Depression ('socialism' concepts, 'prosperity' and 'state intervention' concepts)

The Irish Rebellion 1916–21 ('nationalism' group of concepts)

The women's movement ('change in attitude' concepts).

Second Half-year

'Thematic' approach

World War II, the Arab-Israeli dispute and Vietnam ('war' group of concepts)

Chinese Revolution and China since 1949 ('socialism' and the economic concepts)

Labour movement, Britain since 1945

African nationalism, Indian nationalism ('nationalism' and 'socialism')

Black people in USA since 1945 ('attitude changes' group of concepts)

We now have an outline syllabus. Apart from the rather careful matching up of the two halves of the year, it is not a particularly unconventional one except in one respect, that it leaves quite large gaps. For instance, there is nothing on the rise of Hitler or the origins of World War II.

At this point you could do one of three things:

(1) You could recognise that your initial working-out of the five main areas of concern was faulty, and that it is essential to add in say, the rise of Hitler. Bear in mind that we have already about twelve major areas to do. Postulating a 36-week year, that gives about three weeks per area. Some of the areas, like America and the Depression, for instance, seem to contain a large number of difficult and important ideas, which we will be hard pressed to deal with adequately in three weeks.

(2) You could put in the rise of Hitler, take something else out and reorder the plan.

(3) You could decide that one mark of a syllabus that tries to make careful provision for concept learning and concept strengthening is that it cannot be over-stuffed with content. Selection, therefore, has to be very ruthless, quite simply because worthwhile, structured learning takes a lot longer than just covering historical ground. So Hitler's rise is best left out.

We now know how to work out a concept list to form the basis of our planning for teaching in either of two situations; from scratch, or from the 'givens' of a syllabus written by somebody else.

There is one more thing we can do to provide ourselves with a fairly complete answer to the question, 'What concepts are we going to be dealing with?' Giving an explanation of an abstraction often involves using other abstractions. In a moment we shall deal, under the heading 'Giving Explanations of Concepts', with ways of reducing this difficulty, but there is no complete way round it. You might, for example, find that you just cannot sensibly explain 'revolution' without using the term 'government'.

So we should take our concept list and as our last preliminary planning move, rough out brief explanations of all the concepts. If explaining an abstraction throws up other abstractions, then add those abstractions to the list and try explaining *them*. Keep up the process until you are confident that there is no concept left that you cannot explain in concrete terms or at least in terms you are quite confident your student will understand.

Exercise

Try explaining complex abstractions like 'revolution', 'capitalism', 'nationalism', or a similar idea of your own choosing, noting the abstract concepts you have to use in explaining the original concept. Then try explaining *those* concepts in their turn until your get down to ideas you can explain without using abstract language.

Giving Explanations of Concepts

The safest rule is to become as skilled as you can in explaining abstract concepts by reference to the concrete, avoiding reference to other abstractions as far as possible. The following illustrates the point: the first 'explanation' in each case involves a tangle of further abstract concepts, perhaps more difficult than the idea being 'explained'.

Tactics

(a) 'Tactics are the mans employed by a commander to defeat the enemy in a given situation.'

(b) 

'Look at this diagram. We would say that General C's *tactics* were to send some of his men to attack the enemy (B) from the front, and others to attack from the side.'

(c) 'Suppose you had a soccer team planning their next match, deciding things like how many men to have in defence, what to do at corners and free kicks and so on. We could say that they were planning their *tactics.*'

Unrest

(a) 'Unrest is manifestation of discontent—it can be social, or political, or both.'

(b) 'People saying the government is no good, people attacking the police, or not paying taxes, people being very unhappy about something going on in the country, that's *unrest.*'

(c) 'Suppose they brought in a new school rule that everyone had to wear ties. Suppose a lot of kids wouldn't and people wrote 'down with the tie rule' on walls, some people even broke windows and things because they were so upset by the rule. Then we'd say there was *unrest* in the school.'

Radical (nineteenth century)

(a) 'Radicalism involved making more fundamental attacks on institutions and putting forward more far-reaching plans for reform.'

(b) 'Suppose a man had the idea that, say, Wales ought to have its own Parliament and make some of its own laws and suppose a second man said Wales ought to be entirely separate from Britain and make all its own laws. We would say that the second man was taking a more radical line.'

(c) 'Suppose the bus fares went up a lot. Suppose some of you said, "Let's write to the council and complain the fares are too high" and suppose others said "No, let's write and say that school students should travel free on the buses anyway"—we could say the second lot were being *radicals.*'

Notice how in 1 (b), 1 (c), 2 (b), 2 (c), 3 (b) and 3 (c) the explanation does not start with the words in question. The word occurs near the end, or actually *at* the end of the explanation. This is a good piece of technique to copy. Research indicates that it is often the more effective method to 'build up' to the newly-learned word in this way.

Now try your hand at explaining the following terms: peasant, revolution, dictator, emigrants, investment.

In the above examples, we have imagined the explainer speaking as if the concept in question as quite new to his audience. Sometimes this is how we have to do it if the pupil has no grasp at all of the new concept, or is completely mistaken (for example, if he thought that 'radicals' meant 'Frenchmen'). Very often, though, the pupils have *an* understanding, but not an adequate one.

Let us take the 'Parliament' examples of imperfect understanding discussed in this chapter. The ideal to aim for is to accept and use whatever understanding the pupil already has. So in the case of student 1, we would not say 'No, no, it's nothing to do with the King, it's like this . . .', but rather on these lines:

> Suppose there was something we wanted to tell the King, like there's a great many robbers round here causing trouble—we wouldn't all go to London to tell him, we would choose one of us to go, perhaps the best talker. The one chosen would go to London and talk to the King and tell him about the robber problem; all the other towns would send a person too, to tell the King things he ought to know. The whole gathering of men from the various places, talking to the King, was called 'Parliament'.

In the case of student 2:

> Yes, that's right. Another thing you should understand is that to be allowed to be chosen, you had to be fairly rich. And it was not everybody who was allowed to do the choosing. Usually you had to be fairly rich to choose (or vote for, as we say), someone to go to Parliament. And you had to be a man, women could not choose.

In the case of student 3:

> Try it yourself—the understanding shown in the extract is defective in that it does not mention the role of the King, nor

that 'Parliament' was not a monolith, but rent by disagreement. Try to write a brief explanation aimed at giving student 3 a better understanding of 'Parliament', accepting what he already understands.

Now have a look at these following statements about concepts. Try to decide where the understanding is defective and then write a brief 'further explanation' in each case, designed to build on the understanding he already has.

Deciding what the *main* defect in understanding is, is for you to judge. In the example above, of student 2, I decided that the most important thing for him to add to his understanding of the seventeenth-century Parliament was the unrepresentative nature of the Commons. You might have decided that what he needs to learn next is that there were two chambers, only one of which was elective at all. That would be a perfectly defensible alterative approach.

(1) *Dictator* is when you only have one person for a ruler, as England has only one Queen.

(2) *Knights* were soldiers.

(3) *Middle classes* (nineteenth century) were shopkeepers and traders.

(4) *Imperialism* is when people go to another country and start colonies there.

(5) *Empire*–is a big place, a big country.

(6) *Revolution* is when people rise up against the government and overthrow it.

Pre-tests of Students' Understanding of Concepts

Before we start teaching a topic, we need to form at least a rough idea of the understanding the students already have of the concepts we want to deal with. The quickest and most reliable way to do this is to give them a test. Your intuitive assessment of their level of understanding might be correct, but it is quite likely to be wrong. Experience indicates that teachers of young children (i.e. under eleven) greatly underestimate their children's level of understanding. From about twelve up, there seems to be a tendency greatly to *overestimate* it.

By way of illustration, a certain group of history students, when tested, showed a significant level of misunderstanding of the meaning of the political term 'left wing'. To be precise, about half of them thought that it meant something like 'against the government of the day'. Two or three indicated that they had no idea at all. You might like to guess what the average age of the group was, and what, in general terms, was their level of ability. The answer is at the end of this section.

Which Concepts to Test

Suppose our topic was the Irish nationalist movement, 1912–23. We have worked out a list of concepts something like this: conscription, nationalist, rebellion, suppress (as in 'suppress a rebellion'), party (political), Sinn Fein, Black and Tans, guerrilla, martyr, propaganda, civil war, treaty.

As a rule we could say that we would test understanding of all these except Sinn Fein and Black and Tans. These terms are very specific to this topic and you would not expect students even to recognise them.

How to Test

The important point to remember when devising the test is that we want to know what students understand. We must, therefore, give them plenty of scope to put down what they know. We, therefore, do not set questions like 'Define nationalism'. Such questions could produce blank returns from students who had some understanding of the idea, but knew that their definition was likely to be imperfect and so were unwilling to write it. What we want to get are revealing answers such as these on nationalism:

> 'Nationalism is when the banks and airlines belong to the government.'
>
> 'Nationalism is people who are against the government.'
>
> 'Nationalism is like being patriotic. But it does more things, like fighting.'
>
> 'Nationalism is ideas about freedom and government.'

To encourage this kind of useful, revealing response, we do four things:

(1) Set questions in the following sort of 'encouraging' form: 'Write a sentence to show the meaning of "nationalism", or explain any other way you like what it means'.

(2) Vary the style of question, using some which call for the student to use the concept in a context, like 'Can you think of an example from history of a nationalist? Try to explain about the example you give'. (There will be much more about the using of concepts in the sections on 'Intellectual Skills'.)

(3) Tell students directly that incomplete, 'rough idea' answers are quite acceptable, in fact, welcome. Never ridicule students' answers to a pre-test, even gently, even indirectly.

(4) Make clear to the class what the purpose of the pre-test is and that it will in no way count towards any kind of assessment.

Some people use objective tests, where the students have to tick the correct answer out of five choices. These are a lot of trouble to make up, and a tick is not really a very revealing response. The main virtue of those sorts of tests is that they can be done quickly.

Interpreting the Answers

It is important to be very clear in your own mind about the meaning you, yourself, attach to a term; and not to be misled by poor expression. Look at this example of an answer on 'nationalism'—'It's what people think about other countries'. This does not look like a very impressive response, but, in fact, it contains two of the fundamental elements of the idea, i.e. that it is a set of ideas and attitudes ('think about') and that it has to do with 'countries'.

How many of the fundamental elements of the idea in question are there in these responses, would you say?

Party Political

(1) 'Parties is if people get together to talk on what the country should do.'

(2) 'Parties run the elections.'

Conscription

(1) 'Men in the Army.'

(2) 'When men have to write down what job they do (in a war).'

(3) 'If they went round and they had no more men they might get people.'

Martyr

(1) 'To get killed'.

(2) 'A good thing, like something they looked up to or a person.'

(3) 'Fighters.'

Civil war

(1) 'A war somewhere else from where you live.'

(2) 'Wars between people in a place that are all one people.'

(3) 'When the sides do not want really to fight but still do.'

Treaty

(1) 'What you have to do like you sign.'

(2) 'Signed papers by someone.'

(3) 'If you promise to do something and don't do it that is broken.'

Implications of the Results

(a) *If all the scores are high.* You can clearly proceed with your plans and, most important, look for chances to build on existing understanding to develop higher levels of abstraction. For instance, in this case, good understandings of 'martyr' and 'propaganda' could be a safe basis for the further, difficult concept of 'myth' as a political idea. Terms like 'propaganda' and 'guerrilla', if well understood, might make a basis for the idea 'terrorist' and for considering the whole question of emotive language, the way in which the same man is described as 'terrorist', 'guerrilla' or 'freedom fighter', depending on your point of view.

(b) *If all the scores are low.* You will need to reduce the number of concepts that you plan to deal with. Also, in the case of the most difficult abstractions, like in our Irish example, 'nationalism', you would probably do best not to attack the idea directly, but go through the move described in this chapter, the procedure of writing a simple explanation of the term and noting the abstractions you use in the explanation itself as, for example with nationalism:

If a person thinks the most important thing in *politics* is trying to make his own *nation independent* of others, we call him a nationalist. If his country is *independent* to start with, a nationalist might *vote* for things like a *strong* army, or not letting *foreigners* own land in his country.

In other words, if explaining 'nationalism' is really beyond a student's powers, it is probable that the trouble lies in a faulty grasp of those ideas needed as tools to explain nationalism—like 'independent', 'politics', 'nation', 'foreigner' and so on.

We could imagine a sort of pyramid of concepts, leading up to 'nationalism' at the top, with ideas like 'nation', 'politics', 'independent' and 'government' in the next level down and below that level a third level of ideas like 'country', 'laws' and 'language'. If all the scores on our pre-test are low, we might well be trying to work in the wrong level of the pyramid altogether. It will be no good trying to work at the top of the pyramid if the foundations are unsafe, any more than it would be profitable to discuss quadratic equations with someone who does not know how to do multiplication. So, if our test shows general lack of understanding of abstractions at the level we have set them, we must modify our original learning goal and come down one level of the pyramid, at least to start with, so far as we can see how to.

(c) *If there is a mixture of score.* This is the most probable result and in a way the most satisfactory. It shows that you have pitched your planning at a level that is neither consistently too high nor too low. With luck you might also get good guidance on which particular concepts to emphasise, if, say, 'propaganda' is generally well understood, but 'guerrilla' is not.

2

Techniques in Action

In this chapter we deal with two matters that have not been touched on at all, except very lightly; the use of books, and history field-work. These are activities which offer such special problems, and which are so central in a history teacher's work, that they deserve separate treatment, for the sake of clarity. We also deal at some length with the question of putting together our various techniques and types of tasks and questions into the sort of fairly lengthy teaching sequences in which teachers actually try to organise their work.

First, though, we turn to a matter which has been referred to more than once already, but which is of such basic importance that it must, now, have a separate and more leisurely treatment—the question of students' differing abilities.

Planning for Mixed-ability Groups

Throughout the sections on the various intellectual skills, we have mentioned the problem of allowing for students' greater or lesser abilities. Most explicitly, in the section on translation and interpretation we suggested three rules of thumb for setting tasks at an easier level without abandoning the learning-goal: shorten the task; simplify the language in which the task is set; break the task into its component parts. In the section on application we added to the simple idea of 'shortening' the idea of reducing the number of factors of which the student is required to take note in historical problems.

We need to have a separate review and pull-together of this question of abilities, though, away from the context of any specific skill, for two reasons. First, the fundamental importance of this question in a teacher's work: virtually any class of students, anywhere, can fairly be described as a 'mixed-ability group', whether they are allegedly 'streamed' or not. In any case, we may well sometimes be teaching the same historical material with two or more different age-groups. So no teacher can avoid this question. Second, at the moment of writing, there is a noticeable shortage, in the history-social studies area, of answers to this plain question: 'What makes a task harder or easier than another task?' Defeatist approaches to the question, of the order 'let the less able ones draw pictures' are still being publicly propounded.

First, let us consider what we mean when we say John is 'less able than Debby'. Suppose someone set John and Debby the same task—how might their response differ? Take the case of the task 'Account for Hitler's rise to power in Germany.' If John is 'less able' we might expect him, compared with Debby to:

(1) *Write less.*

(2) *Write less well* from the angle of grammar, spelling, syntax, and so on.

(3) *Write less relevantly*—he might put something like' Adolph Hitler was born in 1889; first he was an artist in Vienna, being born in Austria, and then a soldier in World War I. He got the Iron Cross'. He might write this way for one of two main reasons—he may not understand the task, and so may actually think his response appropriate. Or he may just be so slow and incompetent at writing that what was meant as a preamble turns out to be the whole 'answer'.

(4) *Give some factors which are relevant undue prominence*—for example, 'There was great fear of Communism widespread; mass unemployed set in about 1930; people were afraid. Afraid of Russia, and revolution and all thought the Treaty of Versailles was unfair. Also Hitler's party of the NSDAP was well ruled and organised with propaganda, played up for fear of the "Reds". 'Here again, the response gives (arguably) too much space to the Communist threat because John is inept at the skill of synthesis, or possibly because he does not understand

that Russia, 'the Reds', and revolution, and Communism, are virtually the same thing said in different ways. Or may be he just writes slowly: if the response was twice as long (and the rest of it did not mention Communism) the thing would look less badly balanced.

(5) *Stick in passages from books verbatim*—i.e., without trying to translate or interpret them.

(6) *Give wrong interpretations of books or of the teacher's statements*—Sometimes teachers call this, confusingly, 'getting the facts wrong'. Suppose John put the following, though: 'All the other parties like Centre and Social Democrats were in favour of Hitler so, he got in easily'. The most plausible explanation for this error is misinterpretation by John of some teacher—or book-phrase like 'Centre and S.D. parties played into Hitler's hands by . . . and so inadvertently helped him'. It is not the same kind of error as saying, 'Hitler became Chancellor in 1931', a factual-recall error about a date, and it is much better to think of it as a failure of interpretation than to confuse it with such factual-recall errors.

(7) *Show unmistakable signs of not grasping concepts*—Suppose John puts 'The first thing Hitler did in 1933 was set himself up with camps for enemies as a Dictator. And plans for war on the world. The first country he attacked was the Rhineland from France. Then Czechoslovakia and Austria'. He has plainly not understood the idea 'rise to power in Germany' and his lack of understanding is not, this time, obscured by his slowness in writing or lack of synthesis skill.

We could obviously take this analysis further, but we have said enough to show this: when we say 'John has given a less good answer than Debby', it could mean any or all of at least seven things, ranging from merely a less complete answer by John to an answer by John showing various fundamental misunderstandings. Another thing is also clear—that in several of the examples of John's responses, it is not easy to tell exactly what has gone wrong—lack of actual writing skill and speed, or lack of understanding, or what.

So we need a policy for setting John an easier version of this task which will do three things. First, keep him to the same basic learning task as Debby: 'Draw a picture of a swastika-flag' is not the sort of task that will help John to improve. Second, make it easier for him to write a good response. Third, if he cannot write a good response, at least make it clearer to the teacher exactly where he is going wrong.

Let us start with the original task: 'Account for Hitler's rise to power.' If we apply to it our basic three-part technique: 'Size of task; language of task; break task into parts'—we might get something of this sort—'Make a list of four main things that helped Hitler to rise to power: think of the way things were in Germany, and also of the things that Hitler did to help himself.'

Let us work through the seven-point list of John's deficiencies again, and see if this revised task will meet the three criteria we have set ourselves.

Points 1 and 2—volume, grammar, syntax, etc. Asking for a list should certainly put less strain on John's writing powers than the mini-essay of the original task.

Point 3—the list-format lets John off the need for a preamble, so he will not waste time on irrelevancies like Hitler's date of birth, etc. If he does, at least we know for sure he does not understand what to do.

Point 4—undue prominence to certain factors. If John really is not seeing that 'Reds' = Russia = Communism, this new task will not help him to be more successful than he was with the old one. It will, though, make his error easier to spot with certainty.

Point 5—verbatim quotations from books. The new task makes it quite difficult for John to make the 'verbatim quote' response at all. He is virtually driven to use his own words, and so be more successful in this respect at least.

Point 6—wrong interpretation of books or teacher's words. As with *Point 7*—failure to grasp concepts—the element of 'clue-giving' in the new task (think of the way things were in Germany: think of what Hitler did to help himself) might help a little bit to point John the right way. Basically, though, the new task probably just makes the misunderstanding clearer to the teacher.

To sum up: the new task will make it a great deal easier for the teacher to make out what is going on in John's mind. In so far as it simplifies the organisation of the end product it helps John to give a better answers, by letting him concentrate on essentials. It is, in other words, a genuinely 'easier' task of real usefulness to John and his teacher—provided John has understood the central concept, 'rise to power'.

If he has failed to grasp the main concept, what can we do?

Well, one thing we can do is not get in this fix in the first place, that is, not set tasks involving difficult ideas like 'rise to power' before making sure the students have grasped them, through short exercises involving translation, extrapolation, etc.

But that is pretty unhelpful of course. Nobody can head off every possible difficult idea that way and however well we teach consciously for concept development we are going to find ourselves needing to know how to present a concept in an easier form because some students cannot handle it in the form we first thought of it. 'Easier form' in this context means 'nearer to the concrete'. In the case of 'rise to power' that means going down to, say, 'persuades people to let him be leader'.

It is very important to be able to do quickly and easily this sort of transformation 'Hitler's rise to power'—'Hitler persuading people to let him be leader'. It is at the centre of the teacher's art of simplification and, in class, you might have to do it at any moment, orally, when a student asks you for an explanation of an abstraction. The key is that the 'easier' form has concrete nouns in it ('people', 'leader') and, as it were, 'concrete verbs'—like 'persuade', verbs where you can form a mental picture of somebody doing whatever it is. You can't so readily form a mental picture of somebody 'rising'.

Here is a fairly full example, showing how sometimes you can even take abstractions 'down to the concrete' in more than one stage. The key difficult abstractions are emphasised with italics.

Version 1—'How might, *environmental* changes *affect* the *material culture* of a *primitive community*?'

Version 2—'How might, say, changes in the climate change the way of life of, for instance, a Stone Age tribe?'

Version 3—We can still get nearer the concrete with the terms 'climate' and 'way of life' thus: 'Suppose the weather got a lot colder, and stayed cold all the time. With a Stone Age tribe, how might that change (a) the clothes they wore, (b) their houses or shelters, (c) food they ate?' (See how the ideas of 'nearer the concrete' and 'breaking the task down' coincide here.)

We could suppose a version 4, where we make the idea 'Stone Age' even more concrete with a picture and said 'look at the people in the picture . . . suppose where they lived it got a lot colder. . .' etc.

If, of course, students still couldn't give an answer at version 3 or 4, we could presume they didn't understand the whole idea of environment influencing material culture and we would have to introduce it from scratch.

Exercise 1

Here are two tasks. In each case, write an easier version by bringing the abstract ideas involved nearer to the concrete—if you can, make your easier version easier yet. (Both tasks are phrased at a pretty elevated level at the start, to make your task easier.)

(1) What was the impact of the abolition of slavery in 1833 on British-Caribbean society?

(2) What were the economic and political issues in the dispute between Britain and her American colonies?

Summary and Further Example

One way to approach the question of differing abilities is to plan to set different students different tasks according to their abilities. If we do this, an easier task should:

(a) be addressed to the same basic learning as the harder tasks;

(b) be shorter, use easier task-setting language, be broken down into its component parts where appropriate, have fewer factors for students to consider; and

(c) the language in which difficult ideas are expressed should be nearer to the concrete than in harder tasks.

To reinforce the idea of tackling the learning of the same concept in ways suitable to students of different abilities, we should now practise stringing together series of tasks on the same concept, each task at two levels. Here is an example. In the example, the different skills are employed in the same order in which we set them in this book—in real life, of course, there is no reason to have students practise skills in that particular order.

Concept: 'Underdeveloped' (as in 'Underdeveloped Countries')

Translation Task

Version 1—Say in your own words what you think 'underdeveloped' means.

Version 2—Say how the people in an underdeveloped country might live differently from how we do: think about food, schools, sorts of work they do, houses.

Interpretation Task

Version 1—Read this passage and say why the writer thinks Spain is a 'peculiarly interesting' case of an underdeveloped country.

Version 2—Read this passage and say: (a) why did people think Spain was rich in the sixteenth/seventeenth centuries; and (b) why the writer thinks Spain should really have been seen as an 'underdeveloped' country.

The Passage

Spain in the sixteenth and seventeenth centuries was a peculiarly interesting case of a poor, or as we might say nowadays, 'underdeveloped' country.

Because of the huge masses of gold and silver which Spain got from South America and Mexico, she was able to pay great armies of soldiers, and conduct great wars for over a hundred years. She fought the English, the French, the Turks, the Dutch, the Venetians—and won many great victories between 1520 and 1640. She was able to act militarily exactly like a very rich country.

But all the time, the silver was going straight from Cadiz to the Spanish armies. Hardly anyone in Spain got their hands on any of it.

Spaniards were living in poverty. Spain had a bad soil, some bad farming methods, a harsh climate, not many industries. Useful minerals like iron were not dug out as much as they could have been. So most Spaniards lived in poverty, in a poor country.

Meantime, foreigners looked at Spain's silver, and great armies and said, 'What a great and rich nation is Spain!'

Application Tasks

Version 1—Here are some facts about Sylvania: is Sylvania an 'underdeveloped' country?

(1) About 100 Sylvanians are millionaires (in dollars).

(2) The population is pretty large—80 million.

(3) There is still plenty of spare room in the country.

(4) The capital city is impressive—many skyscrapers.

(5) Most Sylvanians leave school at 12.

(6) Most Sylvanians are farmers.

(7) Average farm size is 6 acres.

(8) There are big oil deposits, just starting to be drilled.

Version 2—Here are some facts about Sylvania: is Sylvania an 'underdeveloped' country?

(1) About 100 Sylvanians are millionaires (in dollars).

(2) Most Sylvanians are farmers.

(3) Most Sylvanians farms are about 6 acres.

(4) Most Sylvanians leave school at 12.

(5) The population is large—80 million.

Extrapolation Tasks

Version 1—Suppose around about 1940, a citizen of one of the underdeveloped countries had made a great revolutionary industrial invention. Sketch in the possible sequence of events—would that country have ceased to be underdeveloped, or what?

Version 2—Suppose round about 1940, a citizen of one of the underdeveloped countries we have been learning about (say Mexico) had invented the jet engine. What would have happened next? Would the inventor have tried to sell his invention in Mexico, or somewhere else, do you think? Would the factories to build the engine be in Mexico or somewhere else? Would Mexico get to be a rich country because of this invention by one of her people?

Evaluation Tasks

Version 1—If an underdeveloped country could direct big extra resources to just one of the following, which should it be?

Technical education—health services—general education—prospecting for minerals—subsidies to farmers—industrial investment?

Version 2—Suppose you were the government of an underdeveloped country like Mexico and you had a lot of money from somewhere which you could only spend on *one* thing from this list. Which ought you to choose, and why?

Schools—money to farmers—building factories—people to go round showing new methods to farmers?

Synthesis Task

Version 1—Write a handbook of advice—about 1,000 words—to somebody setting out to help 'underdeveloped countries'.

Version 2—Write a list of five or six main problems you think an underdeveloped country has. Then write a paragraph saying how you might try to solve any two of them.

Exercise 2

Try to put together strings of pairs of tasks like this, using a concept of your choice as the focus. Try putting the use of the various skills in different orders from the order we have used, to see how it turns out.

Exercise 1—Levels of Difficulty—Answers

(1) 'Impact', 'abolition', 'British-Caribbean-Society' are the obvious candidates for 'taking down to the concrete'. (Slavery certainly is an abstraction, but if that term is not understood, the usefulness of the whole task would be doubtful.) Version 2 might be—'What was the effect of doing away with slavery in 1833 on the people who lived in the Caribbean islands that belong to Britain?'

'Effect' in turn might be expressed in a Version 3 in this way: 'After they did away with slavery in 1833, what happened to the people who lived. . .' etc. Outside the terms of the present exercise, of course, we would *reduce* the task by asking only about, say, Jamaica; and *break down* 'people' into ex-slaves, ex-owners, and so on.

(2) 'Economic', 'political', 'issues', 'dispute', 'Britain' and 'American colonies' are the terms to 'take down'.

Version 2, perhaps—'In the quarrel between the Government in Britain and the people in the American colonies, how exactly did they disagree about (a) money and taxes, and (b) questions of government?'

Version 3, more concrete yet, might perhaps involve making that final phrase 'questions of government' into 'what laws to have, and who should make them'.

Using Books

We have referred in several contexts to students making use of books, most especially in the context of the skill of analysis. Books are so important in a teacher's work, and problems about books loom so large sometimes, that the question of history books deserves at least a small section to itself.

Teachers have two main problems about books—selecting them, in the first place, and, second, using books which they didn't select, don't like much, but have to use because they are the only ones available.

Selecting Books

Books must clearly be scholarly and accurate: but there are other principles of selection.

Before we can have principles on which to select books, we have to have an idea of what we think books are for. So far, in the sections on the various skills, we have assumed a certain function for books in the general scheme of history teaching, but we ought to make that assumption explicit now.

We assume that books are things which teachers ought to use to set specific tasks using the full range of cognitive skills, in order to foster concept development. Books are not repositories of information into which students can dip and ladle out information when they or the teacher thinks it appropriate.

Task A

Read and make notes on the following passage:

> One of the greatest signs of the new spirit of the Renaissance was a growing awareness of the workings of the universe. With the disappearance of the medieval fear that too deep an enquiry into Nature would upset the balance between God and man, there were rapid advances in scientific knowledge.
>
> During the fifteenth century Leonardo da Vinci was the leading scientist of the age. Da Vinci was a man of very wide interests, who was always too busy to put his ideas into actual use. Despite this, he was in every way a scientist, using observation and research to overcome any problem with which he was faced. In order to paint and draw more naturally da Vinci made a careful study of anatomy, dissecting corpses and carefully drawing the actions of muscles and limbs. Having a very active mind he was very interested in the behaviour of animals and birds, and took especial note of winged flight. This led him to study the problems of manned flight, and he drew up the first known plans for a helicopter. In the same way da Vinci designed a paddle steamer. The great weakness of these plans was that there was no power to drive these machines, and for this reason his designs were lost and forgotten for several centuries.
>
> Da Vinci was several centuries ahead of the contemporaries in many other respects. He advanced the theory that light travelled in waves, and experimented with the theory of gravity. To a certain extent he realised the enormous age of the earth, and that fossils were the remains of creatures several million years old. Perhaps his most important scientific idea was that Nature was governed by certain forces, which when properly understood would enable man to use Nature for his purpose. Apart from his theoretical work, da Vinci was an important engineer, designing new towns and fortifications which would withstand cannon fire.

The Beginning of European Supremacy,
Heard and Tull

Task B

Read the passage above and make notes for an answer to this question: 'In what ways was Leonardo like a modern scientist and in what ways was he not like a modern scientist?

Now try the following procedure on other people:

(1) select a fairly long piece of text;

(2) tell people simply to 'read it and make notes';

(3) then ask them a specific question about the text, like Task B;

(4) now give them another text of similar length and difficulty to the first, but this time let them know in advance the question they will be asked;

(5) ask the question, and note the differences in performance compared with the earlier test.

Everybody reads better with a task to focus the reading, and the younger and more inexperienced in reading the learner is, the more he or she needs to have their reading focused by precise tasks and questions. For our purposes, all our students can be thought of as 'inexperienced learners'. So the main question we ask about a book, when deciding whether to choose it for a class, is 'Can I readily set specific, tasks on it?

There are some preliminary questions to ask first, though. The first is about the book's vocabulary, especially its use of abstractions. Books for schools very often fail to state the age-ability group for which they have been written. Even when they do say who the book is for, some authors have surprising ideas about suitable vocabulary in a book for, say, 'average students of 14'. So take nothing for granted.

When we come to assess the suitability of the vocabulary in a book, if we bear in mind our purpose of task-setting, we can do better than merely forming a general impression that a book is 'a bit hard' or 'about OK'. We can ask ourselves: 'How many translation tasks would I feel I had to set on a typical page before I could safely proceed to using the other skills?' Student do not have to be able to translate accurately every term on a page to be able to do useful work on that page, but in the 'Leonardo' passage we just looked at, they would certainly have to be able to translate 'scientists' and 'scientific' to make much sense of any other tasks.

All readers have some facility in slurring over words or phrases they do not fully grasp. You would probably say you fully grasped the whole of the 'Leonardo' passage. But can you really explain the phrase in paragraph one, 'would upset the balance between God and man. . .'? Even if you can't, though, it does not detract significantly from your grasp of the passage, and you probably did not even pause over it. The really important and hard question to answer is 'How often does this author use terms which I don't think my students know or are ready for and which are central to the understanding of what he is writing?'

The second preliminary question is about density. The following passage occupied 7¼ lines of print in a textbook. Count how many names, dates, facts it contains.

> Charles IX dies in 1574 and was succeeded by his brother Henry III (1574–89). When Henry's younger brother died in 1584, the Roman Catholics feared the throne would go to the Huguenot Henry of Navarre. To stop plots to depose him, Henry III had the Roman Catholic leader, the duke of Guise, murdered by a monk in 1589. Henry of Navarre then became King Henry IV and defeated the Roman Catholics.

It is fairly obvious that, although the vocabulary is not notably difficult, it is a hard passage to read, or to set useful tasks on. Usually, however, books are not like this all the way through. So it is usually possible to *avoid setting pupils to read passages dense with names, dates and information.* However, if such passages are very common or actually typical of the book, don't choose it.

The third point to look at is pictures. Good pictures can constitute a reason in themselves for choosing a book. By 'good' we mean, of course, as in the case of the text, 'forming a useful basis for a wide range of tasks'. We could say that a good picture has plenty of activity in it, usually involving people—but you might find that you could set many good tasks on a picture that broke both those rules. The safest course would be to pick a few of the pictures most typical of the book's picture-style, and see if it is possible to think up five or six questions on each one. If it is, that might be a good enough reason to choose the book.

It is possible that you 'pass' a book on the score of vocabulary, density and pictures, and yet when you try to work with it, find it difficult to devise good tasks. This might be because the author's approach or style, or something about the text, puts you off. The time to find this out is before you order fifty copies of the book, not after. In other words, the final test of a book's 'usability' must be whether you can actually use it as the basis for tasks.

Exercise 3

For practice, in assessing 'usability' see how many tasks, using all the cognitive skills if possible you can make up about the 'Leonardo da Vinci;' passage. Then try it on this next passage, which contrasts with it in subject-matter, style and tone, but is broadly similar in length and vocabulary level.

> Japan made a treaty of alliance with Great Britain in 1905, and when war began in 1914 Japanese troops very quickly captured German fortresses and bases in China. Japan also made money by selling munitions to the Allies, and began to increase her factory production of cotton and other goods. As hours of work were usually very long, wage-rates very low and conditions in the workshops poor, the price of Japanese-made goods of all kinds was usually well below those which had to be charged by European nations, especially Great Britain, where work-people were much better treated.
>
> Competition between Japan and other countries for world trade became very keen, with the Japanese leading and gradually obtaining a larger and larger share.
>
> Pride in Japanese achievements and a desire to extend Japanese power led to the building of a large battle fleet and the upkeep of a large army. A 'war-party' of admirals and generals managed to obtain power. Those Japanese who believed in democracy were deprived of power or murdered. Manchuria was attacked and seized from China in 1931. Then followed other attacks, on Shanghai and Chinese coastal cities. At the same time huge quantities of cheap, mass-produced articles and cloths, 'made in Japan', were sold all over the world. The Emperor became the symbol of warlike Japan, which needed new lands for its hard-working, ambitious and constantly increasing population.

In 1937, an alliance between Japan and Germany was joined by Italy under her dictator, Mussolini. Hitler hated Communist Russia. So did the Japanese. In 1940 Japan, Germany and Italy signed a treaty promising aid to one another. The Japanese had long before this ended their friendship with Britain, partly because the Chinese received help and trade from the British through Hong Kong and the Burma Road. The United States were also hostile to the Japanese, and stopped Japanese settlers from entering California or the Hawaiian islands. However, the Japanese signed a non-aggression pact with the U.S.S.R., in April 1941, and did not fight when Hitler invaded Russia two months later. They were still fighting against Chinese guerrillas in China itself, and they took over northern Indo-China and air bases in French Indo-China after the French collapsed in 1940, and refused to withdraw.

While meetings between the Japanese and Americans were being held to discuss these and other questions, Japanese aeroplanes and submarines were secretly brought close to American bases in Pearl Harbor and the Philippines; they prepared also to attack Hong Kong, Malaya and the British. Without declaring war, the Japanese suddenly attacked Pearl Harbor on December 7th, 1941, and quickly gained startling successes.

History for Today,
T. H. McGuffie, Macmillan, 1967.

Using Unsatisfactory Books

For all sorts of reasons, teachers have got stuck with books they would not have chosen, but have to use with a class none-the-less. Nothing can make such a situation satisfactory, but there are a few ways of making it less bad.

One way is to avoid use of the unsuitable books as much as possible by writing your own information sheets for students. This is a particularly suitable move if the problem with the book is that its vocabulary is too difficult. It is also a lot of work. If it is not to be an overwhelming task, you will need a very clear idea of what is the minimum information content necessary for the work you want to do. One way of approaching that question is set out below, taking, say, the case of the 'Leonardo' extract; supposing we wanted to write an information sheet as a substitute for this passage, because it was conceptually too hard for our needs.

Stage 1—Work out what the main concept is that you want to work on—in this case, not the concept 'scientist' (or we could use the text as it is), but some more concrete notion. One that would illustrate the case here would be the idea of a 'power source'.

Stage 2—Rough out the tasks we want to set, e.g. 'Say what you think a power source is', 'What sort of power source would a helicopter need?' 'What power-source would do for a paddle-steamer?' 'Which of Leonardo's inventions worked least well? What had they in common?'

Stage 3—Write an information sheet giving as much information as students need to do the tasks: in this case, not much more than a list of his innovatory activities in the field of mechanics might well be enough.

Using Very Small Sections of a Book

If the main problem with a book is that its text is already dense and full of information rather pithily expressed, then summarising it into information sheets is not going to be much use as a technique. So we can use another approach—using very small parts of the book at a time.

Look at how many tasks can be set on even a tiny, fairly dense passage like this one:

> After the German defeat and collapse in May 1945, the whole of Europe was occupied by the Allies. German leaders like Hitler and Goebbels had killed themselves in Berlin; Goering and many German military leaders were imprisoned; Himmler, leader of the Gestapo and S. S., committed suicide soon after British soldiers had hunted him out of his hiding place. The Russians occupied eastern Germany, and the British, French and United States armies had their 'Zones of Occupation' in the west. Berlin itself, the German capital, now in ruins, was inside the Russian zone, but all four main

Allies took over a 'sector' in it; the city was still the home of hundreds of thousands of Germans.

History for Today,
T. H. McGuffie

(1) Say in your own words what a 'zone' and a 'sector' are.

(2) Why do you think the Allies imprisoned some German military leaders?

(3) Why did all the Allies have a 'sector' of Berlin?

(4) Were the Allies right to imprison German military leaders?

(5) What would the Allies have done with Himmler if he had not killed himself?

(6) What might have happened if the Allies had not occupied Germany?

(7) Could you describe the Allies as 'Imperialists'?

(8) What's the difference between a 'leader' and a 'military leader'?

Exercise 4

Suppose that you thought the extract on Japan you worked on in Exercise 3 was so dense that you wanted to give students only very small reading tasks—how many tasks can you make up on just the last paragraph of that extract?

Obviously, you would be in real trouble with a book if you were having to set readings of four or five lines! But learn to see a page or less as being a possible amount of reading to form a useful basis for work, if necessary.

Finally, remember the pictures as a source of tasks, even if all else fails and the text is really difficult and frustrating to use.

An Approach to History Field-work

Suppose we took out a class of students in a bus to look at a well-preserved early nineteenth-century woollen mill, and some well-preserved workers' homes built at the same time, near the mill.

We must first be clear in our own minds why we would be doing such a thing. One good reason for a field visit is motivation.

If the students had been led to work better at some in-school tasks by the promise of 'field-work' then that might be justification enough for the activity, provided that we did not spend much time on it. But there is a lot more that we can get out of it.

The mill and the houses can serve the same sort of function as the exhibits in a museum—they can act as strong concrete referents or hooks for strengthening concept-learning. The procedure for planning a visit to the mill, therefore, is in principle no different from planning for a museum visit, or indeed any other learning activity in the history/social studies field.

First, you work out what the concepts are that are necessary to an understanding of the site, and also what other concepts might be handily strengthened by a visit to the site. You have to visit the place in person, of course, to do this properly.

In the case of our mill, with younger students, we might well concentrate on two main ideas—the concept of a *site,* and the idea that the way buildings and places are is not accidental, but is determined by rational principles which students can figure out for themselves. This is not as simple as it sounds. The trouble with field-trips, as a learning experience, is that they are very confusing; the learner is bombarded with all sorts of quite irrelevant experiences—the journey, the packed lunch, the weather, losing his scarf, and so on. The problem is very well known to junior-school teachers who ask children to 'write about the trip to the beach' and get responses such as: 'We all waited but the bus was late. In the bus we had ice-cream, soda and tomato sandwiches, and we saw a horse in a field. Tony was sick and then we got to the sea and then came home.'

So getting across ideas about the rational sitting of the mill, ideas which to us are pretty obvious, may not be too easy with excited younger students. But we are getting ahead of ourselves. The second main idea we will want to strengthen is the idea of *evidence,* and the understanding that buildings can constitute evidence for things, just like sources can.

We might add one more concept to this list of basic essentials–perhaps in this case the idea of 'cheap' as in 'cheap housing'—the sort of idea which field-work can make concrete in a dramatic way that no other kind of work can equal.

So we have the list: 'site', 'evidence', 'cheap'. Our next problem, of course, is to decide which tasks the students will do, using which cognitive skills. Some teachers, faced with planning a field-visit, fall back on approaches which they would not use in the classroom—a 'guided tour' type of lecture in which the learners are quite passive, or having the students complete a questionnaire about the site which deals only in factual information. So what could we do to do better?

A better way would be to use as our basic device an individual task-sheet for each student. It will contain tasks of interpretation, such as:

(1) 'Why do you think the mill is built where it is?'—broken down for less able students to: 'Why is the mill near the stream?' 'Why is it also quite near the bridge over the river?' 'Why is it not on the river itself?' and so on.

Application tasks such as:

(2) 'In what sorts of ways do you think they tried to keep the houses *cheap?'*—and made easier for less able students by giving clues like 'Why are the ceilings so low? Why are the windows of the houses smaller than those in the mill?'

Evaluation tasks like:

(3) 'We have been learning in class about documents being *evidence*. How useful are the mill and buildings as evidence for what life was like in those says?'—broken down to an easier version in perhaps this form: 'What can you tell from the houses about how people lived? What can you not tell, but would need to read documents to know?

The tasks need not all be of this kind—the students will probably be pleased at finding a slate on one of the houses that says '1811' on it, and want to tell you about it, so set a number of simple information finding tasks like 'When was the mill built?' as well as the tasks directly on the concepts.

The occasion is also a good one for using translation skills of the less usual kind, like sketching and making rough maps on the actual site, so 'Make me a sketch-map, trying to show me with as few words as you can why the mill is built where it is' would be a good style of task.

As with any kind of work, it will be vital to prepare students beforehand and make absolutely clear to them what they are supposed to do and why. The task-sheet, for example, should be given out and gone through, and if necessary explained, well ahead of the trip itself. And if field-work is going to be a regular, worthwhile part of your activities, it is arguably more important to follow up the visit with work obviously connected with the visit. It will be hard for students to take future visits seriously if you don't do that.

Progression in Field-work

It is easy to get on to a sort of plateau of difficulty with field-work, and have students of sixteen, say, being asked very much the same sorts of question about a site as young students of thirteen.

We can try to guard against this in three ways. First, we can try to set tasks involving more difficult concepts. In the case of our mill and workers' houses, it might be possible to set application tasks like this in connection with the visit for older students: 'Look for evidence to support or attack the idea that the owner of the mill was paternalist in his attitude to workers'.

It will not always be possible to think of tasks in this order, because buildings as evidence are not always very eloquent on matters of that kind. Usually possible, though, would be our second move: increasing the number of factors students must take account of, by asking them to compare the mill site with other sites. We could ask, for example, an evaluation plus interpretation task like this: 'Are the workers' houses better or worse than contemporary ones in the town we saw last week? If you can see a difference, either way, try to think of reasons for it'.

The third thing we can do is, again, to make students deal with more factors by taking them to more complicated sites—a complex of buildings of different periods, built for different purposes, for instance.

Unless you live in an area unusually full of settlements, remains and buildings suitable for field-work, it is pretty obvious that your work in this area will have to be planned around those relatively few sites which are available, if field-work is going to be a major part of your approach. That gives rise to questions which only you can answer—building *x* may be available and easy to visit, but that does not make it worth visiting necessarily. Field-work is a 'high-prestige' activity, like discussion or games, and so we are tempted into treating it as an end, not a means, and accepting less cogent answers to the questions, 'What will students learn?' 'Is this the best way of learning it?' than we would in the case of more ordinary work.

On the other hand, field-work has high prestige partly because it deserves to have it. In terms of student motivation and involvement, and in terms of setting up good learning, it can be arguably more powerful than any method, if used well.

Planning Sequences of Lessons and Activities for Different Kinds of Classes

So far we have tried to deal with two main things—how to work out what concepts you want students to learn and use, and how to make up tasks in which they could use them. So far, though, mostly what we have actually worked out is single tasks or little strings of tasks. We now have to work out some principles on which to construct whole lessons and series of lessons, taking realistic note of things like available time, examination pressures, the different attitudes to work of a twelve-year-old and a seventeen-year-old and so on.

Case One

First we will consider a fairly easy case. A class of thirteen-year olds of average to slightly higher than average abilities. No one in the class has special reading difficulties. There are no harsh pressures from examinations, so you have been given a fairly free hand in these terms: 'Try to get through the early days of the American Colonies, up to about 1700 in about ten sessions (each session is 40 minutes long) and cover Drake and Raleigh and the Armada, and all that, at the same time.'

There are some fiercer constraints though. You are told this about the class on reliable authority: 'These kids like to get all the facts, they like to get their note-books well filled. They don't like discussion or fancy stuff.'

Books and other materials are adequate—you can get a few relevant pictures, the main class textbook is a possible base for tasks.

You have written out a list of main concepts to be worked on, which looks like this: colony (colonist, colonise), explorer, pirate, economic, strategic (as in 'economic reasons . . . strategic reasons'), invade, treaty, alliance (ally).

Making the Scheme of Work for the Ten Sessions

What we have is a list of concepts, a set of constraints and a body of historical material. Exactly how we turn all that into a detailed scheme of work depends largely on our individual mental make-up and characteristic style of attack on problems. The following method offers some advantage though, and could be worth trying.

Ignore all constraints to start with—student expectation, time, historical chronology, everything and just write down your good ideas for student activities, as they occur to you. Note down which concepts these activities will be addressed to—(if you have to extend your concept list, do so). You may not use all the ideas, in the end you may not use any of them, but never mind. What you are doing is starting to impose a framework on the material, a framework which is based on your central concern of student learning.

Suppose, as a result of this 'brain-storming' process, you came up with ideas like these:

(1) Comparing Spanish invasion of England attempt, 1588, with English 'invading' America—application tasks—is 'invade' right word? Evaluation tasks—morality of Spaniards and English colonists. Discussion work? Concepts—invade, colony, pirate (Darke).

(2) Comparing Virginia and Massachusetts—'strategic colony' and 'economic colony'. Work on Raleigh—idea of different motives. Classifying exercises, synthesis work. Concepts—strategic, economic, *motive* (new concept—not in original list).

(3) Students choosing sites for colonies, off maps real and invented. Game—discussions on colony sites. Concepts—colony, economic.

Check out the concept list to see if there are any not being dealt with so far, or any new ones. In this case the concepts 'treaty', 'alliance', 'explorer', are missing, and 'motive' is a newcomer to the list. We must now decide what to do about the newcomers and the concepts *not* covered. In this case a reasonable decision would be to add 'motive' to our list of target concepts, decide to work in 'treaties' and 'alliances' with the Indians to the work on Virginia and Massachusetts and drop 'explorer', since the emphasis of our thinking seems to be swinging away from the exploration angle anyway, towards settlements.

We can now make a very rough plan, like this:

(1) Virginia—site—selection, motives of settlers.

(2) Massachusetts—compare and contrast with Virginia.

(3) 'Meanwhile, back in Europe'—1588, Armada, etc.

Assume an equal distribution of time between the three elements, unless there is a strong reason not to. Now think about *lesson one,* in detail.

Lesson One

The first problem is how to begin. To start with the concept pre-test would not be a good idea. We have to work it in somewhere, but no at the start of our contact with a new class, unused to our ways.

Normally, we could suggest this rule for the very beginning of a lesson: always plan for three things: arousing interest, making clear what pupils are to do; involving all pupils in activity other than listening to teacher at an early stage, preferably within ten minutes.

These principles might yield a start like this:

(1) Explain that class is going to hear a story, that the story contains a mystery, and that the class will be asked to try to solve the mystery (1 minute).

(2) Tell story of disappearance of Roanoke colonists (5 minutes).

(3) Class as individuals rough out answers to extrapolation task—'What might have happened to the Roanoke colonists?' (10 minutes).

(4) Answers evaluated by class in terms of plausibility of explanations given.

(5) Pre-test.

There is an important constraint, though, which that procedure would ignore: the class are not used to this kind of work, and 'like to get their notebooks full'. So we must make a modification. Without dropping the three fundamental principles of a good start, we must give the class some, at least, of the kind of learning experience with which they are familiar—note-giving; setting of frameworks by the teacher; and rather more teacher-talk than we would ideally have. The revised Lesson One might therefore go like this:

(1) Explain that for the next few weeks we are going to learn about early days in North America, and about Drake and Raleigh (2 minutes).

(2) Give the class dictated note or cyclostyled note of main data, names, etc., of the topic (5–10 minutes).

(3) Tell Roanoke story, set class to extrapolation task on 'what might have happened to colonists' (10 minutes).

(4) Explain, and give, pre-test.

One vital element in both of these plans may have struck you as a pretty glib suggestion—the telling of the Roanoke story. It may be that there isn't a nice story like that conveniently to hand and that it is impractical to start *every* session with something 'interesting'.

We could helpfully extend the idea of 'tell a story' to the wider idea of 'putting an idea into a concrete setting and introducing actual people'. Then we can see that the technique is really of quite wide application, not very difficult, and not dependent on exciting stories that just happen to be lying about. Take a case—the origins of the American Civil War—not at first sight a particularly easy topic to start off interestingly. Here is how you might do it, by telling this little 'story'.

> Suppose you were in an army, in a battle, and you suddenly realised that the people on the other side you were firing on were friends you used to go to school with, or may be one of them was even your brother or even your own father; well that sort of thing really happened to people in America, in a great war that happened just over a hundred years ago. How could such things be? Well, we are going to imagine that in the year 1861, in Maryland, a man called John Starter, who

was on one side, is having an argument with his brother-in-law, called Christopher Payne, who was on the other. Note down in your books, now, what they said, in a summary form, and I will note it up on the board. First John Starter said, 'Look, Christopher, I'm a Southerner like yourself, but I know that negro slavery is wrong, and has to go, and go without delay'. Christopher said, 'I don't like slavery too much as you know, but I think the question of if it goes and when it goes, and how it goes, is for those Southern states who have got slavery to decide for themselves'.

And so on. What comes out, in the end, is merely a pretty straight-forward summary of the Union and Southern cases; but to put the case into the mouths of two real or imaginary protagonists is a simple, but very powerful, device for injecting interest, and making it 'a story'.

The traditional starting method, 'Recapping on last lesson' is a very difficult procedure to make interesting, and if it consists of putting questions to individuals about what they remember (or probably don't remember) of last time, it can easily destroy all interest at the outset. If you think it necessary to recall the previous session, do it either:

(1) Very briefly—'Last time we learned how the Civil War started—now today I'm going to tell you a story about . . .'

or

(2) more fully, but *not* at the beginning—e.g.,

  (a) *story* about Wolfe at Quebec;

  (b) *work on* (e.g.) problems of conquering a distant, primitive country in the eighteenth century;

  (c) then, well into the lesson, when interest is well established, and pupils have had time to settle to the work and orient themselves, we could say—'Last time we learned about Clive in India—who remembers what *his* problems were—how were they different?'

The basic idea is to plan for any recapitulation you want to do as carefully as for any other element in the lesson and not just 'stick it on the front' of the lesson.

Exercise 5

Write some 'story' type beginnings to new topics, or lessons within topics, on the lines of the American Civil War example above, then try devising some on topics where there is no clear debate to put into the mouths of protagonists, e.g. the industrial revolution, the Great Discoveries. How could these topics be 'personalised'?

Now to get back to our original lesson-series on the early days of the American Colonies.

Lesson Two

The problem has one new dimension now—you have the evidence of the pre-test. Let us suppose that one item 'economic' was particularly badly explained by students and to some students was not apparently even familiar as a word. The pattern of the lesson could be:

(1) Express pleasure at 'results' of pre-test: do not mention poor result on 'economic'.

(2) Say, 'Today we are going to do some interesting and slightly unusual work with maps'. Note that devices for securing interest can be very simple and economical—we have just used two in that sentence, namely:

   (a) claiming that what is about to happen will be interesting and novel;

   (b) promising work with maps, which, on the whole, students like—as they like stories, films, slides, 'quizzes', trips out of school.

(3) Set tasks on colony site-selection (10–15 minutes)

Explaining a Concept—'Economic'

(4) Say, 'One thing a colony had to do was set itself up in such a place as to be safe from attack, as you figured out in the work we just did (stage 3). Another thing the colonists had to look out for was this: they wanted a place that would be good for trade, a place that would grow good crops, that they could sell some day, a place that would grow the kind of crops that people back home would buy, a place may be with minerals they could dig up some day and use or sell, like iron or gold. When people think

about getting rich, making money, selling crops and so on, we say they are thinking about the economic side of things. If we had chosen site B on the map for our colony, because it had gold mines, even though it was hard to defend, then we would say we had gone for the site for economic reasons' (5 minutes).

(5) Set conventional, familiar reading and note-task on book—'Make notes of pages 20-22, note down especially the economic reasons for the Virginia colony, and see if the book says the Massachusetts colony as likely to do well on the economic side of things' (15–20 minutes).

When you have to explain a concept from the ground up, as it were, remember three things:

(a) If you can, try to set up some possibly relevant experience beforehand. In this case, students were working on site selection; not necessarily thinking in overtly economic terms, but probably in terms like 'good harbour, good place for a fort, trees useful for home-building'. The teacher can then refer back to that recent concrete experience, as when he says, '. . . if we had chosen site B on the map . . . then we could say . . .'

(b) Build the picture of what the concept is all about, in as concrete terms as you can, before introducing the term. In this case the student met ideas like getting rich, money, gold, crop, iron, buy' sell before meeting the new word 'economic'. This way is, according to Piaget and others, more efficient than the more traditional fashion of explanation, 'Economic means . . .'

(c) Follow the explanation with work for the whole class using the concept, as soon as possible—in this case there was an application task, and an interpretation task, both based on a book.

Exercise 6

If we were really in the position of having to explain all the concepts in your original list for this lesson series, from scratch, as it were, we would obviously have badly miscalculated the level of thinking of the class. But suppose for the sake of this exercise that you had to explain all the concepts in our original list, i.e.

colony, pirate, economic, strategic, invade, treaty, alliance, motive. Plan out brief but detailed explanations in each case. (You can explain 'ally' instead of alliance, and so on, if you find it easier.)

Lesson Three

So far, our planning of lessons one and two has illustrated these principles: introduce new styles of work slowly, mixed with styles of work familiar to the student; try to plan the start of each lesson with particular care. Three big problems remain:

(1) students' differing abilities;

(2) whether to work in all the cognitive skills over three lesson, or ten lessons, or whatever;

(3) whether or not to stick rigidly to the original scheme of work.

First, differing abilities. We can start taking appropriate notes of differing abilities as soon as we perceive them. By the end of lesson two of the series, for instance, we will have noticed that some individuals write less than others, and that they write less well. It is not probable that we would yet be able to be much more specific than that, let alone designate an 'abler' or 'less able' group in terms of conceptual level.

So we introduce at this stage the simplest of our devices, i.e. we let the less able write less, and yet still be successful. We might rough out an exercise like this: 'Here is an imaginary list of people, with the jobs they did, who wanted to go to the Virginia colony (actor, soldier, carpenter, silversmith, doctor, wagon-driver, shipbuilder . . .): write a little bit on each one, saying if you would let him go on the first colonising voyage, or not'. Thus, we allow the less fluent to write quite small amounts, yet to show by the subtlety of their cases for and against whether their lack of fluency shows lesser understanding or not. The more able can write more on each item, and also get further down the list.

As to problem 2—trying to get all the skills deployed in the course of about ten lessons would not be an unreasonable rule of thumb. Consciously to say to yourself—'They have not had application (or synthesis or whatever) tasks for a while, I must try to think of one, if I can'—is a very reasonable way to approach planning. In the present case we might note that there has not been much application in sessions one and two, and that 'economic' has emerged as a concept of particular interest to us. We could quite deliberately try to think up some application tests on these lines—'Suppose Raleigh planned to use Virginia as a base to attack Spanish treasure-ships, would that be an "economic" use of Virginia?'

Problem 3, how closely we should stick to our original plan, is more difficult. Suppose it emerged already, in lesson two, that students were somewhat thrown by our apparent disregard for chronology, and asked 'Why are we doing Virginia and Massachusetts all together?—Massachusetts is not until 1620, the book says, and Drake and everything and the Armada is before that'. Perhaps that would be a good enough reason to change the planned order to: Virginia; Drake, Raleigh, Armada, etc.; Massachusetts.

However, nobody wants to be a 'headless chicken' type of teacher, running around from one plan to another. Equally, nobody wants to be a robot. The point to hang on to is this—if you make the change which circumstances see to be suggesting, you must still be able to see your way through your original plan, without having to abandon important concepts. On this test, doing Drake and the Armada second, not third, in the sequence looks all right. So we could properly make that change of plan if the students will feel more secure that way.

Exercise 7

Plan lessons three, four and five, of the 'colonies' sequence, *either* sticking to the original scheme of work *or* changing it to the order: Virginia; Armada; Massachusetts.

Case Two

Now let us consider a harder case—a group of fifteen-year-olds, of generally above average ability, working for an external examination.

The first thing we must do is get hold of some examples of the type of question they will be asked in the examination, so that we can work out an appropriate policy. Suppose these were typical examples on our 'set period': European History 1870–1960.

(1) Describe the foreign policy of Bismarck between 1871 and 1890.

(2) Give an account of the involvement of European powers in Africa, 1870–1900.

(3) Why was the League of Nations unsuccessful?

(4) Describe and explain the loss of imperial power by any *one* European nation after 1945.

(5) Why did the USA become so involved in European affairs after 1945?

Clearly, these questions all set a major problem of analysis. Question 4 gives a little more help than the others, breaking the task into 'describe' and 'explain', but generally, the questions are very bald. They do, of course, all involve a formidable synthesis task, and also the understanding of a truly formidable range of concepts.

The first thing we must do, therefore, is pre-test not only the grasp of the class on some of the relevant concepts, but their level of skill in analysis and synthesis.

A test of analysis would look something like this—'Last term you learned about *x*—look up your notes, and write down the points you would make in an answer to this question (set question in form typical of examination questions). Never mind about the order of the points, just put them down as you think of them'.

It might be too hard, if you start work in September, to have the class think back to work done in June, so you may not be able to test their analysis powers until you have covered some ground with them yourself. You can test synthesis, however, straight away. Give them a set of 'points' of your own devising on some question familiar to them and ask them to arrange them into an actual written answer.

It is important to separate skill in synthesis from skill in analysis, and to separate both from a conceptual grasp, so far as you possibly can, if you are to help students effectively. Just giving 'practice in answering questions' will not do much good by itself.

Consider this actual example of a student's work:

Explain the Rise to Power of Mussolini [first two paragraphs only] Mussolini's party, Fascism, was both left wing and right wing. On the left were the socialists and communists, and on the right Republicans and Monarchists and big business. In between were working class. The two sides conflicted with violence, from 1918 to 1922, as many ex-soldiers like Mussolini returned unemployed from War. And Fascism answered their problems.

Mussolini's main ideas were some reforms, like the 'Battle of Wheat', increasing Italy's population. But most of all he looked for glory and battle in wars; Corfu, Abyssinia, Spain and then World War Two.

In this piece so far we can see evidence of failure to synthesise well, and of failure to analyse properly what operations the question wants the student to perform, and also evidence of failure to grasp concepts. But all these evidences are mixed up together, so that the question 'Where would we *start* in helping this student?' becomes a very difficult one indeed—too difficult for a busy teacher with thirty such scripts to sort out very successfully. Such are the limitations of the 'Give practice in answering questions' approach.

Student Attitudes

As well as bearing in mind the urgent need to find out about their powers of synthesis and analysis there are the other constraints to make our task harder than it was in Case One. Notably, and obviously, there is the fact that students are not likely to respond well to work that does not seem to be directly relevant to success in the examination. Their idea of 'relevant' might well be very narrow. On the other hand, we might expect a good response if we make clear exactly how the work we do might help them to pass, and this gives us an extra motivational weapon we did not have in Case One.

Making a Scheme of Work

Suppose we were planning twelve session on the period 1870-1914, as a start. We know we can expect students to be asked questions on diplomacy—probably Bismarck, 'Eastern Question', origins of World War I. Another area fairly sure to 'come up' is European imperialism; possible but not certain are areas like working-class movements, or some question of economic history.

We work out our concept list in this fashion: 'foreign policy', diplomacy, alliance, entente, Power (as in 'Great Power'), economic, imperialism, political (politics), tariff, free trade, socialism, liberalism.

We can make the same first move as we did in Case One, that is, ignore all the constraints and write down good ideas for student activities as they occur to us, then check the ideas against the concept-list to see if we need to add to the list. (We are, of course, now not so free to take concepts out of the list at this point, as we did with 'explorer' in Case One.) Finally, we make a rough plan, may be like this:

(1) How people made up 'foreign policies.'

(2) Bismarck's foreign policy as an example.

(3) How the Industrial Revolution went on after 1870.

(4) Imperialism.

Lesson One

We might get away with starting with a concept pre-test, in this case, introduced by some formula like—'Now we are going to approach this question of doing well at the exam in a really organised fashion. Half the secret of success is having a really good grip on the meaning of a couple of dozen words; also, enjoying our work and getting a lot out of it for our own sakes has a lot to do with how well we understand some of this sort of language—so I want to see first just where we all stand on these words . . .'

After the pre-test, we can start up a system of cycles of work, extending over a period of two or three lessons, which we stick to for a long time, may be the whole year. Here is a possible example:

Phase 1—Take a key term—'foreign policy', explain it, set application tasks in general terms using it (e.g. 'Which of these items would fall under "foreign policy"?'), also translation tasks—'Give examples of items of foreign policy from work you have done before' and other tasks in general terms, for example, evaluation, 'What would a good foreign policy try to do?'

Phase 2—Conventional style work based on books or teacher-provided notes, using the key term, e.g. 'Which of this list of things Bismarck did were "foreign policy"?' 'Was his foreign policy successful?' We can use our original 'good ideas' of the early planning stage, in Phase 1 and Phase 2.

Phase 3—Set medium-scale synthesis tasks using the idea, like comparisons of German and English foreign policy in short essay form.

You can vary the details of the cycle, of course, for instance sometimes taking pairs of contrasted ideas as your start-point, like 'political', 'economic' or little groups of related ideas. If you make sure that the timing of the cycles remains tight, you will secure three good results. First, the students learning ought to be much better if they are meeting ideas in an orderly fashion, explained in simple terms, before they meet them head-on in their reading. Second, making application of the concepts to the material of the course in Phase 2 an inflexible part of your plan, and making synthesis tasks or 'little essays' also an inflexible part of the plan, you will be helped to keep to the syllabus and less tempted to get into large-scale activities, say large-scale simulations, giving undue weight to one or two concepts. This will, in turn, tend to create, students' confidence in you and your procedure. You want them to feel, ideally, that work with you is interesting and unusual, but also purposeful and directed closely to their goal of the examinations. Nobody has to be dull because they have an examination-oriented class. What you have to be, to be fair to such a class, is purposeful, and as keen to 'cover' the syllabus in your way as they are in theirs.

Exercise 8

Take a topic of your choice. Work out what you think are two or three of the main concepts on which the topic hinges. Write brief explanations of each one; and then devise as many short tasks as you can, of as many different types as you can, to illuminate that concept and deepen students' understanding of it. Plan so that the whole thing, including initial explanation, will only take half an hour.

Revision for Examinations

We can make good use of our classifying and reordering of materials exercises at the revision stage. Also at this stage, if not before, students must have practice in analysing what is required by the standard question forms of the examination in question, such as 'How far was. . .', 'Explain . . .' and so on.

Case Three—A Senior Class

For this case we will postulate a class of seventeen-year-olds, of above average to very high ability. They are probably working towards some advanced level examination, though in a more leisurely way and with more teaching time per week available, than in Case Two. One of the traps we might fall into with such a class is to assume, because of their age and ability, that they do not need to practice the analysis of examination questions and the synthesising of answers. This is very unlikely to be true of all such students.

The analysis they will have to do on questions is more difficult than the class in Case Two had to do, in four main ways.

(1) They may have to make more complex analysis, as in a question like 'How have historians' judgements of the peace settlement of 1815 changed over the years?' Here they have to work out what kind of thing to say about the 1815 settlement, and also what kind of thing to say about what historians (which ones?) say about it.

(2) The clues about what kind of response to give get more cryptic, they go from 'describe' and 'explain' at the lower level of examination to, for example, a quotation followed by the gnomic instruction 'Discuss'!

(3) Very high-level abstractions, such as 'significance', 'critical analysis' are likely to occur in the questions they meet in the examination.

(4) The synthesis tasks are likewise large—Hitler and Stalin, domestic affairs and foreign, and so on, commonly having to be dealt with in one question.

It is very probable that the class will profit from small-scale exercises in analysis and synthesis, in just the same way as the class in Case Two. In fact, to cut the matter short, no important element in the teaching approaches we have discussed becomes superfluous just because the class is seventeen years old and bright. Setting a good concept pre-test will be just as important, making a motivating and interesting start to sessions just as important. The problem is that this group differs from the others in the matter of student expectation.

Student Expectation

The class in Case Two probably had developed their own theory of examination-passing and of teaching, expressed in some formula like 'What you need is a lot of facts; a good teacher is one who gives you a lot of facts'.

The class of Case Three will probably have a more refined set of theories, some helpful to you, others not. Their theories might go like this: 'What you really need for the exam is facts. We should be allowed to express opinions, too—so there should be discussions. A good teacher is a good talker—lively, tells jokes, makes things interesting, while getting through the facts. Some of the time, at lest, history is no longer just a school subject to us—the issues are real and emotionally charged; we care about some questions and see contemporary relevance in them. Acceptable work for us to do is—listening to lecturing, having discussions, writing essays. Unacceptable "kid's stuff" is things like tests, small-scale writing exercises, anything with pictures or maps, being asked the meaning of words.'

If the class have a set of opinions like this, it is helpful to the teacher in these ways—you might expect favourable response to discussion work; to games and simulations where the discussion-element is stressed; to the consideration of abstract ideas; to work involving evaluation.

Not so favourably received might be direct translation or interpretation work. If you ask a student right out 'What do you think "Fascism" means?', he might be more embarrassed and defensive about being unable to give a clear reply than a younger student would be. Also he might be more emotionally involved in working out his attitude to Fascism than in trying to define it closely. He may be ambivalent about many highly charged political terms—he wants to use them in argument; he wants to win arguments using them; he could resent attempts to make him define them, and see such attempts as challenges.

Similarly, with books—he will be using adult history books by now, and his use of them is important to him as a sign of maturity. An interpretation exercise that shows that he does not understand large chunks of the books he reads could meet a lot of resentment.

Even in activities of which the class might approve, you could hit snags, particularly in discussion. You will want to set up discussion with learning goals in mind, stressing application of concepts, extrapolation and the like. They will probably see discussion as most people see it—as an occasion for winning arguments. They will want their discussion to resemble adult 'outside world' discussions, and derive satisfaction from taking part in rambling, diffuse, emotional exchanges such as they see on television, even though you don't think much of them as learning occasions.

To sum up—they will have by now their own ideas about what ought to be happening in history classes, ideas connected with their perception of their own dignity and status as near-adults. These perceptions are not illegitimate—just not always helpful. What to do?

To get over this problem, it might help to think in terms of a cycle of activities, as in Case Two. One way to plan a cycle might be like this. We could work it out backwards. Session 4 could be the 'target session' as it were, in which the class will discuss at length some question such as 'Were Metternich's politics justified or not?' Also round about session 4 they will be embarking on a major piece of written work with a little similar to the question put to focus the discussion. In sessions 1 to 3, we prepare for this grand debate. As individuals or groups, the class work basically on analysis and synthesis tasks on a small scale, working out arguments and counter-arguments on aspects of the debate. They also work on translation and application tasks, involving the major abstractions which will come up, e.g. liberal, repression, censorship, nationalist, conservative, middle class. We present these tasks not as bald challenges to the student, but in forms such as—'The other side, the anti-Metternichs, are going to accuse Metternich of being "repressive". Let's figure out a good definition of that word, then read about what he did in Austria and see if we can't show that it didn't amount to much repression. If we can't show that, may be we can look at the 1848 revolutionaries, and see if we can make out that they were as "repressive" as Metternich.'

We can use all our 'good ideas' in this phase, trying to work in extrapolation work, evaluation work, or whatever. When the great debate arrives in session 4, the debate should be of higher quality because of the preparatory work, but we need not worry too much about that, we will have managed to get what we want—intensive work on small-scale tasks—in sessions 1 to 3.

Setting up a debate as the 'target' is just one method, the principles are the important thing which we might review in this way:

(1) The students need to do small-scale tasks with clear goals, just like any other students.

(2) We need to take serious account of the hostility they might feel to doing such tasks 'like kids'.

(3) We need to set up as it were dignified short-term 'targets', like a debate, to establish a need for the small-scale tasks.

(4) The whole little cycle of tasks and 'target' must produce conventional visible outcomes, like essays and notes, which are plainly useful in terms of the examination to come.

(5) As in Case Two, we should make the cycles short, so that we are seen to be covering the syllabus at a reasonable speed.

Exercise 9

Plan a cycle of work for seventeen—to eighteen-year-olds on the lies just described *either* with a 'debate' or some other activity as the 'target' for the final session.

3

The Use of Quantitative Methods

There are many ways of attempting to quantify what happens in the classroom. Some observers use *rating scales,* others prefer some kind of *category system.* There are now thousands of published systems as well as unknown numbers of home-made approaches. Rather than gratefully seizing a category system or rating scale simply because it is available, it is better for observers to ask themselves why they might want to quantify something, as well as what might be the focus of their attention.

There are numerous instances when quantities can be informative, especially when these are related to intentions. If the teacher wants everyone to have a turn using a micro-computer during a particular day, then it is useful to know whether all the class did in fact have an opportunity, or whether it was only a half or even a quarter of the pupils. It would also be valuable to know which pupils did and did not manage to obtain a turn, as well as more qualitative information, such as why some completed the assignment and others did not. Similarly, if a teacher believes that children should sometimes give longer answers, rather than short one word replies, it is important to known how often this aspiration is fulfilled, and any explanation of the outcome. Quantitative and qualitative approaches need not be seen as polar opposites as they can often complement each other.

Systematic analysis of lessons has often concentrated on a number of matters in the classroom. They include the following, some of which overlap with each other:

Personal traits	The traits of either the teacher or the pupils—for example, whether the teacher is warm or aloof, whether certain pupils appear to prefer collaboration or disruption.
Verbal interaction	What teachers and pupils say to each other, who does the talking and about what, question and answer, choice of vocabulary and language register.
Non-verbal	Movement, gesture, facial expression like smiles and frowns.
Activity	The nature of the pupils' tasks, what the teacher does.
Management	How the teacher manages pupil behaviour, the use of resources, the organisation of group or individual work.
Professional skills	Questioning, explaining, arousing interest and curiosity.
Teaching aids	The teacher's use of audio-visual aids, such as television, slides, tapes, or other materials and equipment, like the micro-computer.
Affective	Teachers' and pupils' feelings and emotions, interpersonal relationships.
Cognitive	The nature and level of thinking in the classroom—for example, the level of reasoning necessary to answer a question, or the degree of understanding a pupil appears to have of a topic or concept.
Sociological	The roles people play, norms, codes, the effects of social background, status, power.

All of these aspects of classroom life can also be studied by qualitative methods, and indeed have been, especially such matters as relationships, emotional tone, the use or misuse of power, status. However, this chapter will concentrate on attempts to quantify what is witnessed, a matter which raises interesting philosophical and ideological issues. In order to determine and record how often or to what degree something happens, it is usually necessary to have decided in advance what is to be quantified. The main strength of this rational *a priori* view is that it allows the observer to concentrate on elements of classroom life according to procedures carefully worked out in advance. The weakness is that it is less easy to respond to the unexpected, or to retain the flexibility to follow one's judgment about what is important in the lesson in the light of actual events.

This philosophical dilemma is shown on the continuum below:

Pre-ordained schedule .... *open-minded*

Compare two different classroom observers looking at the same issue, but from different standpoints.

Left on the continuum—Let us suppose that teachers in a school are concerned about the amount of disruption from pupils who misbehave, so they want to see if they can reduce it. Observer A, operating towards the left-hand side of the continuum, might decide to watch classes of pupils counting up how many appear to be disruptive, noting who the disruptives are and what they do. This might be followed by some kind of action programme during which teachers try to reinforce and recognise good behaviour whenever it occurs, or take out pupils who misbehave for special counselling. The observer might then go into the classroom after the programme using the same observation schedules as previously, to see if the incidence of misbehaviour had increased, decreased, or remained the same.

Right on the continuum—Observer B, operating towards the right-hand side of the continuum, by contrast, though clear about the focus on disruptive behaviour, would not determine explicit categories beforehand. It would be more likely that interviews would take place in advance of, or after, observations, to determine what teachers and pupils regarded as disruptive and why. The observer might make extensive notes on incidents that occurred during lessons, and ask those concerned to explain how they saw these. The perceptions of different participants could then be brought together to find agreement or inconsistencies and some kind of action programme could be devised and evaluated in the light of how people interpreted events.

It would be easy to caricature the difference between the two approaches and claim that Observer A is rigorous and systematic, and Observer B slapdash and amateurish, or equally that Observer A is insensitive and mechanistic, whereas Observer B is thoughtful and profound; but in reality the two are simply operating different strategies which they may or may not employ skilfully. It is a little like saying one wants a single 'true' account of someone's wedding. Does one choose a photograph, if so, which one? Would a video be better, or a first-hand account from someone present, or a list of factual information telling who got married to whom, where and when? Which single or multiple record suffices will depend on the circumstances and the wishes of the person seeking the account. It is perfectly possible to adopt a variety of approaches to classroom observation, as well as favour a single one.

Rating Scales

The use of rating scales in classroom observation was widespread a few years ago. Indeed, in many cases a list of ratings was the sole outcome. Typically pairs of bi-polar opposites, often based on assessment of the teacher's personality, were scored on a five, seven, or even ten point scale. Some ratings focussed more on manifest classroom traits, rather than individual personality features, and dimensions such as 'well prepared—badly prepared' were commonplace. Mostly the features of a rating schedule were based on commonsense assumptions, rather than the results of research, though Ryans (1960), in a substantial evaluation of teachers' characteristics, used traits that appeared to be related to 'success' in the classroom, like the ones below:

Warm	1	2	3	4	5	6	7	*aloof*
Stimulation	1	2	3	4	5	6	7	*dull*
Businesslike	1	2	3	4	5	6	7	*slipshod*

This approach was criticised for a number of reasons, some self-evident, others more technical. The most frequent comment is that one rater's '4' may not mean the same as another rater's, though it is possible to train observers until they show quite high agreement with each other. Another set of criticisms applies to rating scales generally. The *halo effect* occurs when the rater is tempted to make a general judgment that the person concerned is a '2' or a '6' type person and award roughly the same grade on every scale. *Recency* is the tendency to be influenced by what has happened recently, and give the person a low rating on some trait such as 'businesslike' if something happens to go wrong with the organisation of the lesson at the very moment when the observer is deciding the grade. *Central clustering* is often the result of uncertainty, and it leads raters to score everything at points 3, 4 or 5 for fear of stepping out of line if they utilise the whole range.

Rating scales are often best employed by observers who will see many classrooms, as they are more likely to be able to build up experience at assigning the grades in different contexts, whereas those who see only one or two teachers may not be sure how to use a particular scale. Sometimes observers will use a measure of frequency, rather than intensity, and concentrate more on actual behaviour instead of personality. A typical scale might involve the rater in circling a numbers from 1 to 5 to indicate how often something seemed to happen in a lesson. The range might be 1 = never, or almost never, 2 = rarely, 3 = sometimes, 4 = often and 5 = always, or almost always. The observer would then score items like the ones below using this scale.

Teacher praises correct answers	1	2	3	4	5
Teacher deals with misbehaviour	1	2	3	4	5
Pupils distract other children	1	2	3	4	5

In order to address questions about the subjectivity of rating scale, there is a development which attempts to relate categories to specific acts of behaviour. It is known as *Behaviourally Anchored Rating Scales (BARS,)* and the numbers correspond to what teachers or pupils actually do on what is seen to be a rising scale of intensity or desirability. This approach is often preferred in the appraisal of employees in industry and commerce when the intention is to give feedback about performance which will steer people in a direction thought to lead to greater productivity or effectiveness. For example, on a ten point scale for sales managers, a low grade like 2 might have a cluster of items such as 'criticises sales assistants in front of customers', or 'acts unsympathetically when dealing with genuine complaints', whereas a high grade like 9 might include 'encourages commitment of sales staff by giving them responsibility' or 'arranges regular in-store training'.

An equivalent in the observation of teachers in classrooms might, in the case of a low grade on a dimension like 'pupil response', include 'children inattentive' or 'few responses to questions', wherpas a high score would have items attached to it such as 'discussion of work often initiated by children themselves' or 'pupils appear disappointed when lesson ends'. The essential difference between this and the traditional rating scale is that the observer has plenty of clues about the criteria for each point on the scale, and it is not simply left to subjective judgment.

One of the major problem with rating scales is that they appear objective, but are in practice heavily laden with the values of those who conceived them. They can be misused, becoming a crude device for overriding teachers' individual professional judgment and making them strive to achieve the goals of their superiors, especially if the observation takes place in the context of assigning merit awards or carrying out appraisal.

An item like 'teacher sticks to lesson plan', for example, can be placed at the *hurrah!* or *boo!* end of a rating scale, depending on whether the deviser wants to encourage flexibility or rigidity. As an item in itself it is neutral, for there can be occasions when teachers quite rightly keep close to their original intentions, and other times when to do so would be disastrous in the light of what actually happens in the lesson. It is often the context which determines the desirability or otherwise of a certain piece of behaviour. Rating scales, therefore, can be useful in classroom observation, but they are best employed by experienced observers seeing numerous teachers, and they should never be used automatically, only when the context seems appropriate, and then with considerable caution.

Category Systems

Rating schedules that require the observer to exercise considerable subjective judgment are often referred to as *high inference* measures. By contrast *low inference* measures involve the observer much more in recording whether or not something tool place. If someone wanted to see how healthy an environment a particular classroom offered, then a high inference approach would be to rate it for 'cleanliness' or 'health-conscious behaviour'. A low inference approach, however, would concentrate on the occurrence of discrete pieces of behaviour thought to be associated with good or poor health, and could involve the observer noting down how often a pupil sneezed or coughed without using a handkerchief or covering his face, or whether children washed their hands after visiting the toilet.

ACTIVITY 3.1

Imagine you are going to study a teacher's class management with a view to compiling a record of how well children appear to follow her classroom rules, like 'raise your hands before answering a question' or 'don't leave your seat without permission'. Write down briefly the following:

(1) How would you draw up and construct a high inference approach?

(2) How would you draw up and construct a low inference approach?

In your response to Activity 3.1 you may well have devised a set of categories, in particular for your low inference approach. This is not always an easy matter, and there are a number of guidelines that are worth following. Take, for example, the question of pupils raising their hands to answer a question. It would be possible to use a category 'child raises hand' and then tick the name of any pupil who raises a hand when asking or responding to a question. This is a better approach than phrasing the category as a negative, like 'child fails to raise hand', as you would be recording a tick against most children's name every minute of the lesson, unless the context were specified. A category description should, wherever possible, be unambiguous and easy to assign during what can be a busy observation period.

There are other common errors that are made when category systems are constructed, such as the following:

Pupil happily reads book	(covers two types of category—'action' and 'mood')
Teacher shows interest	(too vague, target of interest not clear, better to qualify it)
Pupil misbehaves and is told off	(two consecutive acts, should be coded separately)

In view of the difficulty of devising home-made categories, many observers prefer to use someone else's schedule. The classroom observation literature is now full of published category systems, some devised for research projects, others for teacher training or appraisal. However, even using a published system should involve a degree of reflection, rather than the uncritical application of an instrument constructed by someone with perhaps a quite different focus or purpose. Whether choosing a readymade set of categories or devising one's own, there are several considerations which must be take into account, such as the main purpose and focus, the sampling period, the nature of the record and the use to which the data will be put.

Specific Focus

An observer watching a foreign language lesson in a secondary school might want to highlight features quite different from someone looking at a reception class in a primary school. The former might be concentrating on the oral parts of the lesson and so devise categories such as 'pupil answers teacher's question in the foreign language' or 'teacher gives command in the foreign language'. The latter might want to study social behaviour amongst children starting school, and so draw up headings like 'child snatches toy' or 'teacher praises good behaviour'.

One way of deciding the aspects of classroom interaction on which to focus is to undertake a pilot study of a few lessons in the field under observation and make notes, not only about events which catch the eye, but also about routine matters which can easily be taken for granted. Some classroom observers are influenced by a particular perspective or theoretical influence, so this will often partially determine the emphasis. Consider some of the following contexts and perspectives:

Science

If the observer wanted to see the extent to which the aims of a particular curriculum emphasising *investigation* were being fulfilled, then one matter of concern could be whether pupils did experiments, recorded their findings and discussed the outcome. Categories might include 'pupil makes hypothesis or speculates', 'teacher asks about findings' or 'pupil formulates scientific law or proposition'. The focus might be on what the pupils do, what the teacher does, or both. For example, there might be a category split into three options: 'Summary by teacher/pupil(s) both'.

Modern Languages

Interest in the use of the foreign language in the classroom could produce a set of categories that were identical for the native and foreign language parts of the lesson, with a special code or suffix for the latter, for example:

4 Teacher asks question in English

4a Teacher asks question in the foreign language

6 Teacher gives command in English

6a Teacher gives command in the foreign language

8 Pupil answers in English

8a Pupil answers in the foreign language

9 Pupil asks question in English

9a Pupil asks question in the foreign language

Physical Education

An observer might want to see how active different children are in physical education lessons. A log of individual children's activities could be constructed with categories such as 'runs slowly', 'runs quickly', 'jumps', 'uses piece of gymnastic apparatus (specify which)', 'plays ball', and this might then be related to other measures of activity, like the monitoring of heart rates during exercise.

Behaviour Modification

Someone influenced by behaviourist learning theory (Skinner, 1954) and wanting to apply it in the classroom would want to ensure that the principles were applied in a consistent manner. According to the tenets of behaviourism the teacher should ignore misbehaviour, on the grounds that this will lead to its extinction (an assumption by no means wholly agreed upon amongst practitioners), and reinforce 'good' behaviour, so that this will occur more frequently. Categories might include, therefore, 'teacher praises pupil' as well as different types or degrees of what is perceived to be misbehaviour, such as 'illicit talk', 'movement without permission' or 'physical aggression towards another pupil'.

This kind of programme is often controversial, and the use of category systems–alone is usually insufficient to evaluate it properly. For example, it is easy to demonstrate whether the incidence of misbehaviour is reduced after an action programme, but figures about the degree of decline do not, by themselves, address questions of value, such as the effect of the programme on pupils and teacher. Nonetheless quantitative data can be an important part of an analysis.

Reading

A teacher might want to know how frequently she hears individual pupils read. An individual pupil log filled in by an observer, therefore, could offer categories such as 'teacher calls out pupil to hear reading' or 'pupil solicits teacher's attention to hear reading'. Another focus, however, might be on what the teacher does when the child makes a mistake when reading out loud. In this case the observer may have a category 'pupil makes error' (which in turn could be sub-divided into types of error), followed by others like 'teacher ignores', 'teacher corrects', 'teacher asks child to try again' or 'teacher points to error without speaking'. This would allow the observer to build up profiles showing how the teacher responds when children make different kinds of mistake in their reading.

Creativity

Although some teachers or observers want to concentrate on a particular subject or type of classroom activity, others might wish to address a more overarching notion like 'creativity', or the extent to which children are able to use their imagination and ingenuity, irrespective of the subject being taught. In this case there could be a specific focus on events thought to be connected with this nurturing of children's inventiveness. Teacher encourages divergent thinking' or 'pupil produces unusual idea', and the consequences of these acts, are amongst categories that might be conceived and used in lesson observation.

Grouping

There is often public debate about the use of what are sometimes called 'formal' and 'informal', or 'traditional' and 'progressive' teaching styles. Too frequently the discussion is polarised, as if one style is generally preferable to another, or even as if there is complete agreement about what constitutes 'formality' or 'progressiveness'. More accurately the debate is about the suitability of general teaching styles and specific strategies to particular contexts, whether, for example, it would be more effective to give information or elicit it, or whether it would be more appropriate to use whole class, small group or individual teaching for a certain purpose or activity.

When coding classroom interaction it is possible to record at the same time the nature of the grouping, without adding significantly to the burden of the observer. This can be valuable in highlighting such matters as what pupils do under different conditions, or what happens during the transitions from whole class teaching to group work. Suppose a simple category system were being used which recorded whenever the teacher asked a question or gave a reprimand, then by adding the suffix C = Class, G = Group, I = Individual, T = Transition from one type of grouping to another, an important aspect of context would be preserved. If TQ = Teacher asks question, and TR = Teacher reprimands or admonishes, the following could easily be coded:

TQC	Teacher asks question to whole class
TRI	Teacher reprimands individual pupil
TQG	Teacher asks question to group of pupils
TRCT	Teacher reprimands whole class during transition

The use of simple suffixes like this is a useful way of adding valuable context information to a category system without making it over complex. This will be further discussed below.

Counselling

Not all observations of teaching occur in large classrooms with 30 pupils. Sometimes teachers may be observed during an important part of their day when they are not in the company of the whole class, or when they are talking with individuals. Counselling children about their work, career, behaviour or aspirations is an example of an aspect of teaching that can occur with two or three children or even just one individual pupil. Many aspects of larger group dynamics may occur in this more intimate context, as pupils ask questions, teachers give or solicit information, praise or admonish, but there may be additional elements that are more likely to occur in a one-to-one exchange. A category system for these purposes might note down such matters as when the teacher gives advice and whether the pupil appears to accept or reject it, or whether it is not possible to judge. There are other examples of teacher-pupil interaction away from the classroom—in the playground, library or dining room, perhaps where certain additional categories may be needed.

Physical Environment

When the location of an activity needs to be preserved, for instance, if an individual pupil's movements during the school day are being noted, then it is easy to devise a simple set of categories to note where the activity under scrutiny actually takes place. The following is a simplified example:

L Laboratory

RC Reading corner

G Gymnasium

H Hall

P Playground

DR Dining room

A study of several individual young children might discover which pupils go to the reading corner and which do not. Another observer might focus on the differences in social behaviour in various parts of the school, where and when disruption is most likely to occur, or whether a school's policy on discipline appears to be consistently applied in different locations and contexts.

Pupils

Many category systems concentrate on logging the teacher's behaviour or movements, but others focus specifically on, or take into account, what the pupils do. A good example would be the observations of, say, differences in behaviour between boys and girls, or between children from different groups. An observer studying individual children to see whether the teacher's interactions with boys were similar to, or different from, those with girls, could add the suffix *B* or *G* to each teacher question, praise, reprimand or whatever to show whether it was addressed to a boy or a girl. It is also possible to code teachers' and pupils' behaviour in an even-handed manner by using a *reciprocal* category system, that is one which has exactly the same categories for both. Thus, TQP could be 'Teacher questions pupil', but equally PQT would be 'Pupil questions teacher'. This can lead to some categories that are commonplace and others that are rare, like 'Teacher praises pupil' and 'Pupil praises teacher', but nonetheless it does not weigh down the observer with as many assumptions as some systems.

Theories and Ideologies

Just as behaviour modification is rooted firmly in the traditions of behaviourism, so too teachers and observers with particular beliefs and concerns may prefer to use a category system influenced by some theoretical or ideological perspective. The main problem here is that any record of observation can become self-fulfilling, merely confirming the prejudgments of the people concerned. For example, a loaded category like 'Teacher works hard' or 'Girl ill-treated by boy', if not counter-balanced by other different categories, could giv- a very distorted view of classroom events.

An interesting example occurs in the observations of teachers' questions. Some category systems assume that certain kinds of questions are superior to others, and it is easy to assemble a hierarchy which does precisely that, such as assigning levels to questions which require different degrees of mental effort:

Level 1 Recall of facts

Level 2 Grouping facts

Level 3 Evaluating facts

Level 4 Making inferences from facts

Though it is legitimate to assume that making inferences from facts can represent a greater cerebration from the learner than merely recalling them, this does not stand up in all circumstances. If you call on friends hoping to have a chat with them, then using the two facts that the house door is locked and a sign on the door says 'Gone fishing' to make the inference that the people you are visiting are not at home, is not three levels higher than recalling the formula of DNA. Some observation schedules have been influenced by such perspectives as the theories of child development of Jean Piaget (1954), the taxonomy of educational objectives formulated by Bloom (1956), the non-directive client-centred philosophy of Carl Rogers (1970), and the views of John Dewey (1916).

Non-verbal Categories

Many of the published category systems focus exclusively on speech, but some look at non-verbal aspects such as movement, gesture or facial expression. It is possible to use squared paper, for example, to track a teacher's or pupil's involvements during lessons. This might be of interest in an open plan school if the teacher and observer wanted to know how frequently the different parts of the school, like the reading area, or the number corner, were actually visited. Observers looking at gesture and facial expression might use categories such as 'Teacher indicates', 'Pupil raises hand', 'Teacher smiles' or 'Pupil appears puzzled'. Some of these categories clearly require more of a degree of subjective judgment.

In order to record posture and positioning, Hall (1963), an anthropologist, used iconic symbols to note where people sat or stood in relationship to each other.

 Male sitting

 Female sitting

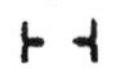 Two people face to face

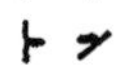 Two people not quite facing each other

Time Sampling

One of the decisions observers have to make is how often to record a category. There are several choices available, and the following are amongst the most common:

Unit Sampling

A particular time unit is chosen, it may be as short as three or four second, or as long as five minutes or more. The main argument for a very short period of time is that it allows for rapidly changing events to be recorded in full, but on the other hand, it can be quite tiring for the observer to tally every few seconds, especially if the schedule is long and complex. When longer periods of a minute or more are used, several events can take place even within a short period of time. There are two common conventions which are used in these circumstances. The first is to note down *every single time* something happens, so that if a teacher asks ten questions in the two minute (or whatever) time segment, all ten are recorded. The second convention is to tick each category *once only* during the period under review, so the teacher asking one, two or 20 questions would produce just a single tick in the 'Teacher asks questions' box. The arguments for and against each of these conventions are finely balanced. Trying to record every instance of an event is exhausting, but does produce a fuller record, whereas coding each event once gives the essential flavour of what happened in the lesson, and is ma?ageable by the observer, but can distort the balance of events by suggesting that they were all equivalent.

Static Sampling

Some observers build up a series of snapshots of a lesson, a little bit like a time-lapse series of photographs. This means that they code what is happening at some regular interval, perhaps at the end of every minute. Suppose the observer were studying four individual children, two boys and two girls, then at the end of each period there would be a record of exactly where each child was and the nature of its activity at precisely that moment. The advantages of this kind of sampling are that it allows 20 or 30 such snapshots to be collected in quite a short time, preserves the sequence of events, and permits analysis that is not too time-consuming. The major disadvantage is that significant developments can occur between sampling, especially if the time period is a long one.

Natural Sampling

Given the problems of choosing a fixed time period in advance, some observers refer to respond to natural units in which something interesting occurs. Thus, if the teacher begins the lesson with a three minute explanation of what is going to happen in that lesson, goes on to 20 minutes of practical work, brings the whole class together again for four minutes to check out what they have earned, and finally asks the pupils to clear away for two minutes before moving on to another activity, then those would be the observer's sampling units, as they reflect the actual periods of time in which specific activities took place.

OTHER QUANTITATIVE METHODS

There are other ways in which classroom observation can be quantified. Some of these are quite controversial and indeed threatening to teachers, so that they are not always widely used. They include the following:

Quality Grading

Some observers give a single grade of teaching quality as a result of watching lessons. For many years in teacher training there was a widespread use of a five or three point scale for rating the quality of teaching seen during teaching practice. The three point scale was often 'Distinction', 'Pass' and 'Fail', whereas the five point scale was based on the literal grades A B C D E, sometimes with plus and minus signs attached, and C + became the sort of mark that would be awarded to some honest plodder who was conscientious but not too stimulating. Veteran appraisers would confidently pronounce "C minus written all over him", or "B plus, though I could even be persuaded to go as far as A minus if you press me", at meetings of examiners. Members of Her Majesty's Inspectorate have often used similar quality gradings when they observe teaching.

Quality gradings are usually used by observers who see many people teaching, like inspectors and teacher trainers, and their use has declined, though the two categories Pass and Fail cannot be avoided by those who have to decide whether trainers should be given qualified teacher status. One of the reasons for the decline was that teaching became recognised as a multi-rather than uni-dimensional activity, and it was thought that giving a single grade of 5 out of 10, or B+ for several diverse activities might be less effective than drawing up a descriptive profile under various headings such as 'Preparation and planning', 'Class management', 'Relationships' or 'Assessment of children's work'. Nonetheless, numerical or literal gradings of the kind described above are still in use, and those employing them need to make sure they know what their grades mean and what the impact of awarding them may be. It is more common nowadays for grades to have criteria attached, as described above in the section on behaviourally anchored rating scales.

Rank Ordering

It is extremely uncommon for teachers to be rank-ordered as a result of classroom observation. Most observations are for specific purposes, such as teacher training, appraisal or research, so there is very little need to assemble a list of the best teacher seen, the second best and so on. However, where merit or bonus payments are assigned to some teachers but not others on the basis of perceived competence in the classroom, then rank ordering does sometimes take place, especially if the number of merit payments available has not been determined in advance, so that a cut-off point can be decided once the availability of bonus payments is known.

Rank ordering is almost always contentious, whether the rankings are secret or pubic, and all the same strictures apply that are cited for single quality grading: that teaching is not unidimensional, that the judgment is highly subjective, that there are many criteria that can be applied, and that it is difficult to say whether a conscientious introvert should be ranked higher than an extrovert who appears more spectacular when observed. The danger in both quality grading and rank ordering in classroom observation is that too much emphasis is placed on viewable performance and that morale suffers when the outcomes are known. Whether to use this approach in classroom observation at all is a decision that should be weighed carefully, as it is too sensitive a matter to be undertaken lightly, and that is why it has been undertaken infrequently, compared with other quantitative approaches.

Time Lines

Sometimes the observer wishes to preserve some simple information, such as how long a particular activity lasted. One way of doing this economically is to draw a line across the page representing the length of time spent on the aspect of the lesson being studied, using graph paper if necessary. An observer might, for example, be watching a foreign language lesson, and wish to know whether the teacher was talking, or a pupil, or no-one, in which case the time line might look like this:

teacher talks ——— ——— ———

pupil talks ——— ——— ———

no-one talks ———

Target Pupils

If observers wish to study individual pupils using a quantitative approach, whether this is in the form of time lines or other forms of record, it is often difficult to tag the movements or contributions of 30 different individuals who may, during a day, be engaged in hundreds of interactions with their teachers or fellow pupils. One common way round this difficulty is to choose a sub-group and concentrate on observing these alone. Frequently the observer will select a group of six pupils, three boys and three girls, chosen from high, medium and low abilities, hoping that these will be representative of the overall patterns observed in the class. Each child may be observed in turn, or alternatively a suffix may be added to any category system to show which child was involved in the particular event. Thus, if the observer wanted to know about the distribution of questions to different children, or the monitoring and assessment of their work, the letters *a, b, c, d, e* and *f* could be attached to show who was involved at the time. Samples other than six can be chosen, as can criteria other than ability or sex. An observer in a multicultural school might concentrate on perhaps four pairs of pupils from Afro-Caribbean, Asian, British and Hispanic backgrounds.

USING A SYSTEMATIC APPROACH

It is worthwhile learning to use one or two systematic category systems, simply to see how they work in practice. The following section contains details about two contrasting systems, the Flanders Interaction Analysis Category System (FIAC), and the Exeter Primary Class Management Schedule, referred to from now on simply as the 'Exeter Schedule'. The difference between an observation system that notes categories every time they occur and one that tallies each category once only, irrespective of how often the event happens, is sometimes signalled in the name used. The former is often referred to as a *category system*, the latter as a *sign system*. The difference, in simplified form, is shown below. The *category system* has recorded all instances that took place in ten minutes. The *sign system* tallies only once in each of five two minute segments. Both, therefore, represent ten minutes of classroom time. The thicker line separating the first three lesson segments from the next two in the *sign system* is there to help observers remember which segment they are recording in, as it can easily become confusing when using a long or elaborate schedule.

Category System

1. *Teacher asks questions*	//////////////	14
2. *Teacher gives command*	///	3
3. *Teacher gives praise*	////////	8
4. *Teacher uses criticism*	//	2

Sign System

1. *Teacher asks question*	/	/	/	/	/
2. *Teacher gives command*	/		/		
3. *Teacher gives praise*	/	/	/	/	/
4. *Teacher uses criticism*	/				/

There are advantages and disadvantages of each type of system. The category system shows all interactions, but the sign system allows the observer to preserve something of the flavour of each lesson segment. In the section below there is an example of each of these types. The category system, FIAC, involves coding what is happening every three seconds, whereas the Exeter schedule for studying the management of pupil behaviour in the primary school is a sign system which requires the observer to tally once only when something occurs in each of five one and a half minute segments.

The Flanders Interaction Analysis Categories (FIAC)

The work of Ned Flanders (1970), who analysed the verbal interaction between teachers and pupils, was strongly influenced by the positivist tradition in which Withall (1949) and others worked. Indeed, his ten category system FIAC is quite close in concept to Withall's four 'learner-centred' and three 'teacher-centred' categories, and the ideology pervading it was strongly influenced by interest in democracy in the classroom in the United States after the Second World War. The ten categories are as given below, and there is no scale implied by the actual numbers 1 to 10, as they are simply the numbers of each category.

(1) *Accepts feeling*: accepts and clarifies the feeling tone of the students in a non-threatening manner. Feelings may be positive or negative. Predicting and recalling feelings are included.

(2) *Praises or encourages*: praises or encourages student action or behaviour, jokes that release tension, not at the expense of another individual, nodding head or saying "uh uh?" or "go on" are included.

(3) *Accepts or uses ideas of student*: clarifying, building or developing ideas or suggestions by a student. As teacher brings more of his own ideas into play, shift to category five.

(4) *Asks question*: asking a question about content or procedure with the intent that a student answer.

(5) *Lectures*: giving facts or opinions about content or procedure; expressing his own idea; asking rhetorical questions.

(6) *Gives directions*: directions, commands or orders with which a student is expected to comply.

(7) *Criticises or justifies authority*: statements, intended to change student behaviour from non-acceptable to acceptable pattern, bawling someone out; stating why the teacher is doing what he is doing, extreme self-reference.

(8) *Student talk-response*: talk by students in response to teacher. Teacher initiates the contact or solicits student statement.

(9) *Student talk-initiation*: talk by students, which they initiate. If 'calling on' students is only to indicate who may talk next, observer must decide whether student wanted to talk. If he did, use this category.

(10) *Silence or confusion*: pauses, short periods of silence and periods of confusion in which communication cannot be understood by the observer.

The reason that FIAC is described here is not because it is the best system, indeed there have been many refinements and modifications of it, but rather because it is an example of a simple category system that has been widely used in its original or modified form in teacher training, lesson analysis and research. It illustrates very well the strengths and weaknesses of quantitative approaches. The FIAC system is not difficult to learn or apply, though tallying every three seconds becomes quite demanding and an observer can become fatigued after about half an hour, so it is advisable to observe for 20 to 30 minutes at a time, with a gap in between. Observers learn to use the ten categories and then check the level of agreement between each other.

Using FIAC in the classroom involves the following steps:

(1) The observer has a data recording sheet with 20 squares available for each minute of time. Every three seconds the category number is recorded (e.g. 4 for a teacher question, 8 for a pupil reply) which best describes what is taking place.

(2) The observer records *across* the record sheet so that each line represents one minute of classroom time.

(3) Separate 'episodes', such as 'setting up', 'monitoring pupil work' or 'summary', can be identified in the margin, so that it is clear later what kind of interaction occurred during various kinds of activity.

(4) A stop watch, the second hand of a wristwatch, or even a specially designed pocket timer which gives a bleep to an earpiece, can be used to remind the observer to record a category every three seconds.

Let us take a simple exchange which will show how the system works in practice:

		Category tallied
Teacher	Look at the list of cities on the blackboard.	*6* (command)
	Which do you think is the one nearest here?	*4* (question)
	(three second pause)	*10* (silence)
Pupil	It's either Bristol or Birmingham.	*8* (solicited pupil talk)

It is worth looking at some of the Flanders categories in a little more detail:

Category 1

Accepting or clarifying feelings is a relatively infrequent category that occurs more often in lessons such as English than science and more often with younger pupils than older.

Category 2

One weakness of the FIAC system is that it does not distinguish between cursory praise ("Good", "Fine" "Right") which may be as regular and frequent as raindrops, and enthusiastic or effusive praise, such as, "That's a really good answer Paul, well done". Flanders suggests ignoring what he calls 'merely verbal habits' like "OK" or a cursory "Right" or "Yes", and the same would apply to category 3.

Category 3

Accepting and clarifying pupils' ideas is also relatively infrequent, though more common than category 1. Some teachers use it extensively, however, to weave children's answers into the

FIAC DATA SHEET

School ——————————— Teacher ———————————

Class ——————————— Subjective/topic ———————————

Date ——————————— Observer ———————————

TALLY ACROSS

01																				
02																				
03																				
04																				
05																				
06																				
07																				
08																				
09																				
10																				
11																				
12																				
13																				
14																				
15																				
16																				
17																				
18																				
19																				
20																				
21																				
22																				
23																				
24																				
25																				
26																				
27																				
28																				
29																				
30																				

The sequence recorded on the data sheet should, therefore, be *6-4-10-8*.

lesson: "Now, Sally told us that magnets pick things up, and John said that they didn't attract all metals, so can anyone tell me what exactly magnets do pick up?" This would be a good example of the sequence 3-4, acceptance of pupil ideas, followed by a question.

Category 4

Many other schedules which have built on FIAC have created a set of different categories of question, such as:

4a Question involving recall of factual data

4b Question requiring pupil to group or classify information

4c Question involving evaluation

4d Question involving pupils' imagination

The observer also has to remember to code questions which are really commands, like 'Andrea, would you please hand these papers out?" as category 6, not category 4, for even though the command is expressed in question form, it is really an order with which the pupil is expected to comply. As with all category systems the observers using them must clarify first what conventions they will employ, and then stick to them.

Category 5

One weakness of FIAC is that it does not make any distinctions between the many kinds of information that can be given. For example, all the following would simply be coded as category 5, despite their immense differences:

"An orbiting body possesses angular momentum"
"Ich heisse Herr Splutzenheimer"
"Insects have seven legs"

Other category systems often distinguish between information that is factually correct or incorrect, based on opinions or facts, or which incorporates different levels or types of thinking.

Category 6

Commands are rare in some lessons, but frequent in others, especially in subjects like physical education lessons where, in certain teaching modes, teachers may be very directive. Questions that are disguised commands, "Would you please . . .", are coded 6.

Category 7

As with praise, category 2, the use of criticism varies considerably amongst teachers. Some observers attach a pupil code number to identify to whom the praise or criticism is addressed, so that 7c would be criticism addressed to pupil C and 2f would be praise given to pupil F. This then allows a profile of the targets of praise and criticism to be assembled. If six target pupils were observed, three boys and three girls, then the resulting profiles of praise and criticism might appear as follows:

	Praise (category 2)	*Criticism (category 7)*
Alison	11	0
June	2	1
Tracy	5	1
Alan	8	0
Paul	1	5
Simon	3	2

Examples of disguised criticism need to be looked for, especially if the tone of voice emphasises the message. The statement: "That's a wonderful answer, the mark of a true genius" would be praise (2) if genuine, but criticism (7) if intended as a sarcastic reply to an incorrect answer.

Categories 8 and 9

Many other category systems have an extensive range of possibilities for pupil talk, but FIAC offers only two. The observer needs to look out for a shift from 8 to 9 when the pupil goes beyond the immediate solicited reply:

Teacher What was the weather like? (4)

Pupil It was pretty bad. (8)

But I don't think the weather matters when you're on holiday. (9)

Category 10

This catch-all category is one of the weakest features of FIAC, which was not really designed either for detailed analysis of pupil talk, or for non-verbal aspects of classroom interaction. Many other systems sub-divide this category into 'noise', 'confusion', 'complete silence', or whatever else seems appropriate, sometimes using subscripts like 10a, 10b, 10c, 10d and so on.

The following exchange shows how FIAC would be used to code the events that occur. The categories are shown in brackets after each statement.

Teacher:	So can anyone give me an example of an insect? Richard?	(4)
Pupil 1:	I know, a spider.	(8)
Pupil 2:	A spider's not an insect.	(9)
Teacher:	Good, that's quite right Jacky. Er . . .	(2)
	(Teacher distracted)	(10)
Teacher:	It's not an insect, because it's got the wrong number of legs.	(5)
	It should have six legs, not eight.	(5)
Pupil 3:	And it's got three parts to its body.	(9)
Teacher:	That's right, Andrew, its body is in three parts,	(3)
	and the middle bit has quite a hard name—the thorax.	(5)

The sequence of exchanges has ten entries into the data sheet and lasts about half a minute. The observer's list of tallies would look like this:

01	4	8	9	2	10	5	5	9	3	5										
02																				

Ned Flanders devised a neat two-dimensional display for FIAC data which preserves the sequence of events in pairs, so that, in the series of codings given above, the first two events, question followed by answer, 4-8, would constitute the first pair. The display consists of a matrix, 10 × 10, giving a 100 little squares, or 'cells'. Each pair of events is tallied in one of the cells, so that the sequence *question—answer—praise* which is coded *4–8–2*, is entered according to the following procedures. The first pair is *question* (4) followed by *solicited answer* (8), so a tick is put into the 4–8 cell (counting *down* 4, *across* 8). But the pupil's answer is also the first event of the next pair, *solicited answer* (8) followed by *praise* (2), so the next tally is entered into the 8–2 cell (*down*

8, across 2). The full 30 second sequence of ten tallies recorded above in the lesson on the characteristics of insects, *4 - 8 - 9 - 2 - 10 - 5 - 5 - 9 - 3 - 5,* would look like this when entered in the 10 × 10 FIAC matrix:

	1	2	3	4	5	6	7	8	9	10
1										
2										/
3					/					
4								/		
5					/				/	
6										
7										
8									/	
9		/	/							
10					/					

The display of classroom interaction in this form allows the teacher or observer to see not only how much of the lesson was talk by the pupil or the teacher, but also quite a bit about the nature of the talk. For example, a programmed learning format consisting of *information - question - answer - praise - next piece of information, etc.* would show sequences like *5 - 4 - 8 - 2 - 5 - 4 - 8 - 2 - 5 etc.*, producing a build-up of tallies in the 5-4, 4-8, 8-2 and 2-5 cells. The 8-7 and 9-7 cells record pupil contributions which resulted in teacher criticism, and looking along rows 8 and 9 shows how the teacher responded to pupil talk, perhaps with praise (8-2, 9-2), acceptance or clarification (8-3, 9-3), an immediate question (8-4, 9-4), or further information (8-5, 9-5). A great deal of other information is also revealed, but as in the case of any quantitative approach, a considerable amount is also lost with such reductions, so care must be exercised, as there are no omni-purpose 'good' or 'bad' patterns.

ACTIVITY 3.2

Analyse the short extracts below using the FIAC system. The text has been split up into short sections, so enter a tally at the end of each line. As a reminder here is a short-hand version of the FIAC categories:

Teacher Talk

(1) accepts feelings

(2) praise

(3) accepts ideas

(4) question

(5) lecture

(6) command

(7) criticism

Pupil Talk

(8) solicited

(9) unsolicited

(10) silence etc.

Real classroom interaction is craggy, rather than clear cut and unambiguous, so not every statement lasts exactly three seconds. Flanders recommends that the *predominant* activity should be recorded if two events happen in the same three second segment, but he also suggests that both might be recorded where they appear to be of roughly equal prominence, such as a short answer and brief praise. This illustrates the difficulty of being precise, and underlies once more the need for caution with quantitative methods.

EXTRACT 1

Category

Teacher : What happens to your colour (blue) when you add yellow to it?

Pupil 1 : It goes dark green.

Teacher : How many colours have you got here?

They're all green, but they're different, aren't they?

Pupil 2 : I've got two greens now.

Teacher	:	So you have. What did you add to it? Blue or white? What happens when you add white to it?
Pupil 2	:	Light.
Teacher	:	It's a light green, that's right. (To another pupil) That's a super green, how did you make that one?
Pupil 3	:	Yellow and dark green.
Teacher	:	That's like a spring green, isn't it, very bright. . . Lovely. . . Dip your brush in there, make it clean and then take some more powder. Wipe it on the side, then pick up more powder.

EXTRACT 2

Category

Pupil 1	:	Miss, Brian's taken my ruler.
Teacher	:	Brian, have you taken Alan's ruler?
Pupil 2	:	He took my pen first, Miss. I just took his ruler to get my pen back, he started it.
Pupil 1	:	No I didn't, you liar.
Teacher	:	Stop it, both of you. I'm fed up of your stupid behaviour, so will you go over there and sit by Debbie and Alan you can sit next to my desk. (six seconds of pupils moving) Now, let's get back to our topic. Who can tell me something else about levers?

EXTRACT 3

Category

Teacher	:	Is a woodlouse an insect?
Pupil 1	:	Yes.
Teacher	:	Does it look like an insect?
Pupil 1	:	Sort of.
Teacher	:	What about its three body parts? Can you find the head, thorax and abdomen?
Pupil 1	:	I can't find the thorax and abdomen.
Pupil 2	:	It looks like it's got lots of little body parts.
Teacher	:	Ah! How many legs has it got?
Pupil 2	:	More than six.
Teacher	:	More than six, and lots of body parts. Is it an insect?
Pupil 1	:	It can't be.

You probably felt some occasional uncertainty about the use of category 2 or 3, for example when the teacher says "Lovely", leaving the observer uncertain whether to record it as praise, which it is, or acceptance of a pupil's idea, which it also is. Another difficulty may have been the handling of repetition of answers, which may be seen as category 3 if the idea is genuinely accepted, but again FIAC does not distinguish clearly between mechanical repetition of what has just been said and genuine acceptance, enhancement or clarification. Perhaps in Extract 3 you were uncertain when to use command (6) and criticism (7).

Nonetheless, despite the problems, trained observers will agree with each other about category assignment over 80 to 90 per cent of events. That still, however, leaves some 15 per cent or so of disagreement, and it is often over the assignment of a 2 or a 3, an 8 or a 9, that observes disagree. The Flanders system is easiest to use during whole class teaching or when the interactions are public. It is more difficult, though not impossible, to apply when the teacher is working with individuals or small groups, and it is usual to code the teacher's interactions with the individuals concerned, a process greatly helped if a radio microphone is available, or if the observer can stay fairly near the teacher without being too intrusive.

The Exeter Schedule

The schedule devised at Exeter University during the Leverhulme Primary Project for observing how teachers manage pupils' behaviour (Wragg, 1993a) is an example of a sign system. There are two parts to it: the first deals with pupils' misbehaviour and how the teacher does or does not respond to it, the second consists of an individual pupil study which allows the observer to build up a profile of how involved in the task children appear to be, and whether or not they misbehave.

The full schedule would be too long to reproduce in its entirety, so abbreviated sections are described below. It consists of a set of categories which the observer ticks at the end of each one and a half minute period. Once trained, observers need about 30 to 40 seconds to complete the checking of categories for that segment. The blocks of segments are in sets of five with a double line splitting the first three segments from the other two. The observer tallies *down* the page. One section of the schedule deals with different types of pupil misbehaviour. A completed first segment, filled in by the observer after the first one and a half minute of observation, on a selection of categories (the schedule below is abbreviated for convenience) would look like this:

Type of misbehaviour

Noisy or illicit talk

Inappropriate movement

Inappropriate use of materials

Damage to materials/equipment

Taking something without permission

Physical aggression to another pupil

Defiance of teacher

Refusal to move

/				
/				
/				
/				

The above represents a lesson segment in which there was noise or illicit chatter, inappropriate movement, someone took something from another pupil without permission, and then defied the teacher.

Sometimes the observer will tick only one category in a section during each segment of the lesson. For example, the first part of the schedule, which records the type of activity, shows how this works. The observer has to decide the predominant type of activity during the segment, which might have been pupil-teacher interaction, or the pupils might have worked alone or in groups with the teacher monitoring. In each one and a half minute segment only one choice is ticked. The illustration below shows the box ticked in each of five successive lesson segments:

Activity					
Teacher solo	\				
Teacher-pupil interaction		\	\		
Pupils working, teacher monitoring					\
Pupils working, teacher not monitoring					
Transition without movement				\	
Transition with movement					

In the first segment the teacher was talking to the whole class, in the second and third there was teacher-pupil interaction, in the fourth segment a changeover took place and the children began to work in their groups, so 'transition without movement' is recorded, and in the fifth segment the teacher walked round monitoring pupils' work.

Other sections of the Exeter schedule cover pupil misbehaviour, and record whether there were no pupils misbehaving, one pupil only, two to four pupils, or five or more. If misbehaviour does occur, then the observer goes on to code teacher response, whether it was to the whole class, a small group or an individual, and whether it occurred before or after escalation. There follow a set of categories describing the teacher's response, including the following:

Teacher's Response					
Order to cease					
Pupil named					
Reprimand					
Involve pupils in work					
Proximity (going over to pupils)					
Touch					
Humour					
Praise/encouragement					

The next part of the schedule records pupil responses, whether they fell silent, altercated or protested, whether the misbehaviour ceased, lessened, remained the same or increased. The observer ticks each category when it occurs, sometimes checking several, sometimes choosing one from a set of options. After several lesson segments have been observed in this way, the observer can build up a profile of the lesson, or of several lessons.

The first section of the Exeter schedule uses a checklist approach to record classroom events. In order to supplement this picture with information about individual children, therefore, the second part of the schedule requires the observer to study every single pupil in the class one by one. For this exercise a different kind of data sheet is required, with spaces for each individual child. The observer must concentrate on one pupil for

20 seconds before moving on to the next child and eventually covering every pupil in the class this way. In each case the observer makes two decisions: whether the pupil is high, medium or low, in terms of application to the task in hand, and whether the child is not misbehaving, or is mildly or seriously deviant during the period of abbreviation. Below is a data sheet for six pupils, based on a 20 second observation period. In this case the criteria for deciding the involvement level would be the number of seconds during the observation that the child appeared to be engaged in the task: 'low' would be 0 to 6 seconds, 'medium' 7 to 13, and 'high' 14 to 20 seconds. Misbehaviour would be coded either as 'none', or as 'mild' if it included minor matters such as

	Involvement level			Deviancy level		
Pupil	low	medium	high	none	mild	serious
01	/			/		
02			/	/		
03		/			/	
04		/		/		
05			/	/		
06	/					/

noisy or illicit chatter, and 'serious' if physical aggression, threat to the teacher or damage to property were noted. All these conventions have to be agreed in advance by the observers.

This schedule would show that pupil 1 did not appear to be involved in the task, but was not misbehaving, whereas pupil 6 was not involved in his work, but was engaging in more serious misbehaviour. Although highly engaged pupils do not usually misbehave, it is possible to see almost any combination in the two parts of the observation schedule. The observer can study each individual child in the class several times in rotation and build up a profile of the behaviour and application of both the individual and the whole class. Frequently the decision about involvement or deviancy is self-evident, but there are particular problems when pupils are not misbehaving but simply sitting quietly. They might be reflecting on their work or day-dreaming, it is sometimes impossible to tell with any precision. That is why such quantitative measures as are described in this chapter are useful, but should be regarded as rough and ready, rather than precise measure, and should certainly be related to other kinds of information when it comes to interpretation and analysis.

To conclude this chapter consider the following activity:

ACTIVITY 3.3

Read the transcript below and note down some *quantitative* information that might be of interest. At the end of it are a few suggestions.

Teacher : Can you see anything that attracts you about the Island?
Anywhere you'd like to visit, David?
Pupil 1 : Castle Point.
Teacher : Why would you like to go there?
Pupil 1 : It's exciting.
Teacher : Yes, it's exciting.
Have you found anywhere you'd like to go, Emma?
Pupil 2 : I think . . .
Teacher : No, it's Emma's turn. I'd like to hear what Emma has to say.
Pupil 3 : Eastern Moors. There's a creature . . . it's . . . it's . . .
Teacher : There's something up there that Emma's found.
What has she found coming out of the sea?
Pupil 4 : A monster.
Teacher : Yes, it could be.
What's coming out of his hand?
Pupil 2 : Lightning.
Teacher : What else has he got coming out of him?
Pupil 2 : Rain.
Teacher : Rain and thunder,
so it's almost as if he's in control of the . . . ?
Pupil 2 : Weather.
Teacher : The weather, yes, I think so . . .
What would be a good word to describe Darkling Forest?
Pupil 2 : Spooky and creepy.
Teacher : Better than 'spooky and creepy'?
Pupil 1 : Strange and weird.

Teacher : Yes, strange and weird.
How about a word beginning with two e's?
Do you know it?

Pupil 1 : Eerie.

Teacher : Yes. What does 'eerie' mean?

Pupil 1 : Scary.

Using FIAC this might come out as *4 – 4 – 8 – 4 – 8 – 3 – 4 – 9* (different pupil answers)–*7* ("No, it's Emma's turn" is a reprimand) – *8 – 3 – 4 – 8 – 3* (though "it could be" is a little grudging) – *4 – 8 – 4 – 8 – 3* (teacher accepts "rain" and enhances it) – *4 – 8 – 3 – 4 – 8 – 4* (not 3, as the teacher asks for something better) – *8 – 3 – 4 – 4 – 8 – 4* (possibly with an extra 3 thrown in, as the teacher accepts the word offered) – *8*. In addition to this kind of analysis, however, there are many other quantitative statements that could be made about the exchange, if one had all the necessary information, such as:

Pupils participating	4	
Teacher's questions	12	
Open questions	7	(approximately)
Closed questions	5	(approximately)
Statements of approval	5	
Statements of disapproval	2	
Reprimands	1	
Length of episode	68	seconds
Total number of words uttered	164	
Words spoken by teacher	138	
Words spoken by pupils	26	
Percentage teacher talk	84	per cent
Percentage pupil talk	16	per cent
Length of pauses	19	seconds
Length of talk	49	seconds
Number of teacher utterances	12	
Number of pupil utterances	12	

Percentage of talk	72 per cent
Percentage of non-talk (pauses etc.)	28 per cent
Average length of each teacher utterance	11.5 words
Average length of each pupil utterance	2.17 words
Average length of each pause between teacher and pupil talk	0.83 seconds
Number of key concepts	4

(1) Where to visit

(2) Why place attracts

(3) The nature of the creature

(4) The nature of the forest

There are, therefore, numerous ways in which observers can quantify what happens in the classroom, but there are also very important qualitative aspects of the lesson extract above, like gesture, factual accuracy, voice, body language, classroom climate, use of learning aids, understandings, misunderstandings, interpretations, meanings, inferences and numerous others.

4

The Use of Qualitative Methods

Just as there are many ways of quantifying what happens in the classroom, so too there are numerous approaches which try to probe beneath the surface of events, to elicit the meanings sometimes deeply buried, the interpretations and explanations, significance and impact of classroom life. Trying to explain the meaning of a particular incident in a classroom to an intelligent Martian would not be straightforward, as explanations are sometimes easiest when a great deal can be taken for granted, or when there is a background of shared assumptions.

The danger with the taken-for-granted, however, is first of all that explanations are intensely subjective, and second that subjectivity can become compounded, with judgment and assertion repeated and reinforced until they become reified. When a football referee fails to give a penalty kick to the home team, the immediate reaction of 30,000 supporters is to scream abuse, question his eyesight, and even his parentage, and convince themselves that he is at best biased, at worst a complete villain, probably bribed by the opposition. For some people the experience of seeing the video replay and watching in slow motion the unambiguous evidence that he was actually correct in his decision will make little difference. We often interpret events as we wish to see them, not as they are. There can be several filters along the route, as information about an event speeds towards the human brain. Good qualitative analysis of classroom behaviour involves rigorous scrutiny of these barriers to accurate perception.

I once read a dissertation based on several observations of primary classes. Throughout the whole of the lengthy account the writer used the term 'good primary practice', over and over again, without once attempting to define what it was. There was an assumption that the whole community must surely share her view of what was desirable and effective, and there was no need for critical analysis. Yet Ronald King (1978) in his study of infant classrooms *All Things Bright and Beautiful?* spent 600 hours observing lessons and, while he saw a number of features common to more than one classroom, he did not label these 'good primary practice'. Indeed, terms like 'good' and 'effective', though regularly used in everyday conversation, have to be used with care. Classroom observers seen to have a single fixed stereotype of what is 'good' may be met with scorn or contempt, if their views are out of harmony with those of the teacher being observed, or with fear and apprehension if they are thought to be in a position of power and influence.

Observers who use qualitative methods are of many kinds. Most informal and semi-formal observations of lessons, such as teachers sitting in on each other's classes, the supervision of student teachers, visitors to schools who have come to 'watch some teaching', tend to adopt qualitative rather than quantitative approaches. Many observers simply form impressions about the generalities of classroom life: whether pupils appear to be busy; if the teacher seems to know her subject or topic, be in charge; whether the children are behaving well or badly; what is displayed on classroom walls. These perceptions are simply filtered, absorbed, occasionally discussed, sometimes written down, depending on the circumstances. In more formal settings an appraiser might use a qualitative approach, perhaps making notes and then discussing these with the teacher being appraised. Another possibility is that a trainee teacher or a researcher will be observing a lesson with a specific brief, and therefore be compiling notes for a report or action project.

Some observers, like Sara Delamont (1976) who used a mixture of methods, are influenced by George Mead, the American philosopher and social psychologist who taught at Chicago University in the early part of the twentieth century. Mead advocated the study of the symbols that are part of interaction between people, that is their language, appearanc and gesture. This school of thought is sometimes called 'symbolic interactionism', and even those who have not read the seminal texts, like Mead's *Mind, Self and Society* (1934) are often, albeit unwittingly or at second hand, following some of its precepts. *Participant observation,* whereby the observer joins in activities and talks to the other people involved, is a role frequently played not only by researchers studying an institution as outsiders, but by teachers or other insiders looking at the world in which they work.

By contrast, other classroom observers might be influenced by a particular philosophy or school of thought. Those taking a Marxist perspective, for example, like Sharp and Green (1975) who looked at an infants' school in a working class area, will see the classroom as part of a wider social context. Their conclusion that teachers act as agents of social control on behalf of a capitalist society will to some extent be pre-determined by their initial perspective, just as was that of the teacher who sought to confirm her notion of 'good primary practice'. A bell ringing at the end of a lesson may be seen as the normal signal to move on to the next subject by a secondary teacher observing a colleague, but by a Marxist observer as an illustration of the way in which schools prepare working class pupils for obedience to orders in the factory production line. No doubt a bell manufacturer would be concentrating on the penetration of its sound.

In qualitative analysis it is not a pre-requisite that the observer should be a central part of the school. Although some observers wish to become, or already are, enmeshed in classroom life, others working is a similar tradition try to keep their distance. The study by King (1978) of infant school classrooms was a *non-participant* observation. He was strongly influenced by the German sociologist Max Weber (1947), whose action theory put forward the notion that the subjective meanings attached to events by individuals are inseparable from social structure. This view requires the classroom observer to understand and explain how teachers act, usually by first observing and then interviewing. Teaching is such a rapidly moving set of activities that the way teachers, and for that matter pupils, see and interpret what happens is often neglected. Observations and interviews allow the taken-for-granted to be explored in greater detail.

In a later account of what he actually did, King describes how this approach worked in practice. He collected several notebooks of jottings about what happened in the lesson he observed, but did not wish to become part of the teaching staff, though he was an experienced secondary school teacher, a stance which sometimes caused difficulties, especially with young pupils' natural tendency to want to talk to anyone visiting the classroom:

> I lacked the professional competences. I was too old to fit either the student teacher category . . . or become an 'honorary pupil'. . . .In my relationship with teachers I drew upon the social, qualities of polite acquaintance between middle class men and women . . . . Although I felt I was drawing on the anthropological tradition, I was not concerned with the whole way of life of my subjects, which ethnography usually implies. My interest in the teachers was as teachers. . . . I did allow myself to be approached by children to begin with, but I soon found that they treated me as a teacher-surrogate as they did other non-teacher adults, showing pictures, asking me spellings. . . . I politely refused requests for help, referring the child to the teacher, and met requests for approval only with smiles. To begin with I kept standing so that physical height maintained social distance. Most importantly I avoided eye contact; if you do not look, you will not be seen. These measures led to my being, for the most part, ignored by the children. . . . My intended relationship with the teacher was that of an interested, non-judgmental observer.
>
> (King, 1984)

KEY CONCEPTS AND INFLUENCES

In the literature on qualitative research there are numerous overlapping concepts, some of which have been described above. A researcher engaging in a long-term classroom observation project might be deeply interested in the intellectual basis of and justification for each of these philosophies or concerns. Someone simply observing lesson out of interest, or appraising a fellow teacher's classroom 'performance', on the other hand, may have little interest in what may appear somewhat arcane distinctions between different philosophies and vantage points. Yet even those who do not wish to read extensively about ideologies, philosophies or traditions will still need to consider certain issues, such as whether they should be a participant or a non-participant observer. If you are observing in an infants' school classroom and a child asks you how to spell a word, you need to decide that you will either give the answer, or, as King did, refer the child to the teacher. Whether this is done purely on intuition, on the basis of reasoned argument or under the influence of Weber, is a matter of personal taste.

Bryman (1988) has summarised the main influences on qualitative research as coming under five headings: phenomenology, symbolic interactionism, '*verstehen*', naturalism and ethogenics. These are not the only key terms and concepts, but some of their relevance to classroom observation and the issues they raise are summarised below.

Phenomenology

This is one of a number of generic terms used to embrace those people who concentrate on how we interpret our world, the phenomena that surround us. It rejects the quantitative approach on the grounds that this imposes the observer's rational pre-suppositions on to events in a systematic way, rather than seeing them through the eyes of those being observed. Its beliefs were formulated by the German philosopher Edmund Husserl in the early part of the twentieth century and have been influential on psychologists of the *Gestalt* school, who believe that the whole is greater than the sum of its parts, and on literary figures such as Jean-Paul Sartre.

Various methods of observation and enquiry are used and related traditions, like *ethnomethodology*, the study of how people perceive and make sense of their daily routines, and *symbolic interactionism* (see below), are often subsumed under the broad heading of 'phenomenology'. So far as classroom observation is concerned it will often involve making notes about classroom events and interviewing teachers and pupils to see what constructs and interpretations emerge when they talk about the classroom. Often extensive analysis of lesson and interview transcripts is involved.

The major benefit of this type of observation is that it does draw on the richness of individuals' personal insights. Its drawback is that, by putting a premium on the subjective, it may simply report personal fantasies, which, important though they may be, are often at variance with actuality. For example, a teacher of 6 year olds may be convinced she has heard almost every child read every day. The reality might be that she hears, on average, a third to a half of the class and that on only two days in a month did she actually hear everyone. Her belief is important, as is the fact that it is verifiably untrue, but her subjective answer is only one part of a larger story, a single snapshot taken through a lens covered by filters.

Symbolic Interactionism

The accounts of symbolic interactionism vary from those that see it as virtually the same as phenomenology, to those that make significant distinctions between the two. Symbolic interactionism has a strong focus on the self, especially on the symbols like language and gesture that we employ when engaging in interaction with others. Our definition and assessment of how our actions will be perceived by others is influential on how we behave. A classroom observer might, therefore, watch lessons and interview teachers and pupils looking at how both believe their actions are interpreted by others. This could include fellow teachers, fellow pupils, or teachers' interpretations of pupils' actions and *vice versa*.

Verstehen

The verb *verstehen* simply means 'to understand' in German. Max Weber, the German sociologist, used the term to describe both the way in which a particular act is understood and the explanation that goes with it. In terms of watching teachers and pupils the observer might seek to recognise not only that the teacher would use a different voice to convey various messages, but whether that voice was interpreted as signalling impatience, anger, expectation or humour, and what produced these reactions. King (1978) was influenced both by Weber and by Schutz (1972) who amplified Weber's notion by talking about 'because' motives (retrospective explanation of why something happened) and 'in order to' motives (explaining the intent behind an action). King described a number of voices that infant teachers used to establish and maintain social control. They transmitted such messages as 'now we are going to do something exciting', 'don't be silly', 'I am being very patient with you', 'Oh never mind, let's not have a fuss', a slightly aggrieved, sad voice, and a no-nonsense 'do as I say'.

Naturalism

The study of classrooms in what are often termed 'naturalistic' settings means that the observer tries to see life as it really is. That rules out experiments, for example, whereby the teacher might be asked to try out a particular method of working to see what the consequences appear to be. The study in the Leverhulme Primary Project (Wragg, 1993a) in which teachers were given ten minutes to explain the topic 'insects' to small groups of 8 and 9 year old children would be disregarded, even though it was conducted in teachers' own classrooms, on the grounds that it was done partially under laboratory conditions, rather than being in a 100 per cent natural setting. Quantitative methods are also eschewed completely, as they are seen to be further external intrusions into the natural environment, and therefore likely to distort.

One major criticism of naturalism is that it can appear to take no moral stance and condone whatever happens. For example, in a study of classroom misbehaviour the observer may well appear to empathise with the deviants. This is not as controversial as other naturalistic observers looking at violent criminals or drug dealers, where there is an even stronger expectation that the observer will have a personal moral slant towards condemnation rather than empathy. Supporters of naturalism counter this by arguing that there is already too quick a tendency to condemn something like deviance, without looking at how and why it happens. In classroom terms, the 'deviant' may sometimes be the victim; for example, the child who appears to snatch a piece of equipment may have been robbed of his turn on it by others and be desperate to complete his assignment, rather than an embryo criminal. Empathising with the deviant is not exactly new. The nineteenth-century novelist Samuel Butler described an imaginary world in which the sick and unhealthy were punished, and criminals were sent to hospital, in his novel *Erewhon,* though supporters of naturalism might not like the implication that crime is a pathological condition.

Ethogenics

This is an approach to such matters as classroom disruption based on an attempt to study the beliefs which lie beneath sequences of actions. Bryman (1988) described it as follow:

> A central feature of the ethogenic approach is the understanding of episodes in social life. 'Episodes' are sequences of interlocking acts by individuals. It is the task of ethogenics to elucidate the underlying structures of such episodes by investigating the meanings actors bring to the constituent acts. . . . The understanding and analysis of such phenomena facilitate the construction of theories about the resources upon which actors draw when acting.

Although ethogenics is another variant of the view that renounces quantitative methodology, its adherents support the notion of taking a scientific approach to classroom observation and the understanding of what happens there. It simply rejects positivists' use of quantities of achieve scientific rigour, favouring an alternative form which seeks to *elicit* underlying structure by careful qualitative analysis of sequences of events, rather than impose it by pre-determined schedules and other instruments of observation.

All of these approaches and views of the world in general and social interaction in particular have a great deal in common. Even classroom observers who have no intention of reading a single book would do well to recognise some of the precepts on which they are founded. For example, someone asked to carry out an appraisal of a teacher may feel that the notions described above are irrelevant to the particular task in hand, or even that they are simply abstruse sociological theories. Yet failure to appreciate how the teacher may perceive appraisal, or to understand what may be the significance of events in the classroom when the teacher is being observed, would make the appraisal a very superficial and insensitive exercise.

QUALITY AND EFFECTIVENESS

One of the most frequent outcomes of classroom observation is that the observer is expected to provide, or is asked for, a qualitative appraisal of the teacher's competence, rather than a literal grade or a mark out of ten. Some variation of "Was that OK?" must be one of the most frequent opening remarks by a student or experienced teacher after a lesson in which an observer has been present. It is a natural reaction, after being observed, to wonder how the observer regarded what took place and to seek reassurance or feedback, partly because so few such mirrors are available to teachers.

Judging the quality or effectiveness of what happens in a classroom is not, however, a simple or unidimensional matter. "Fine", "OK by me" or "Carry on the good work" may be the sort of remark that is acceptable in potentially strained circumstances, but serious attempts to watch lessons and then draw out evaluations of quality need some thought. Mostly when we talk about a 'good' teacher, an 'effective' strategy or a 'bad' lesson, we are referring to our own subjective perception. Sometimes we may quote what appears to be external evidence: that several children were seen to be misbehaving; that the teacher made a number of demonstrably inaccurate statements about verifiable factual matters, like classifying a worm as an insect; that the quality of pupils' written work was highly praised by assessors who read it, not just by the teacher; that when the bell went several children carried on working.

The judgment of one observer, both about teaching quality and the evidence for it, might be endorsed by others, but it can also happen that disagreements occur. I once showed a videotape of a student teacher's lesson to 35 teacher trainers (Wragg, 1974). The marks ranged from D, which at the time was a near failure grade, to B+, a near distinction, and comments varied from condemnation of what some observers saw as lack of structure, to praise for what others regarded as a sensitive response to individual children. In the nineteenth century, teacher training institutions were called 'normal schools', on the grounds that there was a single approved 'norm' to which teachers were expected to conform. It led Dickens to describe M'Choakumchild in *Hard Times* as being like 'some one hundred and forty schoolmasters . . . turned at the same time in the same factory, like so many pianoforte legs'.

Judgment about professional competence nowadays, when a wider range of teaching styles is accepted than might have formerly been the case, is often founded on different criteria. Those who prefer quantitative approaches might look at test scores obtained by children, but others operating to a different agenda might appraise what they see as the quality of learning taking place, without necessarily measuring it. A field like music is an interesting example to consider. If scores on tests alone were considered, then a teacher whose class could all define sonata form, or translate the word *andante*, might be highly esteemed. Longer term aspirations, like whether the teacher is laying the foundations for lifelong enjoyment of music, are less easily measured. Observers can find, therefore, that they are either ignoring such matters, or having to make an intelligent guess about them on the basis of what they see in the classroom.

Criteria which inform judgment about teaching quality or effectiveness can be grouped under several headings. These include the following:

Preparation and Planning

Particularly in the training phase, but also at later stages, preparation and planning are often given particular prominence and supervisors of students, or heads and senior teachers, will scrutinise some of the artefacts connected with preparation, like work schemes, lesson plans, and the extent to which assessment and monitoring of pupils' work and progress have taken place not only after a lesson, but before it. It is a widely held assumption that pre-planning is an important part of successful teaching, and sometimes teachers can be judged more on the artefacts than the lessons.

Yet there are teachers who claim to be successful at teaching intuitively and responsively, rather than on the basis of a carefully pre-determined plan. This claim may simply mean, however, that they do not operate to a written plan and that their actions are determined by deep, rather than surface, structures. For example, a teacher who regularly makes jokes during a lesson is not operating to a written plan, because many jokes arise spontaneously from unpredicted situations. It is more likely that deep in the teacher's sub-conscious belief system is a conviction that humour can reduce tension and maintain or arouse interest.

Meticulous preparation in itself does not ensure that learning will take place, but the observer can nevertheless focus on an important aspect of the quality of classroom life, namely the extent to which the teacher's original intentions or plans are actually implemented. This focus of concern can apply both in lessons that are tightly structured and presented and in those that are not. Some teachers believe that children should have a considerable say in what happens in lessons and that assignments, procedures and activities should be negotiated, not imposed. Observers can provide valuable feedback about whether or not this aspiration was translated into action. Such feedback can be offered with or without advice about the appropriateness of the pre-planning or whether keeping to or modifying the original plan was sensible.

Process

The judgments that observers with different perspectives make about classroom processes are also of interest when the indicators of quality and effectiveness are under review. Some observers enter the classroom with a clear idea of what processes they favour or dislike. Their personal reaction to a lesson might include such diverging expectations and tastes as the pairs of polar opposites listed below:

Too much noise — *Not enough discussion amongst pupils*

Teacher clearly in charge — *Teacher not too authoritarian*

Good lesson pace — *Not enough time to reflect*

Teacher should tell — *Pupils should find out*

One important aspect of the observer's personal view of quality or effectiveness is his or her role, standing and relationships with the person teaching the lesson. Sometimes the relationship is clearly defined. Head teachers watching a newly arrived colleague, or supervising tutors or teachers observing a trainee, however, they may handle the situation or seek to disguise it, are inescapably locked into a superior-subordinate relationship. Therefore, judgments about quality are sometimes expected, or, if not offered directly, inferred. The remark "I saw some pupils who were not listening to the story" would have a different impact if offered by (a) a tutor to a student on final teaching practice, or (b) a student to an experienced teacher whose lesson she has observed as part of her assignment. The actual or perceived power relationship between observer and observed is not just a sociological concept, but rather a reality that needs to be recognised.

Qualitative subjective judgment can be sharply or loosely focused. During the Teacher Education Project (Wragg, 1984) in which hundreds of lessons in secondary schools were analysed, we began our class management studies by asking teachers who supervised students what they understood by 'effective' class management. Several phrases emerged on numerous occasions, including 'having a firm grip', 'keeping pupils busy' and 'being in charge'. There was often an assumption that everyone shared the same understanding of these phrases, yet when we moved from interviews to asking people to collect and record 'critical events', a procedure described later in this chapter which involves looking for classroom events that illustrate whatever the observer is studying, there was often disagreement between supervisors.

One example illustrates this well. A student teacher, supervised by two different people, was regarded by the first of these as insensitive in his manner towards pupils. This emerged from interview and from the critical events recorded. However, the second supervisor recorded one critical event which looked on the surface to be identical to those reported by the first supervisor. The class was studying a piece of writing from a novel and one pupil was very critical of it. The teacher asked to know why. The boy replied that it was not written in the sort of language that people would employ nowadays. When pressed to explain what expression might replace it in contemporary language, the boy replied, "That funky music from down the road." The teacher went on to say, "That's typical of the answer I'd expect from someone who gets as low marks as you do".

The actual event recorded by the second supervisor was very similar to those recorded by the first supervisor, but what was different was the interpretation and evaluation of the two people. Whereas the first supervisor deplored the student teacher's manner, the second supervisor wrote about the event described above, "What I like about him is that he stands for no nonsense from any potential trouble makers". For him the event was illustrative of the teacher's *competence,* not lack of it. This focus on specific classroom events brought out very sharply the difference in perceptions of quality of the two supervisors reporting on similar looking episodes.

Outcome

One of the factors affecting judgment about classroom processes is the observer's assessment of the likely outcome of what is witnessed. If there is not to be any systematic measurement of the results of the process of teaching and learning, then consideration has to be given to estimates of such matters as whether or not children appear to be learning. In this context learning can include not only factual knowledge, but also skills, attitudes and behaviour. The observer makes an intelligent guess about aspects of learning that can be important, and sometimes easy to appraise, like whether what is being taught is factually accurate, but sometimes more diffuse and less easy to define exactly, like whether what is being done is:

worthwhile	– of value and importance, however, they may be defined
coherent	– links in with other concepts/activities
influential on future behaviour	– like stimulating a longer term or even lifelong interest in the topic/activity
needed by society	– makes a contribution to present and future citizenship
appropriate	– suitable for the particular child or group in the context of the topic/subject being studied

It is often the perceived relationship between process and outcome that forms the heart of any discussion of a lesson with the teacher concerned after it is over. This is when observers may refer to any notes they have made during the lesson. There are numerous possible ways of keeping a record of the lesson observed. Some observers note down as an *aide-mémoire* anything that catches their attention as it occurs, often about process, but also about possible outcome. Examples from observers' notes when lesson evaluation is involved frequently contain comments like the following assorted collection:

'Bright opening with many pupils taking part', 'Teacher reprimands wrong child', 'Pupils work assiduously in groups', 'Teacher consistently mispronounces the *ü* sound in the word '*über*', 'Pupils in far corner constantly distract children on next table', 'Most children appear to have mastered the concept, which was clearly explained', 'The two pupils in the corner were clearly confused about the notion of a *fair test,* and the teacher ought to have gone over and clarified it with them', 'Check with teacher if everyone's homework had been marked', 'Teacher should have monitored children's experiments earlier', 'We must discuss possible follow-up activities', 'Introduction went on too long', 'Excellent response to story', 'Friendly manner', 'Lesson began at 10.15', 'Roughly equal numbers of boys and girls in class', 'Class restless, pace too slow', 'It would have been better to have some practical work at this stage as some children needed concrete experience', 'Teacher allows boys to rush towards microcomputers and girls find it difficult to get a turn', 'Uses language that is too difficult for class if not explained, like *respiration*'.

These comments are of many kinds. Some are fairly neutral, like the comment on the time the lesson started. Others contain a positive or negative judgment by the observer, encapsulated in words such as 'wrong', 'should have' or 'excellent'. Certain remarks deal with several diverse, if sometimes related, elements, like class management (reprimands, monitoring, timing), personality characteristics (friendly), specific content (modern language topic, story telling, science experiment, including, in the case of the comment on *respiration,* language register), teaching strategies (practical work) or pupil activity/perspective (girls not getting to micro-computers), actual events (reprimanding wrong pupil). Some notes flag a possible post-lesson discussion point. Since these comments are often written down as the lesson develops, freehand notes, as opposed to those put down under pre-determined headings, will often be logged in the order of occurrence, rather than in conceptual groups. Part of the art of lesson analysis is to see and explore shape and direction, make and draw out inferences, as well as talk about possible future action.

There is a problem with the legitimate expressions of concern about the difficulty of defining what constitutes quality, the variations in individual beliefs and expectations, and all the other reservations and caveats about the appraisal of quality and effectiveness. Many teachers when observed *expect* some kind of evaluation from the observer, not a series of reasons why nothing can be said. Student teachers, experienced practitioners who rarely have an outsider present, particularly one with professional insights or able to offer and discuss examples of practice from many classrooms, and anyone teaching new subject-matter or breaking fresh ground are sometimes desperate to know what they can do to improve their professional skill. For the moment qualitative observers might bear the following points in mind:

(1) ***The purpose of the observation should be made clear***—Observers must make clear to the teacher being observed whether they are there to offer advice and help improve professional skill, merely to make a private judgment about quality, or, in the case of certain research projects, for example, not to make any kind of personal value judgment about quality, but simply record what is happening for future analysis. Unless the purpose of the observation is clarified a certain amount of confusion is bound to occur.

(2) ***The need to reflect on the nature of quality and effectiveness***—Observers need to think about their own views on what is effective teaching (see Activity 4.1 below), and recognise that there are often several opinions about quality, not just one's own.

(3) ***The different ways of discussing and enhancing quality***—After the lesson observation there is often a conversation about quality between the teacher and the observer. Thought needs to be given about how this might be structured, whether the teacher or the observer should lead, what aspects should be discussed and who decides the agenda.

(4) ***The nature of the lesson record***—What, if anything, the observer should write down at the time or later, whether this should be under pre-conceived headings, like 'class management' or 'relationships', or simply noted freehand as events occur. The extent to which the record should focus on the teacher, the pupils, both, on personal traits, events, strategies, process or outcome, and how evaluative the comments should be.

ACTIVITY 4.1

Prepare for a lesson observation in a particular field which is of interest to you, perhaps an early years infants class, a lesson on writing an imaginative story with 9 year olds, a gymnastics lesson with 11 year olds, a secondary school foreign language class, or an A level chemistry practical session in a laboratory. Decide what sort of qualitative record of the lesson you will keep. Discuss with others, if possible, what criteria of effectiveness you might look for.

Try to carry out one or more lesson observations using the approach you have chosen and discuss the lesson afterwards with the teacher concerned. How closely did you keep to your intentions? If you varied these, why did you do so? (there is no reason why you should not have done, it is just worth considering what led you to change your original intentions). What sort of points did you note in your written record–classroom events? what people said? pupil behaviour? teaching strategies? What words in your account reveal your own evaluation? (look for evaluative words like 'good', 'poor', 'correct', 'wrong', 'appropriate', 'unsuitable', as well as other words and phrases that reveal your own preference, again without feeling that they are necessarily incorrect assumptions, simply to check what are the colourings and hues of your interpretations).

What did you talk about to the teacher afterwards? Who initiated and who reached? To what extent did the teacher's evaluation concur or disagree with your own appraisal? What was the mood of the post-lesson discussion—deferential? dismissive? apprehensive? animated? positive? What have you learned about appraising teaching quality and effectiveness from the exercise?

CRITICAL EVENTS

One approach which allows the observer to capture and preserve some of the essence of what is happening in lessons is the 'critical events' technique. The observer looks for specific instances of classroom behaviour which are judged to be illustrative of some aspect of the teacher's style or strategies, an element of class management, for example, perhaps a rule being established, observed or broken, something that reflects interpersonal relationships or some other indicative event. The 'critical events' approach is based on the 'critical incidents' technique developed by Flanagan (1949). The observer writes down on a pro forma what led up to the event, what happened and what the outcome was.

Critical event number ———— Name of teacher————

Class ———————————— Date ——————

What led up to the event?

What happened?

What was the outcome?

Interview with participants

After the lesson, teachers can be interviewed and asked for their perception of what happened. The interviewer uses neutral language like "Can you tell me about . . .?", rather than loaded or leading questions, such as "Why didn't you. . . ?". Depending on the circumstances the observer may also be able to talk to some children, but it is important that observers act in an ethical manner and ensure that the head and teachers concerned are fully in agreement with children being interviewed. Talking to children either directly or indirectly about their teachers is not something that should be undertaken without permission, and even if agreement is secured, any interviews should be conducted in a sensitive manner.

The following critical event taken from a science lesson given by a student teacher in a secondary school showed up an important aspect of student teachers' class management problems. The student began the science practical lesson in a relaxed manner, describing the sort of experiment the class was going to do. The critical event, noted after about ten minutes had elapsed, happened when he instructed the pupils to begin the experiment working in pairs. "You know what to do, so get out the gear and start your experiment", he said, whereupon several of the boys raced towards the cupboards, seized pieces of equipment, some wrestling with each other over who should have which bunsen burner. The student had to shout to obtain order and reprimand some of the people playing tug o' war with a bunsen burner rubber tube.

The observer noted this down as an example of the teacher's response to what later became a series of disorderly events in an unruly lesson. After the lesson he asked the question "Can you tell me a bit about what happened when you asked the children to get out the equipment?" (rather than "when the children started fooling around"). The student teacher then explained how he was simply imitating the casual way in which he had seen the class's regular science teacher start experiments. However, it became clear that he had visited the school to watch some lessons in December, after the school had been in session for three months. By then the class's regular teacher had forged a well established friendly relationship and was able to be relaxed and ocular. The student assumed that he could imitate this manner, but was unaware of the considerable efforts made by the class's teacher back in the previous September to ensure that pupils did not misbehave, establish ground rules and enforce these in a consistent manner. It was only after he had impressed on pupils how they must behave in a laboratory that he had adopted a much more informal manner. This critical event and the interviews with the student and class teacher highlighted the problem faced by student teachers inheriting styles and procedures whose origins they have not been able to witness.

Critical events need not be spectacular. They are simply things that happen that seem to the observer to be of more interest than other events occurring at the same time, and therefore worth documenting in greater detail, usually because they tell a small but significant part of a larger story. It is not easy to collect, discuss and analyse more than about three such events in an observation session, but intelligent selection can enhance post-lesson discussion or analysis of someone's teaching.

BODY LANGUAGE

Learning to use one's eyes with sharp discrimination is an important part of the craft of lesson observation. Although a great deal of attention is rightly given to what is said in the classroom, there are many other messages put out by people to one another in communication that are worthy of note. Non-verbal aspects of classroom behaviour include posture, movement, gesture, facial expression and eye contact. In making decisions about what to do, both teachers and pupils will rapidly scan faces, bodies, search their memory for information about previous encounters with the same individuals or similar circumstances, and then decide how to act, all within less than a second on some occasions. It is an astonishing example of human beings' capacity to process information at speed.

The term 'body language' is but one expression used to cover non-verbal behaviour. It sometimes focuses exclusively on aspects such as posture, which can be quite important in classrooms, but there are other elements which must be considered. Posture can reveal interest, threat, boredom, excitement, a whole range of human emotions. Teachers of small children usually crouch alongside them to minimise the height difference, but when they are angry they may draw themselves up to their full height, maximising the height difference to establish or maintain dominance.

Posture can signal impending movement, so that people will flinch, for example, if they see someone's posture change, a shift of weight may be, that suggests attack. Teachers sometimes use movement to counter or even offer threat, so they may move rapidly towards someone who is misbehaving. This quick shortening of social distance, and invasion of someone else's personal space, often conveys the suggestion of possible attack, even though children know, rationally, that teachers are not allowed to strike them.

Gestures are also used to amplify meaning, but teachers, use them for different purposes. A moving pointed finger may illustrate the line of a graph or the timing of a musical rhythm. Both hands may be used to indicate the width of an object, to pacify someone who is angry or over-excited ("Calm down"), or to illustrate the movement of a seesaw. In addition to these more low key uses the hands may also signal aggression through the jabbing or accusing finger, suggestive of a club that could physically assault.

Facial expressions convey added meaning, as numerous small muscles twist the face into different casts, illustrating embarrassment, happiness, apprehension or scorn. Some of these facial responses, like the reddening blush, are innate rather than learned (blind people can blush even though they have never seen a red face to imitate). Other facial expressions are learned socially. Eyes are one of the most important elements of non-verbal and verbal communication, and teachers will not only scan across the room to see what is happening, or focus on an individual pupil, but will also engage children in eye contact in an attempt to read from their eyes what they are thinking. Sometimes lack of eye contact can lead to the teacher not picking up that some pupils have lost interest, or that they have finished their work and are trying to catch the teacher's attention.

Lesson observers often do not write down the detail of non-verbal behaviour, but it does inform their judgment. Some people would not record 'Teacher stands with hands clasped tightly under armpits close to blackboard looking insecure', but would reach a conclusion on the evidence of such visual body cues without necessarily articulating it. The same applies to movement. Many observers do not record detail about teachers' or pupils' movements, but some do, especially where they reveal important aspects of classroom life, life that the teacher moved round the room monitoring different children's work, or that pupils were permitted freedom of movement provided they behaved well.

One caveat about the interpretation of body language is that it can be mistaken. Some postures, facial expressions, movements can be ambiguous—the smile that could reveal nervousness or confidence, the pupil who appears to be either day-dreaming or planning the next move, the frown of confusion or the grimace of anger. We often perceive exactly what transmitters of messages and signals want us to perceive, otherwise, were there too much ambiguity, millions of motorists and pedestrians would be killed every day. However, there are major and minor accidents and disasters in life, and sometimes these are the direct result of ambiguities, or of misinterpretations of moods and messages.

ANALYSING TRANSCRIPTS AND LESSON ACCOUNTS

The end product of many qualitative observations is a notebook full of written fieldnotes, a set of sound or video cassettes, a collection of well documented critical events, or simply an *aide-mémoire* of points the observer wants to discuss with the teacher.

The shelves of many an appraiser's or researcher's study groan under the weight of unanalysed notebooks or tapes. In many ways the notes and tapes that remain undiscussed or unheard for more than a week may never again see the light of day, for the more time that elapses, the less likely it is that anyone will either understand the significance of them, or be motivated to revisit them, once direct and immediate memory have faded. Return to qualitative records as soon as possible is the message.

Language in the classroom is a very important issue which has been addressed in major reports and by several writers in the field, including Sinclair and Coulthard (1975), Stubbs (1983) and Edwards and Westgate (1987). Transcripts of classroom discourse can be analysed either qualitatively or quantitatively, and earlier sections of this book have mentioned some possibilities. However, despite the evolution of computer packages for performing content analysis on transcripts, many people prefer the painstaking personal scrutiny of what people have said, which is why so many transcripts remain unanalysed.

Once transcripts are available there are several aspects of language that can be considered. Some observers are interested in the difference between classroom language and the language of the playground or the home. Tizard and Hughes (1984) analysed not only the conversations between teachers and young children, but also those between the same children and their own parents. They found that there was a more elaborate language exchange in the home than in the nursery school, and that if one looked at what happened during story time, either in the home or the school, children asked numerous questions of their parent, but very few of their teacher. Other observers might be interested in dialect, curious to know what happens when pupils use non-standard forms, like "I haven't done nothing", where the double negative is incorrect in standard English, but may be acceptable as a means of emphasis in the playground or the home, as indeed happens in a language like French (*ne . . . rien, ne . . . jamais*).

Teachers and pupils may talk at 100 to 150 words a minute, occasionally faster, depending on how rapid the interaction is. Even in 30 minutes there can be 10 to 20 pages of transcript. Anyone seeking to draw inferences from the transcripts of several lesson observations could be faced with hundreds of pages of text. It is not for the fainthearted, and observers need to be clear in their minds why they might want such detail. There are numerous possible reasons and there are different approaches for different purposes, such as the following, most of which apply to the analysis of transcripts, fieldnotes and critical events.

Purpose Identifying salient points, for comment or discussion.

Strategy Read text and use highlighter pen to identify statements worthy of note, and then group these under suitable headings. This can be done either when discussing a teacher's lesson with the person concerned, or when conducting research to elicit pupils' and teachers' understandings and interpretations of what happens in classrooms.

Purpose Seeing whether pupils had an opportunity to learn.

Strategy Scan text to find instances where topic or concept was discussed. For example, if a child does not know that magnets pick up objects with iron in them, look back at the section of the lesson when magnetism was discussed to see if this was mentioned. It may then turnout that the issue never came up at all, or that it was mentioned, but the child concerned did not hear or could not understand.

Purpose Looking at language register.

Strategy Search text for examples of teacher explaining to child or group to see whether the choice of words and expressions was appropriate to the individual or group concerned.

Purpose Studying classroom episodes.

Strategy Identify what appear to be the beginning and end of an episode, and then follow through the sequence of talk to see what happened and how it might be explained, possibly with follow-up interview with the teacher and/or pupils concerned. This is useful when trying to obtain teachers' or pupils' comments on events, as the actual words can be discussed. However, it needs to be done as soon after the lesson as possible, otherwise memories become distorted, and this is one of the problems with lesson transcripts sometimes taking a long time to be assembled and collected.

Similar possibilities exist when observers have collected together critical events or freehand notes and want to elicit a pattern, extract principles, or select illustrative examples for their account of what happened in the lessons they saw. Empirical enquiry of this kind, where the observer starts with the data, what is seen and recorded, and then elicits the theory or the questions or the propositions, is time consuming and can be extremely subjective. Grounding one's inferences in what as actually observed, as opposed to the approach of the rationalists and classical humanists who begin with theories and propositions and see if the data fit them, is a tradition that goes back at least as far as Comenius, the seventeenth-century education reformer, who advocated studying the heaven, the earth, oaks and beeches before books.

QUANTIFYING THE QUALITATIVE

Many observers working entirely in the qualitative tradition of observation and analysis would not, under any circumstances, wish to quantify what they had seen. Indeed the very thought would be anathema to them. However, some observers do find that they want to put their fieldnotes into some kind of systematic shape which may involve a certain amount of quantification, and there are procedures which will accommodate this. One procedure is to have the observer's notes, often known as a lesson *protocol*, typed out in line format with each one numbered, and then analyse these line by line. It is a technique pioneered by, among others, Berliner and Tikunoff (1976) in the California Beginning Teacher Evaluation Study. There are several possibilities, just one of which is shown below, based on the following lesson, protocol from an observation during the Leverhulme Primary Project.

Protocol	1	School	Midtown First School
Researcher	ECW	Teacher	Mrs A (and supply Mrs M)

Date — Day 1 of school year — Observation — 8.30 am onwards

Setting — First Encounters Study
City of Somewhere, Midtown Estate
Midtown First School Room 2
Reception class, first day arrival of new pupils
23 children (12 boys, 11 girls)
Six tables for children, two tables for equipment, teacher's desk

(1) The school is a large nursery and first school for 3 to 8 year olds in the

(2) middle of a huge working class estate. From 8.30 onwards children arrive,

(3) some alone, some in twos and threes, sometimes with, sometimes without

(4) their parents. Whole families appear, mother, grandma, grandad, the child

(5) starting school, often a younger brother or sister, may be two, with one in a

(6) push chair, even the family dog. It is a big family occasion. By nine o'clock

(7) most children are in school and the street outside is deserted apart from the

(8) occasional passer-by or late arrival. Mrs A has about two thirds of her class

(9) present. She sits in a chair with the children around her feet. They talk about

(10) dinners, classroom rituals, who knows who in the class and where children

(11) might sit. Every five minutes or so a parent appears at the door with a child.

(12) An extra teacher, brought in for the first week, is on hand to feed in the

(13) latecomers. By 9.30 the class appears to be complete and children are

(14) assigned to tables where they choose an activity from several possibilities . . .

(15) At 10.20 there is an ear-splitting yell from down the corridor. The last arrival

(16) has appeared. She is clearly not enamoured of the idea of coming to school

(17) and her cries of "No, mummy, I don't want to go", are joined in counterpoint

(18) by her mother's audible threats, bribes and oaths,, "I'll come and fetch you at

(19) tea time", "You've *got* to go to school or I'll get into trouble." Outside Mrs

(20) A's classroom the extra supply teacher attempts to soothe parent and child.

(21) "What's her name? Tina is it? Well, come with me Tina and I'll take you

(22) into Mrs A's room." Tina kicks her violently on the shin.

(23) The supply teacher brings Tina and her mother into the classroom. She sits

(24) Tina down at a table and starts to do a jigsaw with her. "I'm just going to

(25) have a word with Mrs A, I'll be back in a second." Meanwhile, Tina's

(26) mother slips gratefully out of the room. A brief ten second conversation

(27) between the supply teacher and Mrs A follow, in which the supply teacher

(28) says she will leave Tina to get on with the jigsaw. She returns to the table and

(29) crouches alongside Tina, "Oh well done, you're good at jigsaws, aren't you,

(30) Tina?" With that she mutters a vague, "I'll be back soon" and leaves the

(31) room. A couple of minutes later Mrs A goes over to Tina. "You've nearly

(32) finished that Tina, well done. Here's a box of building bricks. When you've

(33) finished see if you can build something nice and then I'll come and have a

(34) look at it . . ."

(35) For the whole of the day Tina worked assiduously alongside the rest of the

(36) class, slightly reserved, but indistinguishable from the others, doing the

(37) activities, eating her lunch, playing in the playground during breaks.

(38) The supply teacher made a brief return visit to see how she was, but by then

(39) she was immersed in constructing an elaborate arrangement of building bricks

(40) and barely looked up. At 3.15 she listened attentively as the teacher read the

(41) class a story, congratulated the children on their good behaviour and said she

(42) was looking forward to seeing them all the following day. At 3.30 the bell

(43) rang for the end of school and parents clustered outside the classroom to

(44) collect their children. Tina's mother appeared, pale faced and anxiously

(45) asking how she had got on. "Fine", replied Mrs A, "see you tomorrow Tina",

(46) whereupon Tina burst into tears. Her mother may well have been convinced

(47) that she had spent the day on the rack. The following day, however, Tina

(48) came to school on time, was calm in appearance and manifested no outward

(49) signs of distress about school.

A pair of raters can then read the protocol independently, attempting to bring out important aspects of it, depending on what the observer or teacher wants to consider. It could be 'dimensions of teacher effectiveness', 'pupil behaviour' or 'personal relationships'. The dividing of the protocol into lines allows the readers to compare their interpretations. Suppose, for example, they had both separately identified 'violence towards teacher' as an event to note, then they could check that they were both referring to line 22, 'Tina kicks her violently on the shin'. It also allows each separate line to be coded in some way.

The two readers, in looking for examples of effectiveness, might both highlight lines 23-24 and 28–30, which describe how the teacher sits with Tina and helps her become interested in a jigsaw puzzle. This might lead to categories such as 'involving pupil in task' being noted. Each line can be scrutinised to see if it occurs. A seven point scale could then be used to see whether such features as had been identified appeared to be significant in a lesson or not, using 'less' and 'more' as the dimensions of significance:

Involving pupils		1	2	3	4	5	6	7	
Warmth	*less*	1	2	3	4	5	6	7	*more*
Reprimanding		1	2	3	4	5	6	7	

Study of several such protocols might then find that in lessons thought to be effective there was more likelihood that pupils who had become distracted would be re-involved in their work, or that there would be more personal warmth from the teacher, or a greater tendency to reprimand. The advantage of quantifying in this way is that it can sometimes lend shape to a large amount of descriptive text about what happened in lessons, and also give a certain degree of objectivity by asking readers to make judgments from the same protocol, but independently of each other. The major disadvantage is that it can reduce valuable evidence from a sophisticated and detailed account written by an intelligent observer capable of detecting fine nuances, to a set of crude categories and ciphers. Many observes in any case prefer to use a mixture of methods.

5

Teaching Intellectual Skills

We now move into the area of intellectual skills. In the next six sections what we are trying to do is to get students to develop worthwhile intellectual skills and simultaneously to reinforce their understanding of specific concepts by using them, applying the, writing them, talking about them in many different situations.

At the centre of these six sections is the notion that pupils ought to be active in many more ways than the traditional system of listening, reading, making notes and writing essays allows. Students ought to be engaged in a large number of different sorts of tasks, using different sorts of skill, and using those concepts which the teacher wants them to develop. This is not just a matter of preference, it is an indispensable strategy if students are to develop their grasp of concepts. Consider for a moment how subtle your own understanding of the concept 'democratic' is. It allows you to take in your stride very diverse ideas like '. . . the democratic way to settle this would be a show of hands', or 'the American Democratic party', or the 'East German Democratic Republic' without being confused by these subtle shifts of meaning.

At some stage in your life someone may have tried, well or badly, to explain to you the concept 'democratic', but that explanation probably played really quite a small part in developing your powerful grip on this concept, compared with the thousands of times you have *used* the concept—written it, said it, argued about it, read it. Similarly, we must get students to use concepts as often as possible, in the largest possible number of ways and situations, or our explanations of concepts, useful first steps though they are, will do little good.

The idea of 'using' a concept is virtually inseparable from the idea of 'practising a skill'. If we get a student to use the term 'democratic' in even the simplest of ways, that will involve the student in the practice of one or more intellectual skills. Even, as our first section 'Translation' shows, the simple operation of saying in your own words what 'democratic' means can be done well or badly and is usefully seen as involving a skill—the skill of translation.

There is no conflict between 'developing concepts' and 'developing skills' as teaching aims. We develop concepts by getting people to apply a range of skills to the concepts we want developed.

One difficulty about intellectual skills is that there are several different lists of such skills, published in various quarters and using different nomenclature. For example, suppose we put the following question to a student: 'Why do you think Britain did not fully join either of the great European alliance systems before 1914?' This book describes the principal skill which the student must use to answer that question as the skill of 'interpretation', that is the skill of interpreting the two given facts: there were alliance systems; Britain did not join them. It would be equally reasonable to describe this particular skill, as indeed some people do, as the skill of 'drawing inferences', or 'inferential thinking'.

It is perhaps unfortunate that there is not a standard way of referring to skills, but as teachers the most important first steps are to have a serviceable, comprehensive check-list of intellectual skills and a full understanding of the kind of tasks by questions for students which might promote them. When we have those two things securely, we might then reasonably think about adding to the check-list, or reorganising it, in the light of further reading or of experience and reflection.

The first skill we will consider, that of translation, gives rise to tasks which are of very obvious usefulness in concept development. It involves literally translating information from one level of abstraction to another, for instance, from the relatively abstract language of text-book to the probably less abstract 'own words' of a student and also from one medium to another, for example, from a graph to words.

1. Translation

Suppose we have been dealing with the Australian gold rush of the 1850s, and particularly the miners' rebellion of 1854. We have tried to explain the concept 'rebellion', but we want to reinforce it by setting students some suitable tasks. Here are three very straightforward ones.

Task A: 'Say in Your Own Words What a Rebellion is.'

We might feel fairly pleased with a response like this: 'If people are unhappy like about taxes and a lot of them get guns and start an army to force the rulers to have less taxes'. This answer is inelegantly expressed, but it makes four major points essential to the concept:

(i) rebellions are about expressed grievances—unlike, say, the activities of bank robbers;

(ii) rebellions have to be at least fairly big to count as rebellions;

(iii) rebellions involve weapons—unlike petitions or demonstrations;

(iv) rebellions have large-scale aims—they are not mere protests.

Also the language used sounds like the student's own—we could have good hopes that this student is incorporating the word and idea in his permanent vocabulary—'accommodating' and 'assimilating' it, as Piaget describes it. About the next answer we might be less confident: 'The rebels first obtain weapons, then attack police or soldiers, then go on to proclaim a republic'. Although the writing is much smoother, the idea of rebellions having causes is missing and we might suspect (we might be wrong) that 'proclaim a republic' is not the student's own language, but a bit of remembered and possibly ill-understood 'book language'. How would you rate this third answer in comparison with the other two? 'If all the people in a country wanted to change something, like a different king or a different flag—it's a rebellion'.

Task B

We could ask for a larger piece of writing, e.g. *'Write a story about a rebellion'*. When we looked at the student responses, the same criteria would apply as for Task A, that is, somewhere in the story, the four major points would be made.

Task C

We could ask students to *'Give some examples from history of rebellions'*. Again, we would be looking for examples which fulfilled our four criteria, i.e., a fairly large armed uprising with roots in perceived grievances and fairly clear political aims. Marginal examples, though, could be useful to us—for example, in the case of Australia students could discuss whether the 'Rum Rebellion' of 1808 might be called a rebellion, or in an American setting whether John Brown's Harper's Ferry raid merits the title 'rebellion', We sharpen our understanding of concepts very effectively by arguing about marginal instances of 'mismatches' as some authorities call them.

In all three of these tasks the students are asked to take an abstraction, 'rebellion', and translate it into concrete terms of their own—guns, police, taxes, and the like. This intellectual skill of translation can be practised in many types of exercise besides the three simple examples we have given, as we shall see in a moment. It is of considerable value in helping students to strengthen their grasp of concepts and make them part of their active vocabulary. The principle it works on is that the learner's own explanation, examples and illustrations of a concept, expressed in his own words, are more secure pegs to hang the concept on, as it were, than the explanations, examples and illustrations of a teacher or a book—however apt, elegant and persuasive the latter might be.

If this theory is true, it ought to apply in our resent case and you might like to test it. So either now or at the end of this section on translation, you might try two things:

(1) Make up an explanation in your own words of this concept 'translation'.

(2) Make up your own examples of tasks you might set pupils involving translation together with some broad outlines of 'good responses' to the tasks.

Further Uses of the Skill of Translation

Pupils can be asked to do the reverse of the process involved in our first three tasks, i.e., they can be asked to translate some information expressed in concrete terms into an abstraction. Like this:

(1) All the soldiers agreed they would not obey orders any more—what is it called when soldiers refuse to obey orders?

(2) What do we do call it when a lot of ships sail along together with worships alongside to guard them from submarines?

This kind of question must obviously be used with a lot of care. The abstraction required must already be known to the students and it must be clear, at least within narrow limits, what the required answer is. We can all too easily slip into the situation of, in fact, trying to get students to read our minds with questions like: 'What do we call it when one country suddenly attacks another?' Reasonable answers to this question could be—war, treachery, blitzkrieg, assault, offensive—and so on. It only gives rise to frustration all round if five or six students have to have their answers not accepted before the lucky winner happens on the 'right' answer and says 'aggression'. Here, as always, the moral is to spend as much time thinking about the possible answers to any question we want to set students as we did thinking up the question in the first place. How many reasonable answers, for example, could you think of to this question? 'What do we call it when very many people have to leave their homes because they can't get work?'

One kind of translation involves taking information in one medium and putting it into another—as with *graphs:*

Here are the figures for cotton production in the 1850s—show these figures in the form of a block graph. . .

or with *maps*:

Look at the map and tell me how far New York is from Boston.

or with *pictures:*

Look at the picture of the Samurai warrior—try to describe his weapon and equipment in your own words.

The ability to translate like this from one medium to another is a very important one in its own right. We can also sometimes usefully combine practice of this skill with reinforcement of concept-learning.

Here are some examples, using translation from words into some other medium.

***With the Concept of Strategy* (American History Context)**

> Here is a short description of the Union Side's strategy for winning the Civil War—see if you can show the strategy in the form of a map using as few words as you can.

To perform this task, the student will have to render the idea 'strategy' into the concrete form of arrows on a map and the like, rather as he rendered the idea of 'rebellion' into his own words in the earlier tasks in this section, and with the same valuable effect of forming his own 'peg', in this case a visual image of his *own* map to hang the concept on. He will also have to solve the problem of depicting visually any other abstraction which the written passage uses to explain Union strategy—as it might be 'naval blockade', 'stranglehold on the Mississippi', 'constant pressure in Virgina' or the like.

With the Concept 'Industrialisation'

> Can you convey to me, using only graphs, that an imaginary country called Fantasia became industrialised between 1860 and 1900?

The special virtue of graphs is that they deal in quantities. So to answer this question a student has to go beyond phrases like 'increased production of goods' which would serve him well enough in a written answer to the question. 'Say in your own words what "industrialisation" means'. When drawing a graph he has to consider, however crudely, how much and how fast 'production of goods' would increase—would the line shoot up near-vertically or what?

So the 'words to graphs' translation question can be useful wherever understanding a concept involves understanding the speed at which things happen—for example, matters like population movements, cultural diffusion, changes in climates of opinion—as well as the economic history field where they are traditionally used.

Using the Concept 'Siege'—A Drawing Task

Draw me a sketch picture of a town being besieged.

We can reasonably demand, even of someone who does not draw well, that their sketch shows three things fundamental to the idea of a siege.

(1) The town will be fortified in some way—besieging places as a military technique is, after all, a response to the problem posed by defensive fortifications.

(2) The besiegers will be all around the town to stop people going in or out.

(3) The besiegers will have some place to live, tents or huts—the thing about a siege is that it usually goes on a long time.

This is clearly a useful exercise for a young students not too clear about, say, the difference between a siege and a battle. It lets him produce his own visual image to hang the concept on, as with graphs and maps. Also it lets him show he has grasped the concept without having to put a strain on his ability to write, for once.

Getting younger students to draw pictures is a much-abused teaching technique. Exercises like 'Copy the picture of the Indian on page 3 . . .', or 'Draw Captain Cook's ship' can be mere time-fillers if nothing is being *translated* by the student, if his picture is not illustrating some concept in concrete form.

It might be useful at this point if you thought over this question: What could you ask a student to draw that would help him to grasp the following concepts: nomadic; colony; frontier; industrial? (You might find it useful to extend the idea of 'picture' to include cartoons, i.e., a series of pictures; pictures with 'pin-men'; pictures that are virtually diagrams—it is not, after all, the student's skill as an artist which is in question.)

So far we have dealt with translating from words into graphs, maps and pictures as a way of mastering concepts. If we try it the other way round, going from maps, pictures or graphs into words, we hit a technical difficulty.

Suppose we are interested in the concept 'colony' and gave students this map (p.124), of the eastern part of America in 1740, showing the European colonies. We could set translation exercises such as 'Put in the main English colonies on the map,' but these exercises would not get us very far in promoting understanding of the concept 'colony'. We would want to ask questions like, 'Why are the colonies sited in the places they are?' 'Why do you think the French colonies seem to go such a lot further inland than the English ones?' We would want to get at ideas like the fact that colonies are sited where they are usually for some good reason, or the fact that 'colony' can describe a small, densely settled block of land like Massachusetts, or a string of trading or missionary posts like French North America—and so on. But in asking questions like 'Why are the colonies where they are?' we have gone beyond asking students to translate information from one form to another, we have started to ask them to interpret the information given on the map.

2. Interpretation

Since the skills of translation and interpretation are close together, we will deal now with interpretation and have a joint section of exercises and summary on the two skills together.

Interpretation, like translation, can serve the ends of concept-learning, as well as being a very valuable cognitive skill in its own right. Here are some further examples of it, to make the relationship with translation clear.

Graphs and Maps

(1) 'Does the graph show that large families have become less common in the twentieth century?'

(2) (With the concept 'slump' in mind) 'Look at the graph of cotton-production in the 1850s. Was there a slump in those years?'

One thing is clear right away from these two examples—you can't ask students to interpret before they can translate—so obviously we must make sure students can, say, read off cotton production figures for one year before we ask them to interpret the graph's ups and downs. This is the important point to remember. For the practising teacher, it is not so very important to be able to categorise tasks as 'interpretation' or 'translation' precisely. Take a task like this: 'Look at the map of the Saratoga campaign—say in your own words what the British strategy was'.

Whether the task is translation or interpretation matters a lot less than the fact that it is an example of a powerful way of

learning the concept 'strategy', and it's a way of using maps to promote learning that teachers ought to be skilled at.

See now if you can make up a good number of tasks involving students in interpreting graphs and maps, with the learning of some particular concept in mind.

Museum Objects

The value of taking students to a museum, apart from the way it might motivate and excite some students, is that it can help in concept development, perhaps better than any other experience. This is because students can 'hang' concepts on to some very strong concrete visual 'hooks'—the objects in the museum. Let us take an example.

Suppose we are in a museum or museum section devoted to communications. There is on display a set of telephones (see picture). Such a display is important because it helps students to strengthen their grasp of the concept of development and of the notion that the shape of things changes for *reasons*, be it discovery of new tools, or of new techniques, or materials, or fashions or people's needs; and that old things are the way they are, not because people in the past were stupid, quaint or mad, but for good reasons. If we apply that idea to old institutions and cultural patterns we start to see what an important idea this notion of 'development for reasons' is.

We can use the telephone display to set various tasks. First, tasks of translation. Before they can talk about telephone 1 developing into telephones 2 and 3, students must have a clear idea of what the differences are between the telephones. So we ask: 'What are the main differences between the phones?' (Translation from objects to words, as it were.) Answers like 'The third one is modern,' 'The first one is crazy,' show that students are not ready to discuss the notion of development very profitably yet, so if we got answers like that we would ask supplementary questions, for example: 'What are the phones made of?', 'How are they held together?'—to direct students to the questions of materials and techniques, away from ideas of 'quaintness' and 'craziness'.

The answers, however, need not be technologically expert: a reply like 'The third is made of plastic and sort of more all one' would no doubt distress a telephone designer, but is good enough for us as a springboard for our next question, involving interpretation of the objects:

> Why do you think telephones got to be made lower as time went by?
>
> Why do you think the new ones are plastic?

Telephones

Picture 5.1

Why do you think the first one is made of metal?

Say why you think telephones have developed the way they have.

Then we could go back to translation and ask:

> Can you think of other things, may be in the home, that have developed in the same sort of ways as telephones?

Other areas where you might finds displays showing development are in fields like transport, weapons, housing, furniture—as long as there are two or more objects reasonably close together we can use this technique of getting students to describe the differences carefully, and they try to account for them using concepts like development in the process. We shall return to the matter of museum objects in the section on evaluation.

Sources

The use of original written source material is one of the most important and distinctive activities of the teacher of history. Let us look at how we might deal with an example (in this case a small passage from *Hakluyt's Voyages*):

> The first voyage of the right worshipful and valiant knight, Sir John Hawkins, sometimes treasurer of her Majesties navie Roial, made to the West Indies 1562.
>
> Master John Hawkins having made *divers* voyages to the Iles of the Canaries, and there by his good and upright dealing being growen in love and favour with the people, informed himself amongst them by diligent inquisition, of the state of West India, where of he had received some knowledge by the instructions of his father, but increased the same by the *advertisements* and reports of that people. And being among other particulars assured, that *Negros were very good merchandise in Hispaniola,* and that store of Negros might easily be had upon the coast of Guinea, resolved with himself to make trial thereof, and communicated that devise with his worshipful friends of London; namely with Sir Lionell Ducket, M. Bromfield, and others. All which persons liked so well of his intention that they *became liberal contributors and adventurers* in the action For which purpose there were three good ships immediately provided: the one called the Salomon

> of the burthen of 120, tunne, wherein M. Hawkins himself went as General: the second the Swallow of 100 tunnes, wherein went for Captaine M. Thomas Hampton: and the third the Jonas a barke of 40 tunnes wherein the Master supplied the Captaines roome: in which small fleete M. Hawkins tooke with him not above 100 men for feare of sickness and other inconveniences, whereunto men in long voyages are commonly subject.

First, some translation exercises are needed, if only to check that the students understand the contents of the passage. They could be asked to put in their own words archaic vocabulary like 'divers' and 'advertisements'. They must certainly be able to put in their own words the phrases 'Negros were very good merchandise in Hispaniola' and '. . . became liberal contributors and adventurers in the action'—otherwise the point of the passage, as concerned with the financing of a slave-trading voyage, is lost.

The concept of slavery could obviously be directly reinforced by a question like 'What are people called who are treated as merchandise?'; and equally the concept of investment could be made very usefully concrete if we asked students to 'Say exactly what Sir Lionell Duckett and the others do when they become "liberal contributors", what their money is used for, and what they get back for themselves'.

Some teachers, perhaps, don't get as much value as they might out of source material, became they stop short at translation and do not go on to ask interpretation questions. One basic interpretation question that ought to be asked about any source material is this—'What is the author's attitude to the events he describes, what is his likely bias, in a nutshell, what side is he on?' The exact phrasing of the question depends on the source; we could ask in this case: 'What do you think the writer thinks of Sir John Hawkins? What do you think he thinks of Negro slavery?' The concept of 'bias' or 'slant' could be brought in directly, of course, like this 'Is the writer biased for or against Hawkins?'

A second basic interpretation question to ask of any source is 'Why, according to the writer, did things happen the way they did?' In this case we could ask, 'According to the writer, why did

Hawkins go to the West Indies?' 'Why did Sir Lionell Duckett and the others pay for his ships?' Again, a concept like 'motive' can be reinforced here, simply by rephrasing the above questions, using the word 'motive'. Or a more difficult concept such as 'exploit' might be reinforced with a question like 'How did Sir John Hawkins and Sir Lionell Duckett plan to exploit Africa and the Americas, according to the writer?'

There are some other very important types of question that ought to be asked of a source, but for the moment we will confine ourselves to translation and interpretation questions in our examples.

Perhaps before we go on to further examples, one important point should be made. Suppose we asked a student this interpretation question—'What does the writer think of Sir John Hawkins, and of slavery?' Suppose he replied, 'He dislikes both Hawkins and the slave business—you can tell because of his heavily ironical praise of "the right worshipful knight". He comes on so strong with his praise, he's obviously being ironical'. We could reply to the student that we couldn't see any evidence to support his assumption that the writer is being ironical, and that there is a simpler view that the writer is just saying what he feels, and that the cool way he writes about Negro slavery, for example, probably shows that he *felt* cool about it—he accepted it. We can rightly say all this—but, of course, what we cannot say is that the student is wrong.

We cannot say so, for a reason which has very often been pointed out, that in history we are not in the business of 'right' or 'wrong' interpretations of documents or events, but of plausible or implausible ones, interpretations which on balance have more evidence in their favour than others; interpretations which are orthodoxy today, but may be overturned next week because new evidence is found. However, often it is pointed out, though, it is hard for a teacher not to feel uneasy when faced with a fourteen-year-old giving an unorthodox interpretation of a piece of source material. We really have to school ourselves not to 'put him right', not to sweep his interpretation aside (or, equally bad, apparently accept it, but in such a way that everybody knows that we are just humouring the student). We must try to respect the student's interpretation and it is vital that we try, because dealing with source material is one of the few places that the school student can easily meet two vital ideas, namely, the idea of what Bruner calls 'the tentativeness of knowledge' and the specific idea that *history* knowledge is largely 'tentative'—is interpretation, not 'facts' handed out by teachers.

In the next example of interpretation questions, consider some answers to the questions which a student might give, which you would not think were the best interpretation, but which are nonetheless possible. How would you deal with those answers in such a way that he can see that interpretations other than his own are possible and yet not be discouraged from going on making his own interpretations?

Here is another extract, from the works of Usama, a Muslim chronicler of the Crusades period:

> Not a single one of those who have recently settled in the territories of the Franks but shows himself more inhuman than his predecessors already established among us and used to the Moslems. What happened to me when I visited Jerusalem is a proof of the hardness of the *Franks* (may Allah crush them!). I was going into the Mosque al-Aqsa. Beside it there was a little mosque that the Franks had turned into a Church. When I entered the Mosque-al-Aqsa, which was occupied by the Templars, who were friends of mine, they told me that I could say my prayers in this little mosque. One day I went in and glorified Allah. I was deep in my prayer when one of the Franks fell upon me, laid hold of me and turned my face to the east, saying 'That is the way to pray'. A troop of Templars rushed at him, seized him and thrust him out. I began to pray again. This same man, escaping from their supervision, fell on me again, turned my face to the east once more, repeating. 'That is the way to pray!' The Templars once again rushed at him and thrust him out; then they excused themselves to me, and said: 'He is a foreigner, who arrived a few days ago from the land of the Franks. He has never seen anyone pray without turning to the east'. I replied: 'I have prayed enough for today'. And I left, surprised at seeing what a contorted face that devil had, how he trembled, and what an impression it had made on him to see someone pray facing the kibla (Mecca).

Again, some translation work is necessary to check that students, for instance, can say in their own words what is meant by a 'Frank'.

Useful interpretation questions could include 'What is the religion of the writer?' 'What is his attitude to Franks?' 'How does he explain the behaviour of the Frank who attacked him and of the Templars who defended him?'

The concept of toleration could be strengthened by direct use, thus: 'According to Usama, what determined whether Franks were tolerant or not?'

Here is another passage from Usama:

> I am going to tell you a few things about the Franks and the surprise their minds often caused me.
>
> There was in the army of King Fulk, the son of Fulk, a worthy Frankish knight who had come from their country to make the pilgrimage and then return. He made my acquaintance and became so attached to me that he called me his brother. We were fond of each other and spent our time together. When he was preparing to cross the sea again to return to his own country, he said to me: 'O my brother, I am going home and I would like, if you will let me, to take your son and show him our part of the world (I had with me my boy of fourteen). He will see our knights there, he will learn wisdom and the science of chivalry. When he returns he will have the bearing of an intelligent man'. These words, which were not the words of a sensible man, wounded my ears. For even if my son had been made prisoner, captivity could have brought him no further calamity than to be transported to the land of the Franks. I answered: 'As you live, that was what I meant to do, but I have been prevented by my son's affection for his grandmother, my mother. She only let him come with me because I swore to bring him back'. Is your mother still alive?' he asked me. 'Yes,' I answered. And he said to me: 'Do not upset her'.

In this second example we might ask the student similar questions to those asked about the first passage and also 'Why do you think the Frankish knight made the offer to take the boy to the West with him?' or 'Why did the minds of the Franks cause Usama surprise—on the strength of this story?' The whole story seems to embody very neatly the idea of cultures clashing through misunderstanding and could give us a good chance to help students to make concrete that 'weasel word' 'misunderstanding', often used very glibly in phrases like 'misunderstanding between nations'. We might perhaps do it through the straight translation questions—'Describe in your own words the misunderstanding between Usama and the Frank' and 'Can you think of other misunderstandings between the Muslims and the Westerners, or between the Byzantines and the Westerners, that happened on the Crusades?'

To take, finally, a much more modern source. 'Bombing in war time' (A world broadcast, 10th May, 1942), Winston S. Churchill.

> Now is the time to use our increasingly superior air strength to strike hard and continually at the home front in Germany, from which so much evil has leaked out upon the world and which is the foundation of the whole enormous German invasion of Russia. Now, while the German armies, will be bleeding and burning up their strength against the 2,000-mile Russian line, and when the news of casualties, by hundreds of thousands is streaming back to the German Reich, now is the to bring home to the German people the wickedness of their rulers, by destroying under their very eyes the factories, and seaports on which their war effort depends, German propaganda has been constantly appealing of late to British public opinion to put a stop to these severe forms of warfare, which, according to the German view, should be the strict monopoly of the Herrenvolk. Herr Hitler himself has not taken at all kindly to this treatment and he has been good enough to mingle terrible threats with his whinings. He warns us, solemnly, that if we go on smashing up the German cities, his war factories and his bases, he will retaliate against our cathedrals and historic monuments—if they are not too far inland. We have heard his threats before. Eighteen months ago, in September 1940, when he thought he had an overwhelming air force at his command, he declared that he would rub out—that was the actual expression, rub out—our towns and cities. And he certainly had a good try. Now the boot is on the other leg. Herr Hitler has even called in question the humanity of these grim developments of war. What a pity

this conversion did not take place in his heart before he bombed Warsaw, or massacred 20,000 Dutch folk in defenceless Rotterdam, or wreaked his cruel vengeance upon the City of Belgrade.

Exercises to translate unfamiliar vocabulary are not so obviously necessary here, except probably in the case of the word 'Herrenvolk', but translation tasks on the concept propaganda, like 'Say in your own words what propaganda is, and give examples of propaganda' would be very useful, in association with this text.

The basic interpretation question—'What side is the writer on?' is plainly hardly worth asking here, but there is still scope for good questions in the second main area, i.e. the writer's attitude to, and account of, the events he describes, for example, 'What is Churchill's attitude to bombing as a way of waging war?' 'What is Churchill's attitude to the German people? What does he make out to be Hilter's attitude to bombing as a way of waging war?' 'Do you think Churchill thinks that the British people might have any doubts or misgivings about the British bombing campaign? How does he try to meet these doubts?'

Answering questions like these can gradually change our perception of this passage, from seeing it as a standard bit of wartime propaganda bombast to starting to see it as a more subtle document—illustrating the political and moral uncertainties set up by the bombing campaign and letting us bring quite young students to a fuller appreciation of the reasons why the broadcast was made in the first place.

To sum up on use of sources so far:

(a) check that students understand the general context of the passage by 'say in your own words' translation tasks on important words and phrases.

(b) Ask students to interpret the passage to establish the writer's likely general bias, for example, his religion, nationality, side taken in a given dispute, and also to establish how the writer sees and how he explains the events he is describing.

(c) Watch out for chances to get students to use and thereby strengthen specific concepts, through translation or interpretation tasks or both.

Setting Exercises on Translation and Interpretation

The reader is invited in this and in the other 'exercises' sections to make up his own examples of tasks to suit his own needs and those of his students. It is a good idea to develop the habit from the start of devising tasks at two levels—one for more able students, one for less able. Let us take the example of the very first suggested translation task to see what we mean—it was 'Say in your own words what a rebellion is'. We have not specified for which age-ability group of students such a task would be suitable; in fact, apart from an occasional remark that such-and-such a task might be suitable for 'younger students', we have not so far stated of any task that it would be 'right for bright fourteens' or 'right for average sixteens'.

The reason for this is that fourteen-year-old students (even sub-categories designated as 'bright', 'average', 'below average' or whatever), are so varied in their knowledge and abilities that to designate the suggested tasks as 'good for fourteen-year-olds' and so on would be mainly guesswork. It is probable that in the case of some of the tasks suggested so far a teacher would say, 'Well, it would be all right for most of class 3T, but too hard for some of them—so what about the ones it's too hard for?' Or the problems of students' different abilities could come up even more awkwardly—you could set a task to a group, thinking that it was of the right level and then find out as they are attempting it that it is too hard for some of them. The big danger in both these situations, especially the second, is that with the student for whom the task is too hard we drop our sights too far and say, 'Well if you can't do the tasks on the causes of the war.' In other words, it is tempting when tasks are deemed too hard to abandon the whole concept/skill learning project that the task embodies and go down to a lower level of activity altogether. That way, your expectations of the students, his own assessment of his abilities and eventually those abilities themselves get lower and lower.

Ideally, what we need to be able to do is set tasks at many levels of difficulty, but at each level keeping the same concept/skill learning in view. As a start, we would suggest that you plan all tasks in just two different forms—an 'easier' version and a 'harder' version. It is not always obvious, however, what makes a task easier or harder than another one. Everybody has a rough idea of what is meant by 'easier'—most people would tend to feel that 'Draw me a sketch picture of a town being besieged' sounds easier than 'Convey to me, using only graphs, that an imaginary country became industrialised between 1860 and 1900'. But appearances can deceive. 'Say in your own words what a rebellion is,' 'Why are the colonies sited in the places they are?' are questions by no means easy to answer well—they could be well worthy of the attention of an eighteen-year-old. They look easy at first sight simply because they are phrased in a way we associate more with eleven-year-olds than with older students. The characteristics of easier and harder tasks is quite a difficult question. As a start, though, we suggest that you differentiate your two levels of task in one or more of three straightforward ways.

(i) *The Language of the Task Itself*—If we take 'Say in your own words what a rebellion is' and make it 'Define a rebellion', we have made the task harder. The actual operation required of the student is the same, but he now has an extra task—knowing what 'define' means. There is quite a lot of, as it were, technical task-setting vocabulary, which we can use if we want to make a task harder, or avoid if we want to make it easier. Some of it is easy to translate into easier language, for example:

What is the technical term= What do we call it when . . .
for. . .

Depict, illustrate. . . = Show me a graph, or a picture . . .

Evaluate. . . = Say which was best . . .

Some technical task-setting language is not so easy to make simpler—for example, 'generalise', which would require a circumlocution like 'look at the five examples, say what they have in common, say what the differences are . . .' and so on.

Some task-setting language is downright mysterious, like that old favourite, 'Discuss' as in 'Discuss the view that . . .' A big extra task, or rather set of tasks, is involved here—the student must know what is meant by 'discuss' in the special sense that it is used here, know how to organise his answer in a special way and be expert at guessing what length of 'discussion' his teacher wants. Even more mysterious is the case where a student is given a quotation from a source or from a modern historian with no instruction at all as to what to do about it, except, may be, 'comment'. Perhaps we ought not to set tasks in this kind of language at all, since they put such a high premium on the skill of knowing your way around the quirky conventions of the academic world.

(ii) The Size of the Task—To ask the student for five examples of x plainly makes the task harder for him than if you asked for two. Asking 'What is the difference between a rebellion and a mutiny?', similarly, is simply extending the number of operations the student has to do, as compared with 'Tell me what a rebellion is'. Asking for a sentence, not a paragraph, reduces the strain on the student's power of organising material, and so on. Reducing the size of the task is an easy, valuable and often overlooked approach to making a task easier or harder.

(iii) Breaking the Task Down into its Component Parts—On the face of it, 'Say in your own words what a rebellion is' does not look capable of being made any easier as a task—not if we are going to stick to the learning aim of improving understanding of the concept 'rebellion' anyway. But consider—one student's answer was quoted as follows: 'If people are unhappy like about taxes and a lot of them get guns and start an army to force the rulers to have less taxes'.

To put this answer together, the student had to set himself at least four sub-questions—

(1) What kind of thing causes rebellions?

(2) Do you need a lot of people to count as a rebellion?

(3) What kind of things do rebels do?

(4) What kind of things do rebels try to get?

In the case of this particular answer, the student has both set himself the sub-questions and answered them successfully.

A less able student might forget some of the sub-questions or think of them in the wrong order and thereby give a less useful response. If he regularly fails in one or both, of those ways, he might well become discouraged and faced with this type of task, give up, say it's too hard—although he actually does know some or all of the answers to the sub-questions and has a potentially good grasp of the concept in question. So, if we presented this question broken down into the four sub-questions, we will be presenting an easier task, with the substance of our aim, strengthening the understanding of the concept 'rebellion', unimpaired. We will also be able to tell a lot more confidently exactly what is imperfect in a student's grasp of a concept, according to the answers he gives to the sub-questions.

Not all tasks will break down like this into sub-tasks, but many will: 'Write a story about a rebellion' becomes 'Write a story about how a rebellion began, what the rebels did . . . etc.' 'Give examples from history of. . .' becomes 'Give examples from the history of America of. . .' or even 'Were there any examples in eighteenth-century America of . . .' 'Describe the warrior's equipment' becomes 'Describe his sword, then his armour' (and 'describe' itself might break down into 'Tell me about the colours, the shapes, . . . etc.). 'Why is the colony where it is?' becomes 'Is there a harbour . . .? Are there rivers leading inland? What do you think the climate is like? Was it easy to get to from England?' 'Why are the later telephones made of plastic?' becomes 'Do you think plastic would be easier to work? Cheaper? Easier to make different colours?' 'Draw a sketch picture of a town being besieged' becomes 'Draw a sketch picture . . .Where will the besiegers be? Where will they live during the siege? How will the townspeople try to keep them out?'

Probably the best way to work out whether a question can be readily made easier by splitting into parts and what those parts are is to adopt a useful practice we have already recommended and, whenever you devise a task, think out the answer, or a good answer, as well. Then ask yourself, 'When I was working out that answer, did I proceed in stages, did I, in fact, break the question into parts and, if so, what were they?'

Exercise 1

Try making these tasks (all translations or interpretation) easier. Make sure the new tasks are still translation or interpretation tasks. (If you can then go on to make your easier version easier yet and get a 'three-level' task, so much the better.)

(1) Say in your own words what a Communist believes.

(2) Depict graphically the fact that imaginary country A has a large 'balance of payments' problem.

(3) On your transport museum visit, do these things:

(a) Write descriptions of ten vehicles.

(*b*) Make notes so you can answer this question when you get back: 'How were methods of transportation developed between 1800 and 1900?'

Exercise 2

Devise translation and interpretation tasks (at two levels of difficulty in each case) on a subject area of your own choice, with students of your own in mind.

You will probably find it most convenient to think of the 'hard' version of each task first and then make it easier. Also, you will probably find it most useful not to stick to the order of types of task that we have used in this section. If, say, your interest is in the American Revolution and you can immediately think of tasks involving interpretation of source materials, then go ahead and devise those first and come back to the other sections later. On the other hand, do try to make up tasks of all the types: you may feel that, say, using pictures as a basis for tasks is just not suited to your style, but give it a try.

Exercise 1—Suggested Answers

(1) 'What a Communist believes' is an obvious candidate for move number 3, breaking down into parts, as, e.g. '. . . what a Communist believes about who should own property, who should run the government . . .' etc.

(2) 'Depict graphically' can become 'Draw graphs to show. . . Also 'balance of payments problem' can break down in some such fashion as this—'Draw graphs to show how the imports cost a lot more than the exports'.

(3) (*a*) 'Ten vehicles' can simply be reduced to, say, five. 'Descriptions can break down to, say, 'Describe how they are driven, what they carry . . .' and so on.

(*b*) Making the dates 1950 to 1900 obviously makes the task shorter and so easier. 'Methods of transportation' could be broken down to road vehicles, ships and so on. 'Developed' can be broken down into 'Got faster, carried more people, got safer' etc.

3. Application

If we were trying to teach a Martian about our world, he might soon conclude that the idea of dividing up the world's phenomena into groupings called concepts and using these concepts as keys to understanding was a pretty bad idea.

If, for example, he got a pretty fair grasp of the idea of a 'pen', using the illustrative example of a fountain-pen, imagine his vexation when he encounters a ball-point and a felt-tip and is assured that these are all pens too, whereas a propelling-pencil, which seems to have a lot more in common with a ball-point than a ball-point does with a quill, is nonetheless a pencil, not a pen. However, if we present him with these various examples of the concept 'pen' at reasonable intervals and in a sympathetic way, he might slowly form an idea of what is central to 'pen-ness' and what is peripheral. He might, in other words, strengthen his grasp of the concept 'pen' in a most fundamental way.

We might, in fact, virtually define 'having a better grasp of a concept' thus, as meaning having knowledge of more instances of the concept; understanding better that examples of the concept can be very superficially different from each other; understanding better that some examples of the concept, as it were, lie towards the outer edges of the concept (like ball-point pens) whereas others are very clearly within the concept-boundaries (like quill-pens). One fundamental way in which this 'better grasp' is acquired is that we bring our existing understanding of a concept to a new phenomenon or situation and ask ourselves, 'How does this new thing or situation match up, or fail to match up, to our existing grasp of this concept?'

Sometimes the problem is easy, as it might be for our Martian if we showed him a pen similar to the pens he had seen already, except, say, as to its colour. Sometimes it is harder as if we ask him whether the idea of 'pen' applies to a ball-point as well as to the fountain-pen he is familiar with already. The great pedagogical point is that these encounters (or 'mis-match situations', as Hilda Taba calls them) should be, wherever possible, consciously arranged by the teacher and not left to chance.

We follow Bloom in calling the skill involved in these 'mis-match' encounters 'application' or, in full, 'application of a concept in a situation new to the learner'. Some authorities call the operation or skill 'classifying'. This is an equally reasonable name, of course, as when we offer a mis-match we are saying in effect, 'Would you classify this new phenomenon as a *pen*?' (or whatever). It is convenient, however, to reserve 'classification' here as a sub-category name for the skill of sorting numerous new phenomena into numerous categories (e.g. 'Sort these ten things into pens and pencils) and to use 'application' for the skill used in those cases where the learner is asked, 'Is this one new thing an example of. . .?' or 'Does the concept label *x apply* in the case of this one new situation?'

Here is an example of how the skill of application might work in practice. Suppose you had been teaching a class the concept 'republic' by various means and you asked the students to read this passage of text:

> Diaz ran Mexico for many years, by getting himself elected President time after time, every four years. His rule was oppressive—the opposition was put down, people were afraid to speak or write against him.

Suppose the nineteenth-and early-twentieth-century history of Mexico was quite unknown to them, you could nevertheless fairly ask students this question: 'Was Mexico in the days of Diaz a republic?' What the student is asked to do by such a question is to apply the newly learned concept (republic) to a situation which is *new* to the student (i.e. nineteenth-century Mexico).

Important points are illustrated by this example. Asking a student to apply a concept in a new situation is a very powerful tool for revealing his level of understanding, as well as improving that understanding. For instance, in this case a student might answer thus: 'No, it can't have been a republic, because there was oppressing and no free speech'.

The teacher may have emphasised that a republic is to be understood as a neutral term, descriptive of a state of affairs in which the head of state, usually called 'President' is elected or re-elected at regular intervals. But one way or another the student may have added to the concept the wrong idea that a republic necessarily entails political freedom, yet he could still have successfully answered translation questions like 'Give historical examples of republics', or even 'Say in your own words what a republic is', without necessarily giving any clue that he had developed this wrong idea.

To answer the question correctly, the student has to match a series of facts against his particular understanding of the concept of a republic. Some of the facts clearly fit the concept well—Diaz was called President; there were elections at regular intervals. Some facts don't fit quite so well—Diaz kept on getting elected; the phrase 'getting himself elected' seems to imply that the elections were crooked. Some facts are apparently relevant, but in fact irrelevant—e.g. that the people were oppressed. The student has to pick his way through this mass of information and decide whether, on balance, the situation described matches up to his vision of the concept 'republic'.

Now, from the point of view of level of difficulty of tasks and setting easier or harder tasks, this is interesting. We can make this type of task harder or easier very simply, and with little trouble on our part, by increasing or decreasing the number of pieces of information in the 'situation' to which the new concept has to be applied.

We assumed at the start that the history of Mexico at the relevant period was unknown to students. But the whole exercise could be made to look pretty meaningless if students happened to know that in those days Mexico was called 'The Republic of Mexico'. This difficulty in finding, in real history, situations which we can guarantee are *new* to the learners is one major reason for making use of games, or imaginary situations.

Before we get into those more complicated realms of making up historical games, however, we should point out that application, like interpretation and translation, can be carried out in quite small, simple exercises. If we have been examining the idea 'revolution' in the context of the first French Revolution, we could ask 'If the French had just changed the King, may be got a cousin of Louis XVI to be King instead of him, would that be a revolution?'

Here 'the situation new to the learner' is just a lightly sketched-in alternative version of the real-life eighteenth-century France he has been learning about. This kind of question, postulating a change in the circumstances under discussion, and, basically, asking the learner to apply and re-apply the concept under discussion, is particularly useful in fairly rapid oral questioning following up, say, a translation task. For example: starting question (translation):

Q. We've talked a lot about Roosevelt in 1901-03 using diplomacy to get the Panama Canal started—now see if you can tell me in your own words what 'diplomacy' means.

A. Diplomacy is when one country tries to persuade another one to give it something, or really bullies another country like roosevelt with Colombia.

Follow-up questions (application):

Q. Suppose Roosevelt had actually declared war on Colombia, would that be diplomacy?

A. No, it's anything except actually going to war.

Q. What if the people in the new state of Panama had had to fight a long war to get free of Colombia and the US had sent them guns to fight with and ammunition and may be volunteers from the states—would we still say the US was doing 'diplomacy'?

A. I don't know. May be there's a kind of half and half between really being at war with somebody and getting at them through diplomacy.

Q. So would you like to add to your definition of diplomacy?

A. Well, you could add that it's not always easy to tell where diplomacy stops and war begins.

Q. What about the Colombians—were they engaged in diplomacy when they tried to stop the US getting into Panama?

A. Yes. They weren't trying to get anything, like I said in my first definition though—so—may be you could say there's 'defensive' diplomacy as well as 'attacking' diplomacy.

By this kind of questioning, giving the student one slightly different 'new situation' after another in which to apply the concept, the concept can be refined, extended and developed efficiently in a short time.

The 'new situation' can sometimes usefully be an old situation, as it were, seen in a new light. Suppose a few weeks ago the class studied Napoleon I but did not use the concept 'dictator' in connection with him. Suppose we are now examining the concepts of 'dictator' and 'dictatorship' in the content of Hitler and Mussolini. We could usefully ask this question— 'You remember Napoleon I, well, was he a dictator?' As long as the class had not looked at Napoleon with that question in mind before, the situation is a new one for them in which to apply the concept.

Looking *back* like this for our 'new situation' to material students have already looked at with different goals in mind has two big advantages; it provides a good reason for students to look at their knowledge of Napoleon and re-examine it—far more useful and motivating than simply saying 'I want you to look over your Napoleon I material for a test'. Second, students already have a lot of knowledge of Napoleon's activities, some of which 'fits' with the idea of him being a dictator, some does not and some of which is irrelevant. So they have quite a rich and complex 'new situation' for application of the concept. This saves us the trouble of inventing one.

The new situation for the learner can also be presented in the form of maps or graphs; for example, students could be presented with a sketch, maps or graphs of some imaginary or unidentified country and asked 'Is the country an *industrial* country?' or 'Is this an *underdeveloped country*?' and so on. Pictures could also be very useful, in this area. The basic interpretation question, with a picture is 'What is going on here?' The basic application question would be 'Is what is going on here an example of . . .?'

Application and Source Material

We can easily ask application questions either about a source itself, or about the events allegedly described in it.

If we look at the source documents in the interpretation section about John Hawkins, we could ask the following question, requiring the student to apply the concepts underlined in the following questions:

Could we call this passage *propaganda* for Hawkins?
Is this a *primary* source?
Would you call Sir Lionell Duckett and the others *capitalists*?

The basic requirements, again, are for students to match their newly acquired concept to the 'new situation' presented by the source and say whether the concept 'applies' or does not—or, best of all, whether the concept has to be modified a little to take account of the new situation. An 'ideal' oral answer to the question 'Would you call Sir Lionell Duckett and the others capitalists?' might go like this:

> No, capitalists use money to build factories and things. Well, I don't know, may be paying for the ships was like building a factory—the idea was to get money, just the same. May be Duckett was a kind of capitalist, after all, only not making things.

(Compare this with the gradual refinement of the idea of 'diplomacy' in the Panama Canal example.)

Interpretation questions can be happily linked with application questions, for instance:

Q. 1. Would you say Hawkins and Duckett were *exploiting* Africa and the Americas? [application]

Q. 2. If you think they were, say how they planned to do it, according to this text. [interpretation]

Sometimes, of course, a student might turn a question intended as interpretation into an application question—for example:

Q. How did Hawkins and Duckett plan to exploit Africa and the Americas?

A. I don't think 'exploit' is the right word to use here, because . . . [In other words, 'I do not want to use this concept to interpret the text with, because I do not think it can be applied'. We would, of course, be pretty pleased with such a response, even though we did not foresee it!]

As with the sometimes fine distinction between interpretation and translation, it doesn't matter too much if we cannot readily characterise a given question as interpretation or application. The main thing is to remember this useful approach to a text—'Do the events here (or the way the writer writes about the events) constitute an example of concept x in action, or not?'—followed, if it is convenient, by the question 'If we have here a case of concept x in action, how exactly does it work out in this case?'

Application and Discussion

'Discussion' is a much-abused term—teachers tend to use it to describe question-and-answer sessions and also sessions in which the proportion of teacher-talk to student-talk is so high as to be not much different from lectures.

A passage like this, for instance, can hardly be called a 'discussion'.

Teacher	:	Who did the pioneers have to fight against?
Student 1	:	The Indians.
Teacher	:	What Indians?
Student 2	:	Sioux, Apache . . .
Teacher	:	Yes, all different tribe of Indians. But they all had one thing in common—what?
Student 3	:	All redskins . . .
Student 1	:	All lived in, er, tents and hunted . . .
Teacher	:	The main thing was that they were all living there long before the white settlers. They had lived there for centuries, quite happily and then the white pioneers came and drove them out. Tell me, do you think the white people were right to do that? [silence]
Teacher	:	Well, were they right to do it, morally, I mean?
Student 1	:	Well, they needed the land . . .
Teacher	:	Sure, they needed it, but so did the Indians; did the Indians' needs not matter? What about the morality of it?
Student 4	:	Some of the, er, pioneers went to dig gold. [silence]
Teacher		May be you think the Indians were cruel in some of the ways they fought, like scalping people. But the white settlers were sometimes cruel too. This whole question

of the rights and wrongs of the settlement of the West is a fascinating one.

[silence]

Teacher : All right, let's move on . . .

The failure of teachers in situations like this to 'get students to discuss' can lead to teachers underestimating the capacity of a group of students to carry on discussion and also to an underestimate of the group's general intellectual capacities.

Let us briefly consider the probable causes of failure in the example above. The teacher first asks factual questions—'Who did the pioneers have to fight?' He then moves on quite suddenly to realms of moral judgement, but by means of a question in such a form that students have no way of knowing what he's getting at. ('What did all the Indians have in common?') He then states the moral issue openly, but in such a way as to make quite clear where his own sympathies lie and with the question 'Do you think the white people were right to do that?' virtually defies the students to disagree with him. Their silence leads him to rephrase his question, not in an easier way, but a harder way, introducing the difficult abstraction 'moral'.

Student 1 then volunteers an answer with which the teacher does not agree. He is verbally smashed down for his pains.

Student 4 then says something about gold-miners. It may or may not contain the germ of something relevant and valuable, but the teacher does not investigate it. He ignores it, elaborates a further point and then abandons the discussion.

It is easy to laugh at 'teacher' in this little scene—not quite so easy actually to do better at discussion in real life. Perhaps the first two things we ought to get straight in our minds are the questions of what we mean by the term 'discussion' and what the purpose of having discussion is.

On the first question, we might say that a discussion is different from a question-and-answer session in that the students frequently address *each other*, including asking each other question. Certainly, in daily life, if six people were described as 'having a discussion', we would think it pretty strange if everybody always addressed the same member of the group and if that same member of the group was the only one who asked any questions, or took any initiative in moving the discussion along.

As to the purpose of discussion—sometimes as teachers we are tempted to think of 'having a good discussion' as a goal to aim for, rather than a method of achieving other goals. Sometimes this way of looking at discussion leads us unwittingly to the position apparently adopted by 'teacher' in our discussion passage above, who seems to see it mainly as an occasion for making his views about the world clear to his students and inviting them to agree with him.

Can we see discussion as having clear learning-aims like other activities, such as questioning students? Well, one thing discussion can do effectively is to help make a student feel at home with a concept and adopt it into his active vocabulary, especially by means of applying it to new situations. Look at this passage of discussion:

Teacher	:	Look at the map here—which would be the place to start a colony? Take a minute to think about it.
Student 1	:	On the bay there. [points]
Teacher	:	Why?
Student 1	:	The ships they . . . the people come in would be safe there.
Student 2	:	Not if the wind blew a different way. [pause] They had only sailing ships.
Student 1	:	Well, most of the time it would be safe.
Student 3	:	Ships in those days would sink easily in a storm, they were wood.
Student 2	:	What about there [points to map] by the big river?
		[pause]
Teacher		What's good about the river?
Student 2	:	You can . . . go up . . . go inland along it.
Teacher		Why is that good?
Student 1		Trade. Trade with Indians and . . .

Student 3 : People in that pace . . . er, the colony, the colony would want to grow bigger and they can go up the river.

Student 1 : Do people in a colony do trade?

Teacher : What do people think about that?

Student 2 : Only with England . . . or somewhere.

[pause]

Student 3 : They'd have to trade with the Indians, too, to get some things they would need. They could trade up the river in boats.

Student 2 : Or go up the river to live when more people came to the, er, colony. And it gets too big for it's place.

Notice the term 'colony' gets used four times by students, once as part of a question from one student to the group at large. In all four cases, the term is used spontaneously, as it were, *not* in response to a teacher-question such as 'What is a colony?' This is important both as a sign that the concept it being assimilated and as an actual aid to the process of assimilating itself.

Also, notice that the group are, as they talk to *each other* as much as to 'teacher', setting themselves application tasks at their own level in their own language. For instance, student 1 in effect asks the group, 'Does the concept colony apply in the case of a group of people who engage in local trade?' Student 2 thinks that it does not. Student 3 thinks it does.

Research indicates that students at all ages will both put questions and give answers to each other with much greater freedom than they will with teachers. However, kindly and encouraging 'teacher' might be, student 1 was more reluctant to put that revealing question, 'Do people . . . trade?' to the teacher than he was to ask his peers. And students 2 and 3, equally, would have been less likely to give those answers to a direct question from the teacher.

Third, we can notice how revealing discussion can be about students' level of understanding. On the question of trade, for example, the teacher might never have thought of putting the question 'Do colonies trade?' simply because it never occurred to him that anyone might think they did not.

Discussion is a unique sort of privileged eavesdropping for teachers, in which they can learn about students' levels of conceptual understanding from the world's top experts on that subject—the students themselves.

Discussion can serve other purposes as well, notably in the area of the skill of evaluation, as we shall see in section 5. But we can sum up the case so far—if we can get students talking to each other we can look for three benefits. Spontaneous use of concepts by students, applying them to new situations, freer discourse on the part of students leading to more chances for application of, and general use of, the new concepts by students, a lot of evidence for the teacher of his students' levels of understanding.

Discussion—Techniques

If we are going to try for application of a new concept via discussion, the students must have done some work on the concept beforehand; a discussion is no place to spring a new concept, as our first teacher seemed to do with the idea 'moral'.

General reading on a topic is not a very satisfactory preparation for discussion. Many of us must have set work in this way and suffered disappointment—'Read up chapter on the Revolutions of 1848 and come prepared for an informed discussion about it in Tuesday's session'. An unformed mass of information is really no use as a basis for discussion—far better would have been to give the students the actual question on which the discussion was to be focused and say, 'Read chapter Revolution of 1848 to help you make a case in the discussion about this question on Tuesday'.

It is best to start off with a clear focus for the discussion—a clear question to answer like 'Where to start the colony?' or 'Why did the 1848 revolts fail?' and preferably also some concrete material to refer to—a map, picture, text, source. 'Let's kick around this idea of "colony" for a while' is not the way to go about it.

It is also a very good idea to give people time to think, both at the start (as the teacher in the 'colony' discussion does) and also from time to time as the discussion goes along. The teacher in the 'colony' discussion could have continued the discussion like this:

> The idea of more people coming to live in the colony—take a minute or two and write down on scrap paper about what kind of people might come out to the colony.

That is much more likely to get a good response than—'You say more people would come—well, who for instance?'—expecting an answer right away. If you were to be asked to discuss, with a group of other teachers, the future of education in the Western world, you would probably appreciate five minutes to get a few thoughts together. Twenty-four hours to prepare would be even better. But we are a little prone to ask students to discuss pretty difficult ideas just when we tell them to, without notice.

If students still don't talk freely, there are two main rules to observe. Train yourself to endure longish silences. If you can make yourself sit through, say, fifteen seconds of silence, you may be surprised how often it is a student who breaks the silence, with a useful contribution. If *you* are always the one to break the silence, students will come to expect it of you and not develop what Stenhouse calls a feeling of responsibility for the quality of the discussion. Don't be punitive. Try not to sound impatient, or say things like 'Come on, this isn't hard, just think a little. . .' Don't pick on individuals—'Come on John, you haven't said much' is well calculated to freeze John and everyone else. Use general phrases like 'What does anyone else think?', to encourage involvement.

If an individual hogs the discussion the formula 'What does anyone else think?' is useful, to get other people into the discussion.

Sometimes discussion is quite lively, but doesn't go the way we want it to. For instance, in the 'colony' discussion, the discussion at the start seems to be going off on to a tack about sailing ships which is not what the teacher wants. There are two points here. First, learn to endure a certain amount of formlessness and irrelevance, especially at the start of a discussion, in the same way as you learn to endure longish silences. Apparent irrelevance may be giving students a chance to settle into the situation, at their own level. Second, don't be punitive. Suppose the 'colony' group had gone on talking about ships, masts, rigging, etc., the teacher could then have said, 'Well, we seem to have a little problem about the bay site—because of this problem over the ships—anywhere else on the map we might go?' To have said, 'Look, group, we're getting nowhere—now try to stick to the point' would be likely to freeze the discussion in its tracks.

Above all, don't give people 'the answer' or make clear by your conduct what you think 'the answer' must be. Notice the actual words of the teacher in the 'colony' sequence. 'Why?' 'What's good about the river?' 'Why is that good?' 'What do people think about that?' He does not let the discussion wander on unchecked and undirected—he uses two basic moves 'What do people think?' to keep the discussion going, and 'Why?' (in various forms) to secure full exploration of the ideas. But imagine the consequences if, when student 2 said 'What about going there, by the big river?', the teacher had said 'Yes, good—we could use the river for inland trade and, in due time, we could expand up it as our population grew . . .' Pretty soon the teacher would find that his discussion had become a monologue. Equally, even if he had only said 'Yes, a site near the big river, now that sounds really interesting'—he would have made very clear that he thought the river site was the best one and made it hard for any student to go against the teacher by opposing the river site or suggesting another one.

It is very helpful if the students can see each other's faces during a discussion and worth the trouble of moving furniture so that they can, as far as possible, do so.

As with any activity, students must see the point of discussion, or they will be less co-operative in doing it. It is rather easy for 'discussion' to seem like a separate thing from 'work', so try to make the connection clear. We could say, in the 'colony' example for instance, 'In a little while you are going to have a thorough discussion so that when you write, your written work will be that much better'. More explicitly, yet, we could say, 'We are meeting this pretty complicated idea "nationalism" quite a lot—so we're going to get better understanding of it by discussing this question . . .' At the end of any discussion, it is essential for the morale of all concerned that there is some summary or other written product to show for the work done.

Small Groups

One of the big obstacles to student discussion is the teacher. As teachers we have strong tendencies to want to guide students, rephrase their awkward utterances, offer clarification, think of better examples than they can and generally behave in ways which may be praiseworthy in other contexts, but which can greatly inhibit discussion.

One way to get round this is to break a class into groups of five or six and give them a problem to discuss in those groups while you sit in on only one group (or may be not on any). There are some useful rules to observe if we try this.

It is even more important than with class discussion to set a small group a very clear task to focus their attention on. The great drawback of the small group method is that you cannot guide the group if it wanders off into irrelevance or frivolity. So—make the task clear and require a short piece of written work at the end of the discussion, preferably from all members, not just a group 'secretary'. Set a strict time limit to the discussion, and, especially if you or they are new to the technique, make the time *short*—so it's—'I want you in your group to look at the map, figure out among yourselves where the colony site should be, with reasons. You can have ten minute for that. Then at the end you will all have five minutes to write down where you personally think the colony should go, with reasons'.

Sometimes individuals seem to get 'frozen out' of small groups, or even whole groups just don't talk freely to each other. There are three things to look to here:

(1) Make sure the group are in little circles, so they can see each other's faces.

(2) Try changing the groups around from time to time as a regular policy so that if you want to break up a group that just don't seem to get along, it's not so obvious a move.

(3) This is an emotionally demanding way of learning for students—a withdrawn individual could be made pretty unhappy by it, for instance. So introduce it in small doses and never let it become the dominant teaching method unless you are sure that nobody is being made to feel socially inadequate by it.

One great benefit of organising discussion in small groups is that it allows us to take account of differing abilities among our pupils, by setting the initial focusing task in different forms to suit the ability levels of different discussion groups within the class.

Suppose the concept we wished to strengthen by means of discussion was 'party' (i.e. political party). We might set a basic task like this—'Suppose your discussion group had to set up a political party, in Russia around 1890, to oppose the Tsar and try to get democracy—plan out how you would go about it'. The group have to think up their own range of possible activities to engage in and decide whether the idea of 'party' would apply, say, to a group who largely went in for terrorism.

We can reduce the scale of this task and thereby make it easier for a less able group simply by saying something like 'Plan out *three* things you would do . . .' Or we could use our technique of 'breaking the task down'. We could say something of this kind—'Consider which of these things a political party might do—(1) start a newspaper; (2) write pamphlets for people to read; (3) organise strikes for more pay among workers; (4) try to improve the way the peasants farmed the land'.

The technique of breaking the task down, of course, is an essential one in any discussion situation if the discussion stalls because the proposition facing the discussion group is too difficult. Suppose teacher in the 'colony' discussion had been met by prolonged, baffled silences right at the start, when he asked, 'Where do we put the colony?' He could then have started to break the task down and set a sub-task like 'Well, where could be a good, safe place to land in the first place?' or 'Where can you see a good water supply?'

We should always have an easier version of our basic focusing-task, ready to produce if needed, either in small groups or whole-class discussions.

Application—Classifying

Here is a list of ten of the policies associated with Louis XIV's minister Colbert:

(1) finance controlled by a Royal Council;

(2) East and West India Companies founded;

(3) generally advocated peace;
(4) improved navy;
(5) founded Academy of Sciences;
(6) road and canal improvements;
(7) model factories set up;
(8) many civil servants prosecuted for embezzlement;
(9) indirect taxes increased;
(10) external tariffs increased.

Now we could ask straight application questions on this list—for instance, perhaps 'Was Colbert on the evidence of this list, a *mercantilist*?' But we can ask another kind of application question, which is an interesting and important enough type for us to think of as a sort of special sub-category. An example of such a question would be, 'Classify the ten items listed into foreign and domestic policies'.

Classifying questions like this ask students to apply two or more concepts at once, as it were—with each item on the Colbert list the student has to look at it and say 'Does the idea "domestic" apply here; does the idea "foreign" apply?'

Classifying questions also tend not only to deal with concepts related to a particular context, like our 'mercantilist' example here. They tend rather to involve those concepts of general usefulness for thinking about history, politics and society, concepts which often go around in antithetical pairs or sets, e.g.:

Foreign : Domestic
Economic : Social; Political
Industrial : Agricultural

If we look at the Colbert list we will notice an important thing about some of the items in it. Items 1 is pretty clearly in the 'domestic' category, while item 3, equally clearly, goes into the 'foreign policy' class. Item 10, however, could give rise to debate as to how it should be classified.

The debate could give rise to the useful outcome of students wanting more information, for example, about the size of the tariff increases, whether foreign countries resented them much and so on. And it could give rise to the setting up by students of a third category, may be called 'domestic with strong foreign policy implications'. This kind of moment, where students need to modify the categories they have been using and even invent new categories, is very precious (remember in this context the gradual modification of the idea 'diplomacy' in the Panama Canal example).

This idea of items of information which don't quite fit the categories being used gives us a very handy lead on the matter of progression of difficulty in classification work.

If a student's grasp of the basic classification being used is not yet strong, for instance, if he is hazy about the 'foreign-domestic' distinction at the simplest level, then we should try to keep doubtful, ambiguous items *out* of the material he classifies. When he can handle the basic classification, we can put in the more problematic items in small numbers. We must at this point tell the student that it is all right, in fact, praiseworthy, to find items that don't fit' and to make up new categories, provided he can justify them. (If John comes up with a new category, the question of whether the new category, in fact, is a useful one, would make an excellent focus for a discussion among students working on the same materials as John.) As students become skilled at classifying with the categories the teacher gives them and also get used to the important idea that categories are only tools, not immutable frameworks, they can start to make up their own categories right from the outset.

A useful exercise to do now would be to make up lists of facts of, say, six or seven items, on the liens of the Colbert list, on a subject of your own choosing. Make it a list which you think can be classified into two simple categories without serious ambiguity in any item. They try adding two or three items to the list which might give rise to debate about how they should be classified.

Another feature of the Colbert list is of importance. The items in the list could be usefully classified in other ways than merely 'domestic-foreign'. 'Economic-social-political', 'economic-fiscal', 'traditional-innovatory', are just a few of the classifications that could be applied even to this very short, slight, piece of material. We can make good use of the fact that almost any body of material can be sorted on the basic of many different types of classification, some simple, some more sophisticated.

First, we can use it to make another distinction between the classification tasks using categories like 'economic-political', the other is making use of less abstract but still worthwhile categories like 'foreign-domestic'.

It also helps us in another, particularly awkward, problem. Very many pubic examinations still require students to memorise and reproduce a lot of factual material, as well as showing evidence of various kinds of understanding. The kind of work we have been describing, with a big emphasis on the conceptual content of material and also on using the factual material in all sorts of different tasks will make 'the facts' a lot easier to recall. But we will still come to the point where students need, and want, to revise the material in the final pre-examination period. This revision can be a process involving a lot of boredom and frustration for all concerned. However, classifying exercises can help us to make this revision process more active and efficient, and less tedious. We can work it in two ways. The most straightforward approach would be to get students to classify old material they had not classified before. Even more valuable—they could reclassify material according to new and perhaps more sophisticated categories. So we could say, 'Get out all your old material on America's problems in the twenty years after 1783. Now back in October we did an exercise where we divided the problems into problems with foreign countries, and problems at home. Now I want you to look at the stuff again, and divide the problems into problems that making the Constitution helped to solve and those that making the Constitution didn't help,' or 'We've learned a lot since October so we'll use some harder ideas now for classifying the problems—try dividing them into economic, social, political and military problems 1783–1800, you'll find they break down into different lists from the ones we got in October'. This way, we have students reading their old notes and materials with a clear purpose in mind and yet not feeling alarmed that they are having to 'do new stuff' on the eve of an examination.

Not strictly relevant to the matter of classification, but conveniently mentioned here is the point that all kinds of application tasks that are not just classifying are very useful for revision purposes. The basic move is to get students to re-examine 'old' material in the light of a concept not known to them at the time they covered that material, but learned subsequently. For example, Napoleon was studied in the autumn, *not* using the term 'totalitarian'. The idea 'totalitarian' was used in the context of Hitler in the summer, so for a revision task we could say, 'Go through our old stuff on Napoleon and say whether you think his régime was totalitarian'. (Or 'Was he a dictator?').

Another version would be: 'Check out the Napoleon material alongside the Hitler material and list what the differences between them were and how they were similar—remember ideas we have worked on recently like totalitarian, dictator, party'.

As well as providing a clear and interesting purpose for re-reading of old material, this kind of task might encourage students to do something which examiners endlessly complain that they do not do at the moment, i.e. to go outside the bounds of set questions and make comparisons between historical figures and events.

Application and Pictures

Pictures can sometimes present a very useful basis for work involving the skill of application.

Exercise 3 (Application)

(Remember to try to make up all questions in a more and a less difficult version).

(1) Make up application questions on the line of the one about the concept of 'republic' at the beginning of this section. Make up each question in a more and less difficult version, by *increasing or reducing the number of pieces of information involved.*

(2) Make up application questions using maps or graphs, or pictures on the lines suggested.

(3) Look back at the source material in the section on Sources. Make up some application questions (perhaps followed by interpretation questions) on the line of those suggested for the Hawkins passages, and for the other passages from Usama and Churchill.

(4) Supposing you were concerned with the concept of colony and colonisation in a nineteenth-century African context; can you rephrase in easier form the following attempt to

start a discussion, presuming that it has produced a total silence from the students?

Teacher : How can you characterise the different approaches of the colonising powers to different parts of Africa?

(5) Suppose a passage of discussion, on the same topic, with the concept of imperialism in mind, went like this:

Teacher : Were any African states themselves imperialists?

Student 1 : No, only Europeans can be imperialists.

Student 2 : That's right.

How would you continue the discussion for this point?

(6) We can now start to put together sequences of tasks as whole lessons. Here is an example.

Phase 1 : As part of the topic of the American Revolution, teacher describes Loyalist point of view, using device of a dialogue between a Loyalist and an interested, but neutral, person.

Phase 2 : Students work through a set of six questions, embodying translation, interpretation and application skills, aimed at strengthening grasp of concepts like Loyalism (in eighteenth-century American context), Tory, grievance, economic, political.

Phase 3 Discussion focused by this question: 'Suppose you were a Loyalist in 1775—make a list of what advice you would give to the British government to keep the colonies loyal'.

Select a topic of your own and put together a sequence like the one above, with more detail on the content of the initial exposition and working out the actual tasks for phase 2. Work in the use of pictures, sources, maps or graphs if you can.

Exercise 3—Suggested Answers

Question 3. Possible application questions on Usama extract (concepts applied emphasised).

(1) 'Does this story illustrate the Frank's religions *tolerance* or *intolerance?*' followed by

(2) 'What decided whether Franks were tolerant or not?'

The answer to Q. 1 is really 'both'—a conceptually more sophisticated question could be:

(3) 'Does the story illustrate Usama's *ambiguity of attitude* to the Franks?' followed by the interpretation question—'How does it show it?'

On extract 2 from Usama, the concept of ambiguity of attitude could also be applied, of course, or we could perhaps ask a compound question:

(4) 'Which of these words best describes what the story is about: *religious intolerance, misunderstanding, racialism?*' followed by an interpretation question on the lines of:

(5) 'Do you think Usama sees it as a case of religious intolerance, racialism, misunderstanding, or what?'

On the Churchill passage, a general application question could be:

(6) 'Is this propaganda?' followed by the interpretation (and translation) questions suggested after the passage itself.

A slightly different way of looking at the extract could give us a question like:

(7) 'Does Churchill argue his case on *moral* grounds, or on grounds of *expediency*?' followed perhaps by:

(8) 'If you think Churchill is making a *moral* case, say briefly what it is'.

All these questions can break down into easier ones in the following ways, for example:

(1) 'Were the Templars tolerant or intolerant? Was the Frankish newcomer tolerant or intolerant?'

(3) 'Where does Usama sound favourable to the Franks?

Where does he sound hostile?'

(4) Could most readily be made easier by reducing the number of words to be 'applied' from three to two.

(6) (i) 'Is it easy to tell which side Churchill is on?'; (ii) 'Does he make out that his own side is strong?'; (iii) 'Does he make out the other side is losing?'; (iv) 'Does he make out the other side is in the wrong?'

(7) 'List the arguments that seem to you *moral* arguments'. 'List the arguments from expediency'.

(8) 'What is Churchill's moral case: (i) against the Germans?; (ii) in favour of the bombing campaign?'

Question 4. Easier version:

(a) 'What did the French do with their pieces of Africa?'

Easier yet:

(b) 'Take one piece of Africa—Algeria—what use did the French have for Algeria?'

or

(c) 'Can you think of a part of Africa where Europeans actually went to settle?'

Question 5. First move must be 'What does anyone else think about that?'—in the hope of getting a more accurate view of imperialism from within the group. If that move fails, we could put some question like this: 'Suppose some African kingdom like Ethiopia conquered a lot of neighbouring tribes, would that be imperialism?' This should produce the effect of causing the students to reconsider the idea of imperialism, but supposing it failed and they said: 'No, that's not imperialism, because the Ethiopians would be the same colour as the tribes', we would then present another 'new situation', for example, 'When the British conquered the white Boers people called that "imperialism"—how come?' Eventually, of course, you may just have to tell them that their idea of imperialism is wrong—life is too short for us to build every concept the hard way. But the rule should be, perhaps, like this: before we tell anybody their view of a concept is wrong, try to give at least *one* and preferably *two* chances for him to readjust his view himself, by asking him to apply the concept in a 'new situation'. (And also let us be very sure that it is a wrong use of a concept we are dealing with, not just an opinion from our own.)

4. Extrapolation

The skill of extrapolating involves the student in constructing quite complicated forecasts about how a given situation might develop. It is virtually impossible to make even the simplest extrapolation without bringing into play some conceptual understanding or other; if, for instance, we asked a young child, 'What will your mother say if you mess up your T-shirt?' he cannot begin to answer without some grasp of cause and effect and of appropriateness of response to a crime of the magnitude of a messed-up T-shirt. If he does not grasp these things, he cannot answer.

For older learners, one of the simplest and most interesting ways of setting extrapolating tasks is in the context of a simulation or game, so we will discuss first these particular vehicles for this skill.

Games

Suppose we set students as exercise in the context of Industrial Revolution work:

> Think of an imaginary country called Fantasia, sometimes in the late eighteenth century. It's a poor country with no rich people, only peasants living by subsistence agriculture and making their own simple goods, like shoes and clothing, at home. The only man who is at all rich is the King and he needs all his wealth to keep up his small palace and a few palace guards. (Fortunately, Fantasia is an island with no hostile neighbours, so they manage without an army or a fleet!) One day, an inventor from England turns up, with two marvellous machines, both powered by water-wheels. One machine spins wool very fast and the other is a loom which can weave three times faster than a handloom. What do you suppose will happen next? Will Fantasia be transformed? Is this a turning-point in Fantasian history?

Suppose student A put together an answer like this:

Nothing happened. A society living entirely at *subsistence* level, with a purely *domestic system* of producing goods would have no surplus wealth to *invest* in machinery, no *market* to

> absorb extra goods (unless they exported them), and no readily available *labour force* to leave the land and man the new *industry*. So any *revolution* in the way of making goods is unlikely, unless and until *agricultural* productivity is revolutionised and a *middle class* created.

Student B, however, answers like this:

> The King would buy the invention and set up factories to spin and weave. The new wool *industry* would act as a multiplier, and pretty soon the whole country would have an *industrial revolution*.

What we have asked these students to do is play a small-scale historical game and, by putting the question 'What happened next?' we have made the student use the skill of extrapolation.

The two contrasted answers the students give show us what a potentially powerful teaching tool lies in this simple move of asking, 'What would happen next?' All the concepts emphasised in the two answers have had to be applied by the students in a new situation and in the process the students have revealed their understanding, particularly of the central idea of an industrial revolution, very clearly.

Before we go any further, we could note three things about this little game. First it is very simple. Any teacher could make up a little game like this in a matter of minutes. Teachers sometimes think a 'game' has to be an elaborately worked out thing, in which, say, the complexities of European eighteenth-century diplomacy are faithfully reproduced in fictionalised form. This is not so. In fact, the whole point of fictional situations is that they are much *simpler* than reality. If we had asked our students to imagine the inventor trying to sell his machines in late eighteenth-century China, the complexities of real eighteenth-century China, in so far as the students knew about them, would have obscured the point of the exercise. Second, the teacher who devised this game had a clear idea of what the point of the exercise was. He wanted students to show that they understood that inventions are not enough to give rise to 'industrial revolution', and to use correctly terms like 'investment', 'market', 'domestic system' and so on. Games are fun and students like them, which is one of the good reasons for using them, but it is not enough as a justification for using them.

When we make up a game, we must know exactly what concepts we want examined and used in the course of the game. Third, asking students to extrapolate was the basic task set, but all sorts of other skills were used by the students in putting their answers together. For example, we noted that the student applied a number of concepts. Also, student A, for example, translated the phrase 'making their own simple goods . . . at home' into the term 'domestic system'. To extrapolate well from a given situation to a future situation, we might have to use a whole battery of other skills, as well as that ability to imagine future situations which is at the heart of the skill of extrapolation itself.

So we can sum up now the characteristic features of a good historical game: (a) it is simple, in two senses: it presents a simpler situation than real life and it does not tax the teacher's research resources of time and material to make up; (b) it has clear learning goals in mind; (c) as well as providing for extrapolation, it gives occasion for using other cognitive skills.

Games and Discussion

In the Fantasia industrial revolution game, we simply set a question to answer, but we could also have used the game as an excellent focus of discussion.

Suppose we went back to student B and stopped him at the point where he said: 'The King would buy the invention and set up factories to spin and weave . . .' We could say, 'Good—now where would the King get the money to invest in factories?'

Student B : May be he could sell his palace?

Teacher : All right . . . but who would buy the stuff the factories made?

Student B The people.

Student C But the people don't have any money. They are subsistence people. . .

In a word, a game can be slowed down and each stage discussed, either with the teacher or in small groups. The object, as in any discussion, being to get the main concepts (like 'invest' and 'subsistence' in this case) used, applied, examined and extended.

Sometimes, to get the discussion moving, you might have to change the game a little. This is another, great advantage of the flexibility of fictitious worlds. Suppose this exchange occurred:

Teacher		How could the King get money to invest in factories?
Student 1	:	Sell his palace.
Student 2	:	He couldn't do that, the people would not let him.
Student 1	:	Well, sell just part of it . . .
Student 3		Yes, rent it out.
Student 2		That's crazy.

'Teacher' now could make a move like this, to get the discussion out of thus unprofitable rut: 'Well, we could note that one problem in this story is finding someone with enough money to invest in buying the machines—but suppose the King found a big treasure, just luckily, and had just enough money to build the factories—what other problems could he still have?'

The important point here, as with any discussion, is that we do not express impatience with, or contempt for, the unhelpful little blind alley the students have got themselves into. Instead we dignify it, as it were, with some kind of summary—even if it has to be only, 'Well, we have quite a problem there', and then move the discussion on, by whatever device comes to hand.

Simulation

The distinction between games and simulation is not a very clear-cut one, but we could give a rule of thumb for our own use. In a *game* the students look at a situation from outside. In a simulation, to greater or lesser degree, they play the parts of people involved in the situation.

We could make the Fantasia game into a very simple simulation quite easily, for example, by saying—'Write a letter as if from the English inventor to the King, trying to sell his machines; and then write back a reply as if you were the King'.

Simulations are more difficult to run than games. Suppose we had a fictional medieval king's council deciding whether or not to go on crusade. In a *game* if a student said, 'Well, I think the bishop on the council would vote against the crusade,' the teacher can reasonably ask 'Why do you think so?' In a *simulation,* if someone as it were playing the part of a bishop says, 'I think this whole crusade thing is silly . . . I don't believe in God, anyway,' it is more difficult to challenge the student without implying pretty clearly that you think he is playing his part wrongly.

On the other hand, simulations give a very good chance for extended application of concepts in new situations and for extrapolation. If someone is playing the part of, say, a feudal king, we can present him with one 'What would you do next?' situation after another, in an interesting and motivating way.

Neither games nor simulation need to be entirely fictional. Consider this example:

[*July 1940*]

(1) All Britain's allies were defeated—Germany and Italy controlled most of the Continent.

(2) Russia had to be regarded as an enemy.

(3) Hitler's intentions were not entirely clear–but an attempt at invasion seemed his likeliest course.

(4) The USA was friendly (arms; 'destroyers for bases') but obviously not going to join the war in the foreseeable future.

(5) France seemed to be becoming a virtually enemy power (Vichy).

(6) The army had lost most of its equipment at Dunkirk.

(7) The air force was intact and its fighter branch efficient and well equipped.

(8) It had emerged that the bomber branch could not attack in daylight without being shot to pieces.

(9) The navy was intact but: (i) Norway campaign had shown that big ships were very vulnerable to air attack; (ii) U-boats were being much more successful against convoys than people had expected ('wolf-packs').

(10) Civilian morale seemed to be very high.

(11) British forces faced enemy land forces only in north and east Africa (Italians only).

(12) India, Australia, New Zealand were getting into gear as sources of very good infantry manpower, though not in great numbers.

(13) Japan was looking more and more dangerous and hostile in the Far East (Singapore; Burma Road).

Task A On what sort of basis might Britain and Germany make peace?

Task B : Devise a strategy for continuing the war.

The situation here is pretty near to real history, but simplified just enough to let the learner get to the heart of the problem, without 'real-world' distractions like, say, the position of Iceland, the finer points of American neutrality, or the precise attitude of Vichy.

Competitive Games

Games can be set up like this:

Group A—you have to pretend to be the Tsarist secret police in the pre-1914 period. Your task is to prevent revolution.

Group B—you are the Social Revolutionaries. Your task is to try to bring about revolution.

Each group is allowed ten minutes to plan and describe a move. Then the other side has ten minutes to plan and describe a countermove, and so on.

This kind of game has one great potential advantage—it could be highly motivating. It has two great potential disadvantages.

First, it could be difficult to keep students within what the teacher thinks are reasonable bounds, in the 'moves' they make. For instance, if the Tsarist police said, 'We would secretly poison all the revolutionary leaders'—some pretty unprofitable wrangles could break out over whether that was a possible 'move' or not. To head off these wrangles, the teacher would have to set up some strict rules for the game and could soon find himself involved in a lot of complicated work on forming the rules.

Second, in games we want students to apply concepts in new situations to extrapolate from one situation to another. In a game where two or more 'sides' make 'moves', however, the new situations are devised as it were by students, not the teacher, and so could be trivial, far-fetched, or in some other way not as suitable for good learning as teacher-devised new situations. In the Tsarist police game we would want students to apply ideas like revolution, sabotage, *agent provocateur,* propaganda and so on. But they *might* get into lengthy discussion of invisible ink, pistols disguised as umbrellas and the like, and the teacher would find it the most difficult of situations to guide back to relevance and purposeful learning.

None of these snags has to rule out a use of competitive games, but the learning aimed at should be carefully thought about before we embark on planning one.

Other Uses of Extrapolation

The great advantage of games is that when we put the basic extrapolation question, 'What would happen next?', we can be sure that the student does not know what, as a matter of fact, did happen next.

However, we can get students to use the skill of extrapolating in non-fictional settings as well. Suppose we asked about China in 1945.

> After the Japanese army was defeated and went home, what do you think the Kuomintang and Communists would try to do? Who might help the Kuomintang—who might help the Communists?

The student obviously has to extrapolate from what he knows of the KMT and Communists in the thirties, from what he knows of Russia's attitude to the Communists and so on, to do this task. As with the game examples, he has to use other skills as well, notably application of concepts like political party, movement, alliance, in a new situation. He may, of course, simply already know what happened in 1945—that is the snag with using the skill of extrapolation in a real historical context. But on the other hand, he may not and it's usually possible to tell whether a student is remembering something, or working it out as he goes along.

A very simple and useful extrapolation task with any picture showing action is to ask students what they think would happen next if the picture 'came to life' and the action in it continued.

Extrapolation links rather naturally with graph-based work. Students could be asked simply to extrapolate a graph line and, for instance, work out what unemployment figures for the UK would have been by 1942 if they had gone on rising at the 1931 rate, and there had been no World War II. Or they could go beyond that and be asked, 'If the figures had gone on rising at such a rate, what social and political effects might there have been by 1942?'

All the time, with extrapolation, we are trying to move the student beyond the 'guessing' type of forecast, which takes account only of one factor in a situation, towards a true 'weighing up' of, ideally, all the factors in a situation, and a forecast based on that 'weighing up'. To see what this means, in a rather extreme illustration, we could look back to the student answers on the Fantasia problem at the start of this section. As well as applying a bigger range of relevant concepts, student A has clearly taken a lot more factors into account than student B did.

However, we should recall that students' capacity to take numbers of factors into account is related to their stage of general cognitive development. So, if we're wise, we start off, whether in a game or a straight 'non-fiction' extrapolation exercise, only asking students to take account of a small number of factors, i.e. three or less. As time goes by, we can increase the number of factors to be dealt with and see what happens. This, by the way, gives us an additional, valuable lead on the question of what makes one task harder than another; in the case of extrapolation exercises, as with application, the harder task is one with more factors in it to take account of.

Sometimes, especially with non-fictional extrapolation, you have to think ahead, and actually prevent a group or individual student from bringing up more factors than you think they can deal with. To take a case—suppose you offered a fictional, but very near real-life scenario like this and asked students to forecast the outcome.

> Sometime in the near future, the Arabs, using Russian arms, invade Israel. Soon the Israelis are in trouble and really look like they might lose. What will the USA do?

Now what you intend students to take account of is, say, four factors:

(1) the importance of Arab oil—using concepts like 'economic';

(2) US—Russian rivalry—using concepts like 'cold war', 'strategy';

(3) US—Israel relationships—using concepts like 'historical links', 'domestic politics';

(4) fear of nuclear war—using concepts like 'escalation'.

This would be a useful exercise. But it could run into a snag if students start asking things like 'Is this in a Presidential election year?' 'What do the British and French think?' 'What are the Chinese saying?' The student group itself could bring up more factors, in other words, than it knows how to deal with.

When people have more factors to deal with than they know how to, they obviously get frustrated and confused and eventually don't want to do the work at all. To avoid this, what we can do is make clear to students exactly what factors we want them to take account of, and also what we don't want them to take account of, especially when we are dealing with 'real-world' situations.

Another difficulty about extrapolation exercises is how to use inadequate answers. Let us look at the answer of student B to the original 'Fantasia' problem at the start of this section:

> The King would buy the invention and set up factories to spin and weave. The new wool industry would act as a multiplier and pretty soon the whole country would have an industrial revolution.

Student B has taken account of three factors in the situation—the (presumed) desire of the King to get rich; the existence of the new inventions; the fact that single industries sometimes act as economic multipliers. But he has also left out a lot of factors, and so come up with a projected short-term future for Fantasia which is actually pretty unlikely. Now, suppose this is a *written* answer, not one which can be modified in discussion. We can obviously praise B for a lot—e.g. correct use of terms like 'industry' and 'multiplier'. But how can we progress with the rest of the work from this rather shaky basis? It's possible that three factors is the largest number B *can* take account of at one time—so telling him his answer is interesting but wrong, because of six other factors he has not taken account of, would be both discouraging and not likely to do much good.

There is no easy answer to this one: but two general rules might be suggested; first, retain and accept as much as possible the student's forecast, however, unlikely it might be; and second, introduce those factors which the student originally overlooked or ignored, one at a time. In the Fantasia case, we might do it like this:

> O.K. The King set up the factories like you say. Then one day people came along and said: 'Your Majesty, there are so many people working in your factories, that there are not enough people left to work the farms—we are going to have famine pretty soon—what are you going to do now?'

Whatever answer the student comes up with he will now have to take some account of the previously ignored factor of the relationship of industry to agriculture. When he has worked out a solution we could then set him, say, a reading task on these lines:

> Read pages so and so in the textbook and find out how it was the English didn't have a famine problem when they started up their industries in the eighteenth century.

Perhaps this point has been laboured—but it is of very great importance. Extrapolation exercises are a very powerful tool, potentially, for fostering autonomy, confidence and what we might call intellectual self-respect in a student. Through such exercises he can say to himself, 'History is not just a set of arbitrarily related events, divulged to me one at a time by a sort of priesthood of teachers. It's rational; up to a point it's even structured. Given factors A, B, C, even I can figure out what *might* happen next, at least in a rough kind of way, at my own level'.

Such a state of mind is obviously greatly to be desired. It is also fragile: we can very easily destroy it by treating students' early attempts at rational extrapolation too harshly or dismissively. If we do that, we reinforce the students' idea that it is no good trying to figure things out for themselves, teachers will always know better, so sit back and let the teacher do it all.

Pictures and Extrapolation

Many pictures lend themselves to the simple extrapolation question, 'What is going to happen next in the picture?' Quite often the answer to such a question might be banal and neither foster not reveal a student's understanding of important matters. However, if we look at Picture 5.1 (The Normans enter Lincoln) we can see that the rather simple-sounding 'What will happen next?' formula leads to consideration of important matters like what exactly might have been involved for a given city in a major change of political régime in medieval times.

Picture 5.2. The Normans enter Lincoln, 1067.

It would be interesting now to consider where a discussion might lead if it was started off by the simple question, 'What is going to happen next?' asked about Picture 5.2 (Fall of the Bastille).

Exercise 4 (Extrapolation)

Making up games is not difficult—what is more difficult is making sure they are at the level you want, as to the number

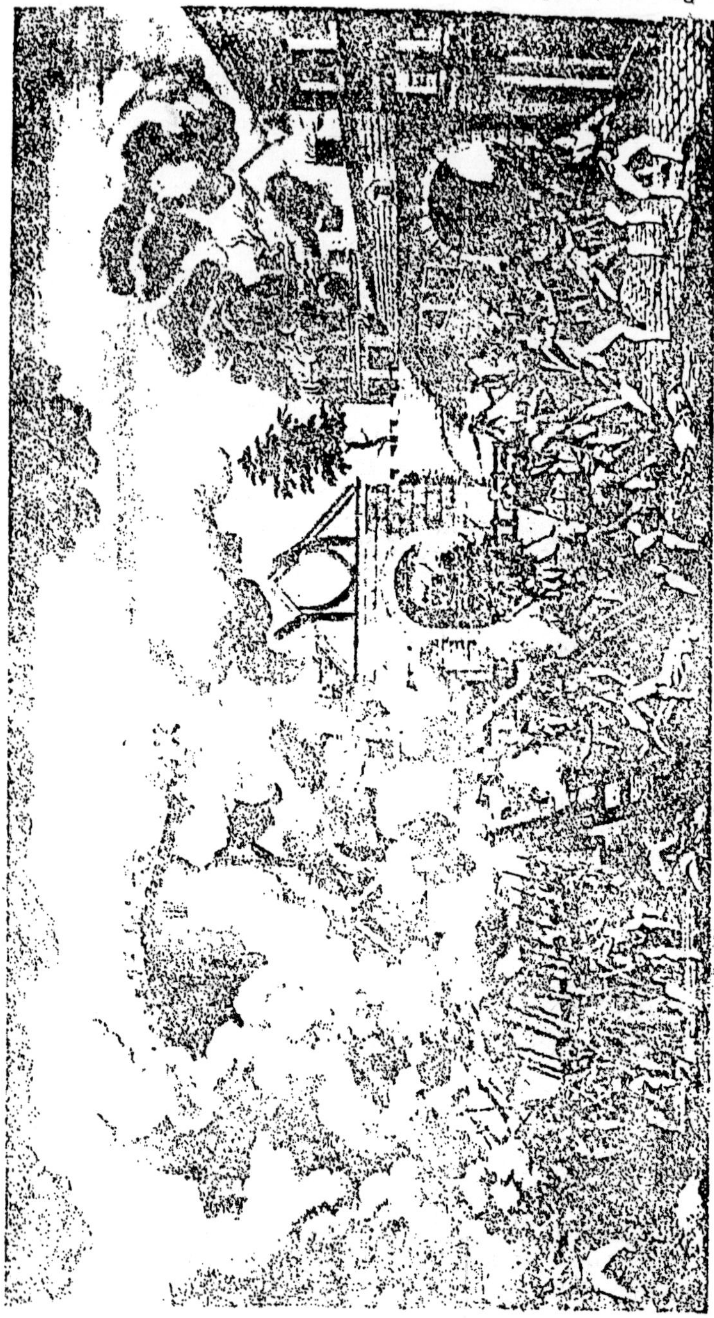

Picture 5.3. The Fall of the Bastille in 1789.

and complexity of factors the students will have to deal with to give a reasonable answer. So let's try an analysis first—what are the main factors students would have to deal with to give a reasonable answer on this game task below?

Concordia Territory Game—This is a map of the territory of Concordia, in the west of North America in 1860. You will notice there are only a few small towns. Concordia is mostly given over to cattle-ranching—every year the ranchers drive their herds to market, far to the south, away from Concordia, in great cattle drives.

Concordia would be good farming country, but not many farmers have settled there yet, because it is so far away and remote.

Politically Concordia is solid for the Patriotic Cattlemen's Party, which backs high prices for beef and low prices for everything else!

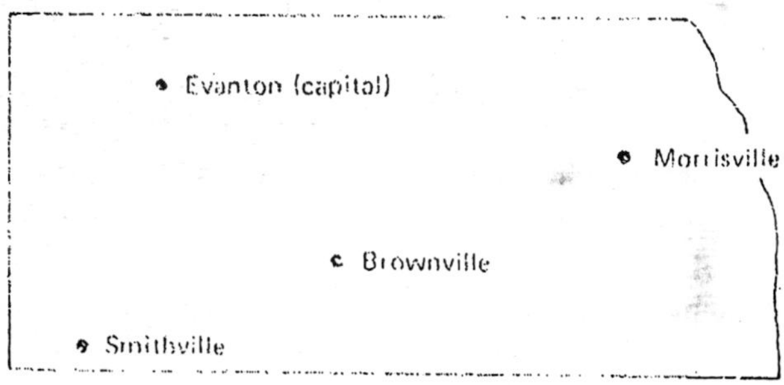

Here is Concordia in 1870 with just one big change—the railroad. How will the railroad affect Concordia in the next twenty years, do you think?

Exercise 5 (Extrapolation)

Look at these written answers to an extrapolation problem—work out what you would say to each student and how you would try to get each student to think the problem through more fully.

The Problem—Borovia is a country in the twentieth century. It is a democracy with two main parties, the Patriots and the Democrats.

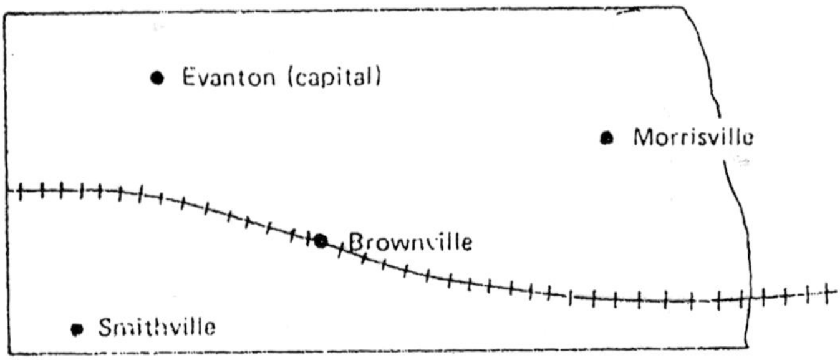

Borovia is developing a manufacturing industry, but so far not too successfully, because of competition from abroad. So the Patriots, who form the government at the moment, decide to put big tariffs on all foreign manufactured goods coming into Borovia. What would be the results of this action over the next five or ten years?

Student A—All prices of manufactured goods in Borovia would increase. Some people, like farmers, might not like this—have to pay more for ploughs, tools and so on. They would just have to put up with it, though, if the Patriots are the government.

Student B—Foreign countries oppose Borovia's action; they might try to persuade Borovia to stop the tariffs and, if Borovia goes on, put big tariffs on Borovian goods and start a trade war. Eventually that might lead to a real war which Borovia might or might not win.

Student C—Farmers and anybody who was not making manufactures would suffer high prices. They would get together and vote for the Democrats at the next election and put out the Patriots and change the tariff back.

Exercise 6 (Extrapolation)

Take the July 1940 extrapolation task on page 165 and try making it easier in two ways.

(*a*) Try reducing the number of factors from 12 to about 6 or 7 main ones.

(b) Try recasting the problem in a fictional form, i.e. as a *game* about invented countries with only four factors in it. It will be interesting to notice those factors you feel you can discard in the fictional game, in the interests of simplicity, but which you felt you could not leave out of the 'real-life' exercise without doing too much violence to historical accuracy.

Exercises 4, 5—Suggested Answers

Exercise 4—A good account of Concordia must take note of at least these *four* factors:

(a) The effect of the railroad on the cattle industry (using concepts like 'railroad', 'industry', 'market').

(b) The effect on the towns, especially Brownville—using terms like 'market', 'industry', 'population growth', perhaps also ideas like 'political agitation' (on the part of Brownville citizens wanting Brownville to become territorial capital instead of Evanton).

(c) Immigration by rail, especially of farmers—using terms like 'immigration', 'agriculture', 'arable', 'diversified'.

(d) Political change—using terms like 'interests', 'election', 'political power', 'party'.

Other factors which we could *ether* include, to make the exercise more complex, *or* firmly exclude at the start if we think the game is already complex enough, could be the Indian question, the presence of gold or other minerals, the links, if any, between 'Patriotic Cattlemen's Party' and the Democrats or Republicans of the real world, whether the immigrants would be Northerners or Southerners—and so on.

Exercise 5—Various lines are possible on all three, of course, but the following are possibilities:

Student A—We can praise the understanding of the relationship of tariffs and prices, and understanding of different economic interests of farmers. A line to follow-up is the apparent lack of understanding that the Democrat Party could be, or become, an instrument of farmer discontent—by questions like 'What might the farmers do at the next election?' 'What might the Democrat Party do?'

Student B—Obviously we can praise understanding shown of complex possible external results of the policy. We need a follow-up question which will give full value to the good answer on external results, and still draw attention back to internal problems—for example, 'So the foreigners won't like Borovia's policy—anyone inside Borovia itself who won't like it?'

Student C—Student C needs to get together with Student A! In discussion together, they could obviously have come up with a pretty full answer on the political side of the question. Failing that, the next probe question to C could be something like, 'Who would still be voting Patriot at the next election, do you think?'

5. Evaluation

The skill of evaluation involves, quite simply, the making and communicating of judgements. When we enter the realm of making judgements and giving opinions, it is sometimes easy for us as teachers to neglect the fact that we are dealing with an intellectual skill at all. A skill in its nature is the sort of thing that is capable of being improved and to talk of improving someone's skill at forming and articulating opinions and judgements sounds presumptuous. It also sounds dangerous, for it would not be a long step from trying to improve someone's skill at making judgements, to 'improving' the judgements themselves in the sense of getting them to conform more closely to one's own.

However, students of all ages are daily called upon to make judgements, to evaluate in historical contexts, so we clearly have a duty to do something about their competence in the matter, on that ground alone. And it is not too difficult in principle (though harder in practice) to separate the idea of a competent or skilful evaluation from the idea of 'an evaluation I approve of'. A practical example will be the best way to approach the question of what makes an evaluation or judgement more competent than another one.

Let us look back at the 'Concordia Territory' exercise (Exercise 4). Suppose we had set students to do more than say how the railroad would affect Concordia; suppose we had asked them to evaluate the impact of the railroad, make a judgement about it, and answer this question: 'Would the railroad coming be a good thing or a bad thing for Concordia?'

Here are some examples of student responses, all giving different answers to the above question on the Concordia railroad. As you read them, try to assess their quality as judgements, as evaluations. You might even try to put them in rank order, before reading the 'comments' section which follows.

Student A—It would be a good thing—only an idiot would not be able to see that.

Student B—A bad thing; the cattlemen would lose their power and may be their land.

Student C—The main thing for a territory was to get more people, and economic development. The railroad is good because it brings in people to settle and economic development. There was no economic development before the railroad.

Student D—The cattlemen would make more money getting their herds east on the railroad, but in the end they would lose to the farmers, who would gain more numbers and get rich and get to control the state. May be their party would be better than the Patriotic cattlemen, may be not. So in the end it would be a good thing, just about.

Student E—Concordia would change from a cattle state to a farming state or industry state. This would be a bad thing for wildlife, with many more people, fences, towns and so on. I think this is the main thing, preserving wildlife, so the railroad would be really a very bad thing, although good for people, especially the farmers.

Comments on Student Responses

Student A—We should not be too hard on student A. He gives no reasons for his evaluation and, worse, supports his case with emotive language ('idiot'), not with argument. Yet his answer has one great virtue, so obvious that it is easy to overlook: it fulfils the prime condition of a good evaluation in that it is clear to everybody what the judgement or evaluation actually is.

Student B—He gives a reason for his judgement, and so ranks above A, but below C, because:

Student C—Does something important, which only one other student, E, does. He states explicitly the basis of his judgement, his premiss, if you like, 'The main thing . . . was to get more people . . .' B does not tell us why it matters what happens to the cattlemen; he just leaves us to assume that he thinks their fate is the over-riding consideration. However, student C's evaluation has a major flaw—it seems to be partly based on a wrong understanding of the concept of 'economic development'. So we are left wondering: if student C understood that cattle-ranching is, in fact, an example of economic development, would his evaluation still be the same?

Student D—His evaluation is the first one which explicitly tries to take account of all the factors in the situation—cattlemen, farmers, politics. To that extent, his is the best answer so far. Also, his final two words 'just about' are important because they show that, unlike the others, he is conscious that judgement involves weighing one factor against another, and so there is always room for at least a little doubt. One weakness of answers A to C is their tone of slam-bang certainty.

D is, however, inferior to C, we might say, because he does not state the criterion or premiss on which he founds his conclusion that the railroad, on balance, is a good development.

Summing up, so far, then, we might suggest these criteria for a good evaluation.

(a) It should be clear what the evaluation is.

(b) The evaluation should be supported by reasons.

(c) The evaluation should not be supported by emotive language ('. . .only an idiot would disagree').

(d) The basis, or premiss, on which the evaluation is made should be explicit.

(e) The evaluation should be based on correct understanding of any ideas which are central to the argument.

(f) All the relevant factors in a situation ought to be taken account of in making the evaluation, not just half the case.

(g) A good evaluation will show some sign of tentativeness, some acknowledgement of the possibility of a different judgement, even if only a phrase like '. . . a good thing, just about'.

If we look at student E's answer on Concordia, we see that it meets all these criteria better than any of the other four.

It also brings us to the problem that makes the area of evaluation so much more sensitive than other areas: what if we, as teachers, or indeed as people, don't like the contents of the evaluation made by a student, however skilfully it is put together? The emphasis of student E on the interests of wildlife may not cause you much discomfort, perhaps, but it would to many people. And how would you have reacted the following situation?

A couple of years ago, a young student-teacher told a story to an ordinary class of nine-year-olds in an ordinary English junior school. The story was about a nine-year-old girl in the 1820s in England who was sent to jail for stealing a penny when she was starving. At the end of the story the discussion went like this:

Teacher : Wasn't that awful, sending a little girl your age to jail?

Child A : She was stealing.

Teacher : Yes, but wasn't sending her to jail cruel?

Child A Not to jail, but she was stealing.

Child B : She has to be punished . . .

Child C Not jail, but could they have branded her?

Child B : Brand her on her hand so people would know . . . ?

Child D : Cut her hand off. [laughter]

Teacher : But she was starving!

Child C Well, they could give her food, some food, just a bit, and brand her and let her go.

These children were nine-year-olds—but the basic problem will still be there when students are sixteen and over: are we interested in improving students' skill in respect of evaluation, when what they might produce is say, cogently argued favourable judgements on Hitler's policy towards the Jews?

We might be tempted to try it both ways—hope that as we increase their skill in evaluating, so we can at the same time subtly make the content of their evaluations more acceptable to us. At the present state of knowledge unhappily (see later section on 'attitudes'), this idea looks like a dead duck. It seems that what students will do if we try it is see through the game; reject whatever opinion we are trying to promote, and become alienated from the whole process, so that even our attempt to improve the skill as a skill tends to fail.

The same applies if we think to try a head-on approach: 'If I don't like what they say in their evaluations, I'll tell them so, right out and if need be, argue them round'. The only difference from the subtle approach is that the likelihood of producing alienation, resentment and, above, all, *even stronger resistance to your point of view,* is a good deal greater. So there is no easy way round this one: if we are going to try to improve students' skill at evaluation, we have to be prepared to hear and, so far as we can, tolerate some things we are not going to like.

Before we move on to consider the business of how exactly to improve students' evaluation skills, there are two further points to consider.

Judging 'In Accordance with the Values of the Past'

A lot of confusion is caused by this idea, which might be crudely expressed as: 'We can't judge the people of the past by our own standards: their values were quite different from ours'.

In fact, of course, we can. Suppose we asked students whether the sack of Jerusalem in 1099 was justified. A student could reply:

> The sack was a horrible event, but to most Crusaders it would be justifiable because they believed they were engaged in just war, the enemy were infidels, enemies of God; and in any case the ideas of the time allowed the sacking of a city taken by storm.

This would be an interesting and worthwhile answer. But it is not an answer to the question, 'Was it justified?' It is an answer to the question, 'Did the Crusaders think the sack of Jerusalem was justified?' and the skill involved would probably be, largely, interpretation. It is not a case of evaluation at all, except in so far as he describes the sack as a 'horrible event'.

A genuine evaluation answer could be given, possibly in this form:

> A massacre of civilians might be justified on two possible grounds—that it was the only way to avoid some even greater evil (e.g. the World War II bombing of Germany), or that the massacring force were saving their own lives in the only way

open to them (for example: the case of policemen surrounded by a hostile mob). In the case of Jerusalem, 1099, neither case seems to me to obtain, so the Crusaders were not justified.

We want, of course, always to avoid sloppy discounting of historical circumstances, of the sort of 'The medievals must have been crazy—they thought the earth was flat!' But there is no reason why students should not evaluate the events of the past, making their own criteria explicit, as well as interpreting the values of the past, essential though that activity is.

Nor is there any reason to suppose that a student's capacity to experience the past imaginatively, to 'put himself into the skin' of, say, a Crusader, or a pioneer, would be impaired in any way simply because that student is adept at making lucid and rational evaluations of past events in terms of his own value system.

Not All Evaluation Involves Moral Judgement

This point is a good deal less controversial than the last one, but very important. When we ask 'Were Roosevelt's New Deal policies effective?' we are asking for an evaluation, but using relatively neutral ideas like 'effective' instead of ideas like right and wrong.

Teachers commonly use this kind of question with older and abler students, but sometimes neglect chances to ask younger students to make such evaluation. This is a pity. Evaluation is a worthwhile skill in its own right and early and frequent practice in evaluating neutral matters like the efficiency of a policy might make students more willing to approach the more highly charged evaluations of moral questions. Questions like 'Was X effective?' are another good tool in our basic task of getting concepts used and made familiar. The Roosevelt example quoted, for instance, would probably call for the correct use of at least these important ideas in the framing of a reply: policy, economic, social, depression, political, agriculture, commerce, investment. Evaluation questions are the handiest single way to reinforce by use one particular set of concepts which are basic to understanding of history, politics and social studies, which are often rather weakly grasped by students.

Just consider the mere *frequency* with which we meet 'weasel' words like the following, in a history or politics setting: 'successful', 'efficient', 'effective', 'useful', 'well-planned', 'important' (and their negatives of course). Then try putting some of them in a context: how firmly do *you* grasp, and how firmly would you guess your students will grasp, the full meaning of these phrases?

An effective President.
Prussia was an efficient state.
A successful King.
Ineffective attempts at reform.
An important event.

Levels of Difficulty in Evaluation Tasks

Let us stay with the Franklin Roosevelt New Deal example for a moment. Suppose, full of zeal for the cause of improving students' skill at evaluation and determined to use evaluation as a method of concept-learning, we put the question, 'Was Franklin D. Roosevelt a good President?' What we might get by way of reply is a blank look, because we have forgotten that evaluation tasks, like any other, can be just too hard for people. Let us try making this particular task easier, stage by stage. Our first move, of course, would be to break the task down. As the task stands, the student has a very difficult hidden 'sub-task'—he has to decide first what areas of Roosevelt's activities it is appropriate to examine in judging Roosevelt and then make the judgements.

So we could suggest areas for the student to look at, for example:

(1) success or otherwise in getting re-elected;

(2) foreign policy and war;

(3) domestic affairs;

(4) dealings with Congress;

(5) Constitution;

(6) how people judge him now.

Right away you will notice a difficulty—that we cannot give a 'neutral' list of 'areas'. Whether, say, 'dealings with Congress' has any bearing on the question of whether a man is a good President, is itself a matter of judgement, of evaluation. Still, if a student is baffled by a question, we have to start somewhere. When the student no longer needs this kind of help in 'breaking a question down', then one of the interesting things we can discuss with him in his answer is just this question—why he chose the areas he did.

To make the task easier still, we could remember from our work on 'extrapolation' the importance of the number of factors in a task and reduce the list of areas to be considered to three or four.

Another useful device to make tasks easier is particularly relevant to evaluation tasks: instead of saying, 'Was Franklin Roosevelt a good President?' we can say, 'Was he a better or worse President than Theodore Roosevelt?'—we can ask for comparison, instead of straight judgement. On the face of it, this complicates matters rather than making them easier. In fact, though, it lets people off the hook of measuring a set of Franklin Roosevelt's activities against the abstract idea 'good', and lets them measure against the concrete—Theodore Roosevelt's activities. Any comparison, of course, has to be carefully chosen. Like must be compared with like and students must have equal information about both parties.

A special point about level of difficulty in evaluation tasks can be illustrated with these two questions:

Was America right to intervene in Vietnam?

Has the Industrial Revolution done more harm or good?

Now, answering these questions would be hard, however much we broke them down into manageable parts. They are hard because they are hard'—that is, because our current value systems are such that very many sophisticated observers would find it difficult to give a straight or simple answer. So, although the first, basic criterion of a good evaluation answer is that it does contain an expressed judgement, sometimes we might want to make clear that an acceptable evaluation might be: 'Can't say'.

One last point on level of difficulty. Our Roosevelt example had one great merit from the outset—it was about a specific President and his specific situation. In questions with a moral aspect, unless we put them in a concrete, specific setting, we can end up with tasks that are dealt with in a disappointingly shallow way by students, because they appear far too easy. Look at this example: 'Were the European Resistance in France. Holland, etc.,' right to fight the Germans in World War II?' The answer 'Yes' would probably be given most times, by most students, after little thought. But look at this case:

> Jean was a fifteen-year-old French boy in 1942. He joined the Resistance. Pierre was also fifteen. He would not join the Resistance because he was afraid that if he was caught his mother and two sisters might be shot or sent to a labour camp. He had known of that happening to other people.
>
> Paul was also fifteen. He did not join, partly because he was afraid for his family, partly because he thought, 'The Resistance in France does not matter—blowing up a few factories and killing German sentries will not affect the outcome of a world war'.
>
> Who was right of these three?

This one is not so easy to answer, certainly not without using ideas like social responsibility, sabotage, effectiveness, importance, patriotism and the like. It also puts a genuine moral problem in something like the way in which in fact it did present itself to people in real life.

The rule is this then—present those problems of evaluation which involve moral problems in as concrete a way as you can devise. What you don't want is glib, general condemnations of war, famine, and wrong-doing that never face real difficulties and dilemmas.

Summary On Level of Difficulty of Evaluation Tasks

With an evaluation task, to make it easier, the same rules apply as for other tasks, i.e.

(a) braking the task down;

(b) reducing the number of factors to consider (the matters of language of task and size of tasks also apply, of course).

An additional, useful device is setting comparison tasks. Some evaluation tasks can sound quite sophisticated, but in fact be too easy if they present moral problems not in a challenging, concrete setting.

Devising Evaluation Questions for Concept Development

We can and ought to use evaluation questions in most topics, as part of a series of tasks and questions. We can use them in two main ways. Suppose we had been working on the ideas of 'investment' in the context of the nineteenth-century American West. We will have possibly used translation questions like 'Say in your own words what *investment* is,' application questions like 'Could you call it *investment* if a man used all his money in a poker game?' Extrapolation questions, possibly in some kind of American West game involving investment decisions, and so on.

We could not ask an evaluation question such as: 'Which do you think would have been the *best* investment round about 1870—gold-mind, cattle-ranch, or the railroads?' As with the other skills, putting together an evaluation answer causes students both to reveal and extend their understandings—as in these responses (which it might be useful to put in order of merit, in terms of the understandings shown of the idea of 'investment').

(1) The gold-mine would be best. You can make more on your investment in a short time, maybe millions in a year.

(2) The gold-mine, gold is a lot more valuable than cattle or a railroad.

(3) Gold-mine might give most in a short time, but railroad would be safer to keep your savings all in a long time. So gold for a short invest, and railroad for long-term investing.

(4) The railroad would still be there if the cattle died of disease, or gold ran out. So railroad to invest in.

Sometimes, though, it is not easy to see how to go for a given concept directly, even though worthwhile evaluation questions seem to be suggesting themselves. Look at this evaluation question, for instance: 'What chance of success did the Irish Easter Rebellion of 1916 have?'

Now this, in fact, is not a particularly good task for developing the most obvious concept embodied in it—i.e. 'rebellion'. To see why not, look at these two responses:

Student A—They had no chance, with not enough men and their only ally (Germany) a long way off. Also the people were not very interested.

Student B—No chance to win, because of the odds and time, but even if they lost they might make people get excited and one day get them on their side.

Neither student investigates, or even directly uses the idea 'rebellion'. Yes student B has shown greater understanding of something or other, we feel, than student A, and the question itself sounds like the kind of question we ought to be asking.

We could get in deep water thinking about exactly what it is that student B has understood better than A—we could say that he has obliquely used the concept 'propaganda victory' or the concept 'political gesture' or 'martyrdom' or 'myth'. But a handy, if less profound way of looking at it is this: student B, we could say, has explored and developed in a worthwhile way the concept 'success'. He has said to himself, as it were, 'success isn't always winning; it can be certain ways of losing, too'. There is a small but extremely important list of such words as 'success', referred to on page 181 and what we can always usefully do, if we cannot devise an evaluation question which goes straight for the development of a specific concept (like 'investment' in our first example, or 'rebellion' in this one) is think out a question which develops one of these central, general ideas—

Was it *efficient?*
Was it *successful* . . . ?
Which was most *important* . . . ?
[and so on - compare page 181]

Exercise 7 (Evaluation)

Try now to make up evaluation questions in connection with the major examples in this book so far, starting with the Australian Gold Rush example at the start of the translation section. (Ignore very minor or obviously unsuitable examples, e.g. 'Look at the map and tell me how far New York is from Boston'.)

Evaluation and Museum Visits

In the sub-section dealing with interpretation using museum visits we pointed out that one great value of museum visits was that three-dimensional objects made concrete and comprehensible, in an unrivalled fashion, the central historical idea of development.

Development is more than change; it involves the idea of a change that has come about for some sort of reason, a reason which can, in principle, be understood by an observer. So, with our telephone example in the museum visits sub-section, the key question was 'Say why you think telephones have developed the way they have?' Now suppose we asked, 'Are the new telephones better than the older ones?' and suppose we got these three responses:

Student A—The old ones are better, they are prettier and a lot nicer to look at.

Student B—The new ones are better—they would not fall over so easily.

Student C—The old ones look nicer to me, but the newer ones would not get knocked off so easily, so I think the new ones are better.

Student C has plainly done the best evaluation, because he has taken two factors into account, unlike A and B. He has also stumbled on more fundamental truths about the notion of development, i.e. development in something almost never involves just one change—even with a simple item like telephones, changes making for greater stability involved changes in appearances as well. This is very often the reason why a given development is evaluated differently by different people—they are actually using different criteria. If you are making an evaluation of the goodness or otherwise of a given development, it could save a lot of unnecessary argument if you make clear which criterion or criteria you are using and at least show signs of knowing and understanding the criteria used by people who don't agree with you. (Think how much political argument in the Western word consists of one side arguing about individual liberty and their opponents arguing about social justice.)

This sounds like a lot of solemn weight to put on some kids looking at old telephones, but in fact it's very hard to think of a better way of making these vital points about evaluating developments, than through the use of actual tangible objects in museums. So when we plan for questions in connection with a museum visit, whenever possible, our questions should include evaluation questions about whatever developments the exhibits illustrate and embody.

Evaluation and Pictures

Pictures can provide a basis for evaluation questions, particularly when the picture seems to have been drawn or taken with some purpose in mind. At a much more concrete level, students can be asked to evaluate the effectiveness, usefulness, and so on of pictures of machinery, weapons, buildings, sites. It would be useful now to attempt to devise an evaluation question on this picture of Lincoln Castle in its early form and map out the discussion that might be sparked off by quite a simple evaluation question.

As this is our last look in this book at the teaching possibilities of pictures, it would probably be worthwhile at this point to do one further exercise on pictures, with absolutely no guidance on what questions or tasks might be set, or even what particular skills might be involved. Picture 5.3 presents a lively and interesting scene: what questions or tasks could you set on it involving interpretation, application, evaluation or any other skills?

6. Analysis

So far, we have been devising tasks for students based largely on giving the students the relatively small amount of information needed for the task. When we have given students a fair amount of prose to read, we have been telling them very precisely what to do with the information, e.g. in interpretation using sources—telling them to translate emphasised terms in a passage and so on.

Obviously, though, someday students will need to be on their own with books, or a lecture or a project. They might have only a relatively general instruction like, 'Read and make notes on . . .' or answer this question, 'What were Washington's main concerns as President?' What they will have to do, as well as translating, evaluating and so on, is use a further skill— 'analysis.

Analysis can be explained like this: it amounts to knowing, in the case of a given body of information, which bits it is appropriate to translate, exactly what to evaluate, what to interpret, and so on.

This is rather a specialised use of the term, but a justifiable use. Sometimes you will see the term 'analysis' used to describe,

Picture 5.4 : Miners in Wales, 1780.

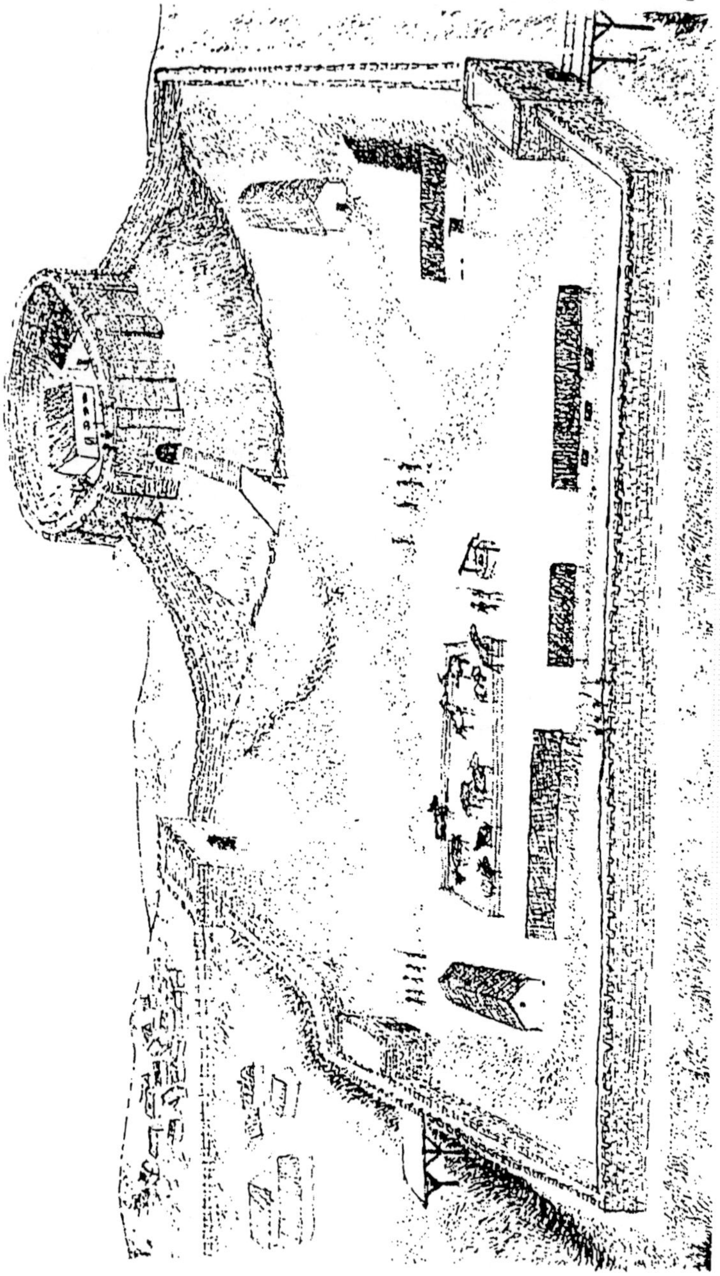

Picture 5.5 : Lincoln Castle about 1100

for instance, what students do, or should do, with a historical source, or with a passage of secondary text. In such cases, however, you will probably find that ideas like translation and interpretation and evaluation are more useful and specific, which leaves us free to use the term analysis for this vital skill of knowing when to use the other intellectual skills.

Let us look at a case. Suppose we gave students this passage to 'read and make notes on'.

> *The Soviet Period*
>
> Since 1917, the movement of Russian history has been from west to east. The capital was moved back from St. Petersburg to Moscow. The Soviet government shrank from contacts with the West. New industrial centres were built up in the eastern parts of the country. After nearly fifty years, Russia's withdrawal eastwards and into herself may be coming towards its end. We shall see.
>
> *The Bolshevik Revolution*
>
> Lenin had been in exile in Switzerland throughout the war. Now the Germans allowed him and other revolutionaries to go back to Russia. The train in which they passed through Germany was sealed in order to prevent any contact between such dangerous people and the German population. But the German government judged that it was in their interest that Lenin should be in Russia and at liberty, for he was the leader of the only political party which was in favour of peace with Germany at almost any price.
>
> The mass of the Russian people wanted two things, peace and land. The Mensheviks and SRs were in the Provisional Government, and they wanted peace, but not at the price of a German victory. They believed that if the Kaiser's Germany won, the Russian Revolution would soon be finished. A majority of the Provisional Government wanted the peasants to get most of the land, but they insisted that this must be done by due process of law and that meant delay. Moreover, the Russian peasant's experience of law was that it usually ended by cheating peasants.
>
> The Bolsheviks, also called Communists, were not in the government, and they had no difficulty in outbidding the other

parties. They had no use for legal forms, they said 'Let the peasants take the land at once'. They were prepared to risk a German victory; so they could also promise peace at once. They believed that in any case no socialist revolution could survive in Russia unless it spread to other lands, and also that there would soon be a Communist revolution in Germany. Events showed that both these calculations were wrong, but that did not effect the immediate issue.

J. Lawrence, *Russia,* Methuen, 1965

Normally, of course, teachers would set much longer passages for students to read but this piece will serve to illustrate the point. Now, suppose we have given the students this task: 'Make notes about why Lenin and the Germans co-operated in 1917'. This will direct their work much more usefully than just saying 'make notes'—but it still leaves them a lot of analysis to do. Here are just a few of the sub-tasks they have to analyse that basic task into.

Translation

They have to recognise that they ought to translate into their own words, either in their heads or actually in their written notes, terms like:

(1) movement of Russian history has been from west to east;

(2) Soviet government shrank from contact with the West;

(3) such dangerous people;

(4) due process of law—and others.

Interpretation

They have to set themselves, and then answer, this interpretation question— 'Why, in the author's view, did the Germans help Lenin—and why did Lenin go alongwith them?'

Evaluation

All items of information have to be evaluated from the point of view of their relevance and importance to answering the main question. In the first paragraph, for example, the student must make a judgement about whether anything in the paragraph is important at all in answering this question.

Application

The student has to decide whether and how the concept 'co-operation' applies to the relationships of Lenin and the Germans.

Now, clearly, a student might analyse the task correctly and still do badly. He might give poor translations, wrong interpretation, and so on. At least we would know exactly where he was going wrong, and be able to help him. But how would a student's work look if he was failing to do the analysis itself properly for this particular task?

The grossest way he could show failure to analyse would be to copy down all, or long bits of, the passage verbatim. All teachers have seen students, even college students, act in this way when they fail to analyse well.

Or he might do some of the analysis correctly, but not enough of it. Look at this response, for example:

Student A *(notes):*

(1) Russia cut itself off from 1917.

(2) New industrial cities built in East.

(3) Lenin in Switzerland 1914 to 1917.

(4) Train sealed through Germany.

(5) Mensheviks in Provisional Government, also SRs.

(6) Provisional Government, wants peasants have land.

(7) Bolsheviks also called Communist.

(8) Thought there would soon be a revolution in Germany.

Again, all teachers have seen work like this. Faced with this kind of thing, it is easy to feel confused about what to say to a student, not know where to start, and finish up with some lame and unhelpful advice like 'Try to be more relevant' or even 'Think harder'.

However, using the idea of analysis, it might be possible to describe more constructively where the student has gone wrong. Let us try to work out how well or badly he has analysed the task and the material.

(1) *Has he translated where appropriate?* Sometimes, at least, he has. He translated, for example, from the highly abstract '. . .the movement of Russian history. . . contacts with the West'

correctly into the simpler idea '. . . cut itself off'.

(2) *Has he interpreted where appropriate?* Clearly not—there is no indication of what he thinks the author's view of the question might be, it is not even clear that he thinks the author has a view at all, from the notes.

(3) *Does he evaluate?* Well, he may have done. He may really think that the eight points he gives us actually are the most important items, in which case he has simply made a bad, hard-to-defend evaluation. On the other hand, the way he has spread the points evenly, taking two points from each paragraph, might indicate that he is not clear that he should be evaluating the information by the criteria of relevance and importance.

(4) Similarly, the failure to interpret the author's view brings in its train a failure to consider the *application* of the concept 'co-operation' in this context.

The importance of being able to analyse properly is pretty obvious from this cursory look at this student's work. If we do not know when it is appropriate to translate things, or evaluate, and all the other processes, then using a book or lecture as an information source becomes very difficult. Our notebooks become useless to us: imagine student A coming back to these notes after six moths and trying to use them to make sense of the relations of Lenin and the Germans in 1917!

So, how could we help student A to improve? First, we could apply our two simple principles: make the task smaller and break the task down. We could set shorter passages of reading to students having difficulty making notes on books, or in the case of the Lenin/German question ask only half the question, i.e. 'Make notes on why Germany helped Lenin in 1917'.

Also, of course, we could avoid the analysis task altogether, if we chose, by setting very specific tasks— 'Read the passage and say in your own words what the following words mean . . . say why the writer thinks Lenin went alongwith the Germans . .list the three most important points the writer makes and say why they are important', and so on.

That is all right where a student really cannot handle analysis and you need to get on. But we should realise that if we do that, we are just putting off the problem, and that admirable and useful as the specific tasks are, someday a student will be in the position of needing to do his own analysis.

More positively, we can do three simple but helpful things.

We can give students models. We could, for instance, give a model of good notes on the Lenin/German co-operation, like this perhaps:

(1) Lenin in Switzerland 1914–17.

(2) Germans in 1917 let him go to Russia through Germany.

(3) Germans did not want him to talk Communism to German people, so train sealed.

(4) Germans wanted Lenin to win in Russia because Lenin would make peace with Germany if he got in power.

(5) Lenin did not mind stopping the war even if Germans profited. Thought there would be revolution soon in Germany anyway. Other people in Russia were scared Germany would stop Russian revolution if she won war.

(6) Germany-Lenin not allies like Germany-Austria; did not really like each other at all but only 'co-operated' for time being.

We could now go through the example with students and make the most important move towards improving students' skill at analysis, i.e. *make explicit what is required of them*. Our explanation might be:

> Notice first how my notes are in my own simple words. Always try to use your own words in notes; never just copy down a phrase just because it sounds good. Never put down anything you don't understand. If you come to something important in hard language, try to explain it in your own language.
>
> Second, notice how in points 3 and 4 and 5 I try to answer the question set, 'Why Lenin and the Germans were co-operating in 1917', just like in an essay. Notes ought to try to answer the questions, like you do in essays.
>
> Third, notice how I don't have any notes at all on that first paragraph. That's because I judged it was not important for answering the question. All the time when you read things in the book, you have to *judge:* 'Is this important to the question?' If you think it is not, leave it out. Sometimes there

might be a whole page you want to leave out. If you like, you can show me you have not just forgotten to read that page— you can put in your notes— 'page 12—nothing important on that page', or even 'page 12—a lot of stuff about the Duma— not sure how it's important, so I left it out'. I won't mind if you are wrong, just so long as you are *trying* to judge what's important.

These are the three main things you always should do making notes—use your own words (translate), say what the book's opinion on the set question is (interpret), and judge which parts are important and which not (evaluate).

There was another thing I did in point 5—I compared this bit of history with another bit and said how it was different—in this case how 'co-operate' meant something a bit different with Lenin and Germany from what it could mean talking about Germany and Austria. You can't always do this with notes, but you can sometimes, and it's a good thing to do if you can.

So we can give models and we can try to give explanations of what we want. The third thing we can do has already been briefly referred to, and the necessity for it is obvious from the suggested explanations of note-taking to students. That explanation refers more than once to 'the question', i.e. 'Why were Lenin and the Germans co-operating?' Whenever students set out to acquire information through note-taking, they ought to have a focusing question. They could be given it by the teacher, or make it up themselves, but a question of some kind they must have.

Before we move on, we should now consolidate a little: with each of the following extracts, try to do two things:

(a) Make up a question for students to use to focus a note-taking task. Remember to keep the question short: do not do the whole analysis task for them.

(b) Draw up a set of model notes on the passage to illustrate to students three main aspects of note-taking— translation, interpretation and evaluation.

The Inter-War Period, 1921–39

In the Treaty of Lausanne of 1923 which established the independence of Nationalist Turkey and regulated her relations with the Western Powers, she had to concede the demilitarisation of the Zone of the Straits: the warships of all nations, with slight restrictions, were free to enter the Black Sea. This was obnoxious not only to Turkey, as limiting her sovereignty, but also to Russia, as exposing her Black Sea coast to the threat of an enemy navy, and in 1925, while Turkey was involved in the acute dispute with Britain and Iraq over the possession of the villayet of Mosal, Russia concluded with her a new Treaty of Friendship and Neutrality. Though official relations between Russia and Turkey remained cordial, and the Russians gave more technical help with the industrialisation of Turkey, there was little contact or cultural interchange between the two people. The Turkish dictatorship permitted the works of Marx and Lenin to be read, but imprisoned active Communists under laws which forbade associations with the purpose of propagating ideas of class distinction, or of class conflict, or with internationalist intentions.

In 1936, when Italy had emerged as the aggressive naval power which threatened the *status quo* in the Mediterranean, Turkey proposed to the signatories of the Treaty of Lusanne that the régime of the Straits needed revision, and obtained important concessions in the Montreux Convention. She was now allowed to fortify the Straits, and in time of war to close them to the warships of all Powers, unless acting under the Covenant of the League of Nations.

G.E. Kirk,

A Short History of the Middle East, Methuen, 1964

No account of twelfth-century English commerce would be complete without mention of the Jews, who formed another community of 'foreign' merchants, as important in their own specialisation, money-lending, as were the Italians or Flemings in the wool trade. To lend money at interest ran counter to the teaching of Canon Law, and in Northern Europe, where the influence of the Church was not tempered by any secular commercial traditions, Christians could not practise usury, though they had begun to see its advantages. This need was therefore met by small groups of Jewish financiers, tolerated rather than welcomed because of the services they could render to kings, barons and even Churches in want of ready money. Successful Jews became extremely wealthy and as such doubly the object of popular envy and hatred. Legally they were counted personal serfs of the King, and so long as he protected them, they were secure. But when that protection failed, they were liable to become victims of savage outbursts of mass-hysteria: at York, for example, on Henry II's death in 1189, some local barons in debt to the Jews incited a city mob to murder a large number of them and pillage their houses. Yet if it had not been for the Jews, many enterprises requiring large amounts of capital, especially the construction of some of the great Cathedrals and monastic Churches, could hardly have been carried through. By the end of the thirteenth century, Christians had found it possible to engage in usury without cost to their consciences, and in 1290 Edward I actually expelled all the Jews from England, a small and unlamented community which had first attained much wealth, had then suffered prolonged persecution, and had finally, in the Crown's view, outlived its usefulness.

G.W.S. Barrow,

Feudal Britain, Edward Arnold, 1956

The Western Allies held democratic elections as early as 1946, to elect parliaments for the *Lander.* The rebuilding of the physical and moral ruin of German education was put in hand, and the teaching profession was purged of Nazis, perhaps more thoroughly than any other. New textbooks, free of the distorted fantasies of National Socialism, were rapidly produced.

The Allies divided the Nazis' single trade union into twelve new unions, with a simplified union structure. Most important, the Western Allies encouraged the growth of a free press reflecting many shades of opinion. Finally, a limited number of industries with export potential were started up under military guidance.

The Western Allies governed Germany during the years of the worst shortages and difficulties and gave the Germans time to recover before they tried, once more, to govern themselves democratically. The prime movers in this were the Americans. Whether they were motivated more by a genuine love of democracy, or by a fear of Stalinist Communism, it is impossible to say. The British in any case agreed with them, and the French were too weak to oppose them.

Germany, 1870–1970, R. Morgan (ed.)

BBC Publications, 1970

In the great wars between the French and the English for the control of North America, no tribe played a more important role than did the Iroquois of central New York. When the French came into the St. Lawrence Valley the Iroquois felt threatened. For a time the Iroquois had forced the Algonquins and Hurons to accept their supremacy. Now these subject tribes preferred to sell their furs directly to the French rather than to let the Iroquois control their trade with the white man. In short the Iroquois and the French hit it off badly from the start.

In 1906 the great French explorer Champlain invaded the Iroquois country on the lake that bears his name. Fighting between French and Iroquois broke out. In 1615 Champlain's men attacked an Onondaga village. This was fortified. There was a moat or ditch filled with water which ran round the village and a double wall or stockade. But the white men built a platform and moved close to the walls. Then from the platform they could shoot over the stockade and bring terror and death to the defenders. The village was soon taken. So began a long enmity between the Iroquois and the French. This was to cost the French their empire in America.

The Iroquois turned to the Dutch for arms, and got them. They then set out to capture the rich fur trade of the interior of the country. The Hurons and Algonquins controlled that trade, and the Iroquois planned to smash their rivals.

Morris, *First Book of the Indian Wars,*

Franklin Watts, 1959

Pre-tests of Skill of Analysis

With a new group of students, it would be very useful to have a rough idea of their ability to use the analysis skills involved in making notes—as desirable, in fact, as having knowledge of their conceptual levels.

The students ought to be tested on their capacity both to make notes from books and to make notes on information given orally by the teacher. As making notes is such a common activity in schools, you probably need not even announce that the tests are tests at all. It would be a good idea, though, to announce that you intend to take the notes in to look at them and that sometimes you might give them a mark. A very useful preliminary move in trying to improve the quality of note-taking is to impress on students that notes are important pieces of writing, which can be judged bad or good like other pieces of writing. The simplest way to establish this point, of course, is to take notes in and mark and comment on them from time to time.

Analysis and Source-materials

The analysis operation that a student has to perform on a piece of historical source material is similar to the operation he does on, say, a history textbook, but more complicated. For example, consider this passage where the student has been given the focusing question, 'What, were the nineteenth-century Chinese like?'

> *A European in Nineteenth Century China*
>
> In their diversions, the Chinese have much of that childish character which distinguishes other Asiatics. . . The childish mind under a despotism has few of those calls for exertion, among the bulk of the people, which in free states give it manly strength and vigour. Bearing no part in public transactions, and living in uninterrupted peace, the uniform insipidity of their existence is relieved by any, even the most frivolous and puerile, amusements . . . My attention was drawn by several old Chinese, some of whom had grey beards, and nearly all of them huge goggling spectacles. A few were chirruping and chuckling to singing-birds, which they carried in bamboo cages, or perched on a stick; others were catching flies to feed the birds: the remainder of the party seemed to be delightedly employed in flying paper kites, while a group

of boys were gravely looking on, and regarding these innocent occupations of their seniors with the most serious and gratified attention.

J.F. Davis, *The Chinese*, 1854,
quoted in K. Pratt, *Visitors to China*,
Macmillan, 1968.

As with any information-gathering, note-taking task, the student will have to analyse:

which terms he has to translate (e.g. 'public transactions');
which parts are important and relevant (evaluation) to the question;
which parts show the writer's view (i.e. interpretation).

Obviously, though, it's not as simple as that. It is pretty clear from this passage that the nineteenth-century Chinese were infantile and they were that way because they lived under a despotism. Equally clearly, that is merely this writer's idiosyncratic opinion.

What students have to do, as well as the three moves listed above, is analyse which parts are relevant and important: (a) to answering the question ('What were nineteenth-century Chinese like?); and (b) to revealing the writer's point of view about the question. Even before he starts doing that, he must have answered this application question: 'Is this passage a "primary source"?, i.e. the kind of material where I have to take very particular note of the writer's angle on events, as well as of the events themselves'. If he decides that it is indeed a 'primary source' he might well decide also to set himself further application tasks at certain appropriate points, i.e. applying concepts used generally to describe writer's attitudes, such as bias, neutral, tolerant, nationalistic and so on.

Any attempt by students to use source material in which they do not perform these analysis operations will probably yield nonsense by way of notes. Students should have a lot of practice in highly structured and guided work with sources (see section on interpretation using sources) before they are asked to deal with them in a less teacher-controlled way, as in project work, for instance.

Project Work

We have referred more than once to 'project work'. It is time to look at it is more detail.

What makes a project is the way the teacher sets it up. Thus, if a teacher says, 'Here's a little book about Columbus—find out about Columbus from it—I'll check with you in thirty minutes', he has in fact set the student a miniature *project.*

It is a very small project, but a genuine one, because the teacher has designated only a general area of work, not a specific task or tasks. Analysing that area of work into a series of specific tasks to do, concepts to master, and so on, is left to the student. That is the distinctive feature of a 'project'.

Projects can differ greatly in size, time allotted for them, whether they are for individuals or for groups, whether teachers prescribe in detail what books and material to use, or just say, 'The library's that way . . .' They can differ greatly in the kind of end product they have in view, whether a written thesis, a display, a tape-recording, a slide-sequence or whatever. But they all have this in common—that the student must come up with his own specific questions and tasks, by a process of analysis.

When projects go wrong, it is usually because this analysis has been poor, or not done at all. So we get the mass of factual information, the unrelated pictures, the whole sad waste of effort characteristic of the project that did not work out.

There are two main reasons for using project work. First, it is popular as a form of work, with most students, partly for good, and partly for bad, reasons. The good reasons are that many students like the feeling of being able to organise a big piece of work independently—even if they are not doing it very well. Many students also are interested and motivated by the elements of novelty in project work—the sheer size of the enterprise and the end product, compared to a standard piece of class-work; the unusual kind of end product, such as displays; the element of co-operating with other students, if it is a group project. The bad reasons are interesting too because, perhaps, there can be satisfaction arising precisely from the fact that the necessary analysis has not been done. If a student has spent a lot of the time answering that kind of pointed, searching question advocated in this book— 'What does *x* mean?' 'How would you evaluate *y*?'—then it can be a relief to spend time quietly paraphrasing, or even copying, some book about the Aztecs, with no tiresome *task* to think about, no difficult thinking to do at all—and at the end of it, a large, satisfying end product. To follow this point through would get us into some pretty deep water. Perhaps it is enough to say that it is only realistic to recognise that not all students get their satisfactions in school-work from useful thinking. So a student who is happily employed on a project is not necessarily well employed. It would be equally foolish, though, to ignore the good reasons students have for liking project work, and the powerful motivation tool that might put in our hands.

The second main argument for project work is this: it can be an excellent way of developing the skill of analysis and, in later life, after school, that skill will be the key to the successful use of all the other cognitive skills. In adult life, given a book, a newspaper, TV news programme, or whatever, nobody comes along and sets us a series of specific tasks to foster understanding. We analyse the material and ask our own questions, just like students with a project. Life is a project, if you like to put it that way.

The next problem, if we want to persevere with project work, is how to teach students to do it well; in other words, how to introduce them to project work through easy project-type tasks that get progressively harder.

First, we can say that the early tasks will be small, i.e. involve few books and other materials and relatively little time.

Second, we will make it clear to students exactly what sort of analysis task is involved in doing a project, perhaps after this fashion:

Project—American Indians

When you do a project on a group of people like this, you always ought to find out these things:

(1) How did they live?

(2) What did they think?

(3) What happened to them?

and you should break these big questions down like this:

How did they live?—What did they eat, what were their houses like, how big were the groups they lived in, how did they choose leaders?

What did they think?—What did they think about religion, what kind of things did they admire, what was their idea of a good man? What part in life did they think women should play?

What happened to them?—Are they still around, did they get conquered by somebody, did they change their way of life?

We get progression, as students get more familiar with project work, in two ways: increasing the number of main headings in the analysis, and reducing detailed guidance, or sub-headings. As in this example:

Project—Aztecs

Remember to think about six things when you do a project on a group of past people.

(1) How did they live?

(2) Why did they live like that?

(3) What did they think?

(4) How did their thought affect how they behaved?

(5) What happened to them?

(6) How do we know about them?

Remember under (1) to think about things like how they governed themselves, not just the food they ate and so on. Remember under (6) that we might have more than one sort of evidence about them.

In other words, we gradually make more complex demands, and give less guidance on how to meet those demands.

We are by no means out of the wood yet, because even if the students follow the given headings closely, they could still simply paraphrase books, and give purely descriptive accounts. So they need further guidance on analysis, of a similar kind to that we suggested you give them on note-taking (page. 193). That involves you in giving them model examples and explaining those examples.

Exercise 8

Suppose we wanted to set up project work not on a group of people but on a celebrated individual, say Joan of Arc, or on an event, like a revolution or a war. Plan now (a) sets of 'easier' project instructions for those two cases, i.e. giving a few general headings and a lot of detailed guidance under those headings, and (b) sets of instructions for more advanced students, giving more general headings and less detailed guidance.

Exercise 9

Work out how, if at all, the suggested guidance on note-taking on pages 193-195 has to be amended or added to, in the case of advice on note-taking for project work.

Designating Materials to Use

With younger and less experienced students we will, of course, give much closer guidance on exactly what to read, and where to find it, than we would to older and more experienced ones.

There is no reason why a project should not be started off by students working through a set of small tasks designed by the teacher, of the type we are now familiar with. In our American Indian case, we could start with materials, say, about Eastern Woodlands Indians, accompanied by a detailed question-sheet to work through, then put students on to Plains Indians material not accompanied by a worksheet.

It goes without saying, of course, that when it comes to project work we cannot *assume* that any student, of any age, knows how to use an index or can make good use of a table of contents, can find his way round a library, knows that useful books might be found in library sections other than the history section, knows how to use a catalogue. Good students can do poor project work simply because they are unskilled in the mechanics of finding and using a book–let alone non-book materials.

We can do very useful small exercises in this area of what we might call 'library skills', e.g. setting students simply to note down the pages where references to Mussolini occur in a book on twentieth-century Europe; or at a later stage, simply nothing where, in a library, there is material to be found on the Aztecs, apart from the 'History of Mexico' shelves.

Mixed Ability Groups and Project Work

Organisationally, project work fits well into a mixed-ability set-up. It involves individuals or small groupings working pretty much at their own pace, and it is very easy to set up student A to do a project with relatively little guidance, while less-able student B has the thing structured more carefully for him.

We could get into trouble, however, by encouraging student B to do a project which is inherently too difficult for his abilities. Sometimes it's obvious that a topic is too difficult, and we don't set it, or don't let a student choose it. Normally, for instance, a study of eschatological elements in later Hussite devotional writing would not recommend itself as a good field for fourteen-year-olds to try to plough. But it is less easy to decide whether a project, say, on the Ancient Greeks (granted there was plenty of materials available) is harder than doing, say, the Aztecs.

Suppose we take our very simplest, three-part analysis of how to approach a project on a group of people in the past, i.e.

(1) How did they live?

(2) What did they think?

(3) What happened to them?

We can see right away that doing the Greeks properly will involve heavy emphasis on point 2, their ideas; heavy emphasis, in fact, on some very difficult abstractions about science, democracy, and so on. Point 2 will, of course, involve some difficult ideas in the case of the Aztecs, but they at least might not be so central to the work as with the Greeks.

What we have to do before letting a student embark on a topic is work out ourselves what level of abstraction the student might get involved with; decide how central the difficult ideas (which will come up in any project whatsoever) are to the success of the whole; and then judge whether a given student is likely to succeed at the project.

Just because a project might bring up some hard ideas, though, is no reason for putting a student off it altogether. Suppose a student wanted to do Ancient Greece. Suppose we guessed he could handle the material culture side of things, and the 'what happened to them' question, but would probably be thrown by the 'history of ideas' element. It would be reprehensible of us to say 'miss out all that hard stuff on ideas'—the best move would be to change the form of the work at the relevant point.

We could arrange it like this. We could say, 'Find out about the way the Greeks lived from Smith's book—just work on your own the way I told you. When you are ready, go on to Jones's book on *The Ideas of the Greeks*—that's a harder book, and there are some hard ideas in it, so I want you to work through this question-sheet on Jones's book—then you can go back to working on your own again, for the rest of the project'.

A great deal of trouble can be headed off by anticipating in this sort of way at least some of the potential sources of difficulty in a project. Not so good is when the student says: 'Please, I'm getting confused with this stuff about astronomy,' and a teacher has to figure out a strategy for dealing with the problem on the spot. That will happen sometimes anyway, but we can reduce these awkward moment by good pre-planning.

A final point on the inherent difficulty of some projects. Students, especially inexperienced and less able ones, will be more likely to succeed in a project if the project involves similar kinds of operation to those the student has been doing in recent class-work. For example, some teachers commonly deal with a stretch of medieval history in a straight political way—events, kings, battles and the like, and then go on to set up project work on 'The Monastery' or 'The Medieval Village'. Now, working on groups, like monks, involves asking different sorts of questions from the ones we ask about kings or battles. We could help students by not asking them to make this sudden switch; we could do class-work on monasteries, say, and then set up project work on 'The Village'—emphasising that a village is another sort of group, so the same kinds of question will be appropriate for students to ask themselves about it as the teacher asked them about the monastery.

7. Synthesis

The skill of synthesis has a special importance in the context of school and of education generally. As adults, we might read a book on history or politics, making interpretations, evaluations and so on at a very high level, without having to articulate them, without having to put together or *synthesise* a series of evaluations and interpretations into connected written prose or oral exposition. For students, though, most of the time, it does not do them much good (in the eyes of their teachers, anyway) to have understanding, make good interpretations and so on, unless they can make an orderly and comprehensible synthesis in spoken or written form.

It is easy to see why skill or lack of skill in synthesis has come to loom so large in the way teachers assess students, and indeed in the way students assess themselves. Quite often the problems of synthesis are so pressing that the students' strengths and weaknesses in other skill-areas, and even the very existence of those other skills, are concealed from the teacher. The best way to approach the problems of synthesising as a skill might be through some examples of student writing. Let us compare these two pieces of student writing on the early days of the Indian Nationalist movement. (Assume that all the names and dates are correct.)

Student A

The first Indian Nationalist Congress was in 1886, the main leaders were Tilak and Gokhale. At first they were only interested in doing gymnastics and reading newspapers.

They were against the Muslims of India, who were not nationalists. The Muslims only felt nationalist about Turkey, not India, and were sad when Turkey was beaten in the war in 1912. This was when the Italians attacked Libya to get a bigger Empire, to be more equal to other countries with empires, i.e. England. The Indians and Muslims fell out over Bengal in 1905 when the British divided it up in a ways that was better for Muslims.

Also in 1907, the Indians fell out within themselves and had to slit between the Tilak followers who wanted independence, right away—and others who would just settle just for a Parliament in India.

So the Indians had not just trouble with the British for freedom, but with themselves and the Muslims.

Student B

The first Indian National Congress was in 1886. Indian nationalism was affected by things *inside* India, and also *outside* things.

Outside was the Russo-Jap war in 1904 which helped Nationalism because it showed Asians could beat white soldiers. The Muslims did not care about that so much as another thing, though I suppose they would be fairly glad, but not so glad as the Hindus. What the Muslims cared about more was in 1912 when Turkey was attacked and England did not help Turkey. Turkey was a Muslim country and, right from the start, the Muslims were not happy about the Indian National Congress because of all the Hindus in it; although the Muslims wanted freedom too. In 1905, the Hindus and Muslims and British fell out over dividing up Bengal in a way to favour the Muslims. Also, around this time, the Indian National Congress split up into two between Tilak and his friends and others about how fast to try to get freedom or a Parliament.

In 1914, India went to war against Germany, but, before this the British undid the dividing of Bengal in 1911.

To start with student A. He obviously has, in his first paragraph, failed to interpret properly something said by a book, or a teacher, of the order 'The nationalists worked through gymnastic societies and the press'. Paragraph two suggests a major failure successfully to apply the idea of nationalism in the case of Indian Muslims, resulting in a near-nonsense idea that they 'felt nationalistic about Turkey'. (It would be interesting to try to work out exactly what information about the Turco-Italian war had been misinterpreted here.) The sentence beginning 'This war was when . . .' shows a wrong evaluation of the relative importance of the details of the Turco-Italian war in this context of the Indian nationalist movement. We must notice favourably, however, the orderliness of the exposition: paragraph one—foundation of INC; paragraph two—Hindu-Muslim dispute; paragraph three—INC internal strife; paragraph four—an excellent brief final summary of the whole matter. Student A has not done too badly at the skill called synthesis—the putting together of a series of understandings, information, judgements, etc., into a whole which is coherent, logical and clear.

We can see the importance of this skill if we look at the work of student B.

Student B starts off with an organising principle which sounds very useful—classification into 'things *inside* India and things *outside*'. Very soon, though, this leads him into a tortuous attempt to explain the Hindu-Muslim problem in the context of the Russo-Jap and Turco-Italian Wars. He fails, not surprisingly, to do this very lucidly. He then abandons this 'inside India, outside India' antithesis and uses very weak connecting ideas like 'Also around this time . . .' to connect the events. The conclusion is very lame. Notice how this lack of skill at synthesis, at putting it all together, obscures his much superior understanding, compared with student A, of nationalism, of the special problem of the Muslims, of the significance of the Turco-Italian war. His understanding of the split in the ranks of the INC sound to be at least as good as that of student A, arguably better.

To some extent, as with the other skills, we can isolate the skill of synthesis, and take steps to improve students' expertise at it. Before we can go into that though, we must make an important point. Teachers often use synthesis, or rather, lack of skill at synthesis, as a sort of cognitive scapegoat. It is very obvious then students lack it, so people faced with students' writing that seems in some way unsatisfactory, are prone to say 'It lacks organisation', 'It does not hang together', and the like.

Students A and B both devote more space to the Turco-Italian war than seems appropriate. But student A does it, not because his organising, synthesising skill has faltered, but because of a serious lack of understanding about how the Muslims felt about Turkey. Student B seems to get in a tangle about Turkey genuinely because of a bad synthesising tactic—the attempt to introduce the Muslim problem for the first time in the unsatisfactory setting of two remote wars. So they both fall short of excellence—but for quite different reasons needing different remedial efforts.

As teachers, we will many, many times see student writing which strikes us as disordered, confused and badly put together. Always, we must ask, 'Is it confused like this because of lack of understanding of something—is it a failure deeper than just a lack of skill in synthesis?' Poor synthesis is like back pain—one easily identifiable symptom, but many different possible causes.

Exercise 10

Have a look at these two pieces on the question 'How could the English Parliament and Charles I have made peace in 1642 and prevented civil war?' They are both badly synthesised—but one of them might be a mess, partly because the student has misunderstood a fundamental concept, not simply because he lacks organisation. Which student is it, and what idea has he not understood?

Student A

There must be peace with France, because the King must stop all taxes and not ask Parliament for money, then Parliament would not mind him so much. He can get money from France and have to fight on their side. When that was over, France would have to let Parliament fight against the rebels in Ireland—OK, because they are Catholics and the King would not get money from Spain (Catholics). King must let Scots off and let them be Presbyterians (but not Catholics). Spain will be fought against in war by Parliament and King (because of the Catholics), but war against Scotland must be stopped because of Presbyterians.

Student B

Charles and Parliament will agree not to fight each other. They might get soldiers from Sweden or Switzerland to care for the country while they made peace. King Charles will agree to change religion of his, or let Scots have their own religion.

Both King Charles and Parliament must send soldiers home. But they must fight rebels in Ireland. King Charles I must try to makes taxes less and more fair somehow. They could have wars against Spain or Catholics in Germany and Ireland. They will agree on some place to meet and make a treaty.

['Answers' p. 221]

Improving Synthesis

If somebody cannot reliably put together a coherent paragraph, it is not sensible to ask him to compose an essay of a thousand words. The first move we can make in improving the skill of synthesis is to think in terms of building up towards the long piece of consecutive prose, the essay, dissertation or whatever, by way of small written exercises which we make slowly longer and more complex as the student's skill grows. This has been heavily implied throughout this book so far—many of the suggested tasks for students have called for quite small pieces of writing.

Every task we can set, however, small, so long as answering it involves writing more than about five words, also involves a synthesis task. The second basic move we can make to improve performance is to make explicit to students what we want of them, and discuss with them different ways material might be synthesised.

This last point is very important. Even in post-18 education, we meet students who are conscious of, and proud of, their ability to make their own interpretations and evaluations and so on, but accept the teacher as a complete authority on how to synthesise. So we get a teacher who says, 'Well, Mary, the content is good, but as a piece of prose the thing doesn't hang too well together—it doesn't really sock it across to me'. And Mary furrows her brow, and nods, just as if the teacher had said something that meant something to her.

Let us look at an example. Suppose we set a very simple translation task—may be the very first one in the translation section. 'What is a rebellion?' We could work out in discussion in the class that there are five points to make, and write them on the board.

(1) There have to be quite a lot of people in it.

(2) The people involved are not just bandits.

(3) The people fight.

(4) They have some kind of cause, or plan, or grievance.

(5) They fight against a government which is in some sense established.

We then ask, 'What is the best order to make these points in?' There are, in fact, several different orders that make perfectly good sense. Students must learn that there is not usually one 'logical' way to synthesise things; they must practise devising their own 'logics'. They must then practise giving reasons for the way they have arranged the points as they would give reasons for, say, an evaluation or an interpretation.

We could then ask, 'Could we present the answer a different way may be through an invented example, what about if we said, "If there was a rebellion in Barataria, the following three things would happen". Try doing it that way and see if you like it better or not'. With even this very small piece of writing, involving less than a hundred words, there is scope to discuss different *forms* of presentation, as well as different *orders* of presenting points.

There are, in fact, few cases where there is one obviously superior way to synthesise material. Even where straight chronological narrative is involved, this is so. Suppose we set a complex task involving a good deal of writing: 'Why did Australia never rebel against England like America did?' Even if we gave students a great deal of guidance on the lines of 'Remember you will need to use the terms "nationalism, "tariff" and "imperialism"; you will need to be careful on the differences between "economic" points and "political" points,' and so on, there is still scope for choice about how to do the synthesis job. Two obvious ways to present the end product are the chronological, going through potential '1776' moments of Australian history and saying why in fact separatism did not flourish; or setting up some general thesis and illustrating it with incidents not necessarily in chronological order. Or perhaps the whole thing could be done in the form of an imaginary dialogue.

So nearly always, we can sensibly ask, as part of the task-setting routine— 'How do you plan to present the answer?' or, as part of the feedback routine, 'Why did you present the answer like this?'

Although we want students to be highly conscious of taking their own decisions about the synthesising process, it is also a very suitable area in which to present them with models.

The best synthesiser in the room is probably you, by a long way, so let the students see you in action sometimes. Build up different plans for 'answers' and essays, on the board, explaining your decisions as you go along.

Exercise 11

Choose a set of tasks, either out of this book or of your own devising, and practise two things:

(a) Thinking out how many different ways an answer could be put together or 'synthesised' (remembering both the questions of different *ordering* of material and different *forms* of answer).

(b) Plan how you would show and explain to a class some of the different ways of presenting the 'answer' in each case.

Problems with Literacy

It may be that a student's ability to construct even a coherent sentence is very poor; or that his spelling is so bad that you really can't always make sense of what he writes. In such cases our general pattern of working through small, specific-task exercises, where he can use oral responses and a small amount of writing, is better than many strategies: certainly better than the common pattern of extensive teacher-talk; note-copying; 'now write about it'. But the skill of synthesis seems to be about end products, and very largely about written ones—so we must be able to improve the skill of synthesis of someone who cannot even write properly.

There are two basic synthesis exercises: deciding on and justifying the order in which to present material, and similarly deciding on and justifying the form of presentation. The first thing we can get poor writers to do, is do the synthesis exercise, like our example of 'rebellion', without actually having to write down the final version. In other words, we skip round their inability to synthesise *written* language at sentence or phrase level, and go straight on to higher-level problems. This could be pretty important to improving their motivation: you could, in school, meet students who have never successfully tackled a synthesis problem involving more than one paragraph, simply and only because they have never, ever, got past composing the first paragraph of any piece of history writing before the bell went.

Another way to tackle the problem of ordering material, without being involved in extensive writing, is to get students to order pictures, maps, graphs, and so on, which are either self-explanatory, or better still, require some short caption. The important thing here is that there is a genuine ordering challenge—for example: with the Trafalgar campaign of 1805, we could make a simple block graph of the relative strength of the two fleets, a diagram of Nelson 'breaking the line' of the Franco-Spanish fleet, a picture of Nelson's death, sketch maps of Napoleon's 1804 invasion plan, a picture of warship of the time—in other words, material which can genuinely be ordered and presented in different ways, to tell a story.

Most of the materials in this Trafalgar example could have been produced by the students in earlier sessions—this is the kind of economy in use of resources to aim for; you may start off full of picture-gathering zeal in September, but by December you could be running out of both zeal and materials, so the trick is to use simple materials, student-made or home-made and re-use them for different purposes, wherever you can.

Giving Feedback

The two precious things you offer students with writing problems are these: occasions on which they need to compose their own prose, in order to do tasks which they find interesting; and, second, success at composing prose. Both could be greatly undermined if we do not mark their work skilfully.

If we under-mark, as it were, and simply praise work which they know to be badly spelled and ill-constructed, they will rapidly suspect that they are being patronised. If we red-ink every spelling error and every awkwardness of syntax, they could easily be discouraged. What we need is a consistent and reasonable policy on spelling and syntax mistakes.

A reasonable policy—on spelling mistakes—might be this: *never* ignore all of them, and never red-ink more than three on one piece of work. Pick on mistakes in spelling important, common words—'because', 'battle', 'reason'; rather than 'revenue', 'guerrilla' or 'entente'. With syntax or grammar errors, again, take note of not more than two per piece of work—or less if the piece is brief. Never simply indicate that a phrase or sentence is wrong—say what is wrong and write in a correct version. There is nothing more irritating for a student than an indication that a mistake has been made, with no clue as to what that mistake might be.

The policy outlined above for spelling mistakes and grammar or syntax errors could be applied when we comment on any student's work, whether he has a major writing problem or not.

But there is far more to commenting on work than that. The reason why we comment on work at all is presumably to encourage students and to try to improve the next piece of work by pointing out the strength and weaknesses of the piece of work before us.

Certain principles of commenting follow from this. In most circumstances, a comment should contain praise. There are cases where praise would be inappropriate, but they are far fewer than the cases in which praise might be given and is not. Teachers sometimes seem extremely reluctant to praise, which is pity, since praise is the easiest of motivational devices to use, and a very powerful one.

Give the praise *first*. It will have more effect that way, and you are less likely to forget to give it at all, if your first move in planning a comment on students' work is always, 'What can I say here that is good?'

When you have singled out a passage or phrase or word for praise, say what it is you like about it, as precisely as you can. If, say, a student has illustrated a general statement with an example of their own, praise that tactic specifically and they will be much more likely to do it again.

The need to be specific is even greater when you single out something for criticism. A great deal of what teachers write on students' work is not even read by students—possibly because it conveys no clear message. Avoid putting things like question marks and exclamation marks in the margin. Don't just underline passages; don't be sarcastic.

As well as being specific, be constructive. Say clearly how the student might do better next time. Saying 'Try to be more relevant; think for yourself more' helps nobody.

If there are many things to criticise, do not pick them all out. Use the same rule suggested for spelling errors and only pick out two or three main points. A lot of red ink on one's work is a depressing sight, however useful and constructive the remarks are.

Here is an example of how a piece of work might be marked on these principles.

Student A

Total War in World War II

(1) To an extent unequalled even by the massive conflict of a quarter century earlier, World War II was a 'total' war.

(2) The most dreadful thing in the whole of the war's time was the killing of all the Jews in German concentration camps. The bombing of many German cities such as Dresden and Hamburg was also a crime against Humanity, but the killing of the jews came first.

(3) The next worst thing was all the refugees who lost their homes and had to travel to camps where some of them still were many years after the war.

(4) I think the next worst thing was Stalingrad because so many people were killed and the soldiers had to fight in the cold, so cold that when they were wounded their blood froze to the ground where they were. And, equally bad also, was Leningrad where everybody in this whole city was starved.

(5) Fathers and brothers having to go away for years and years and may be killed, was the worst thing for ordinary people.

(6) Rationing, mobilisation of industry and manpower, social change, further change in the roll of women were also terrible parts of this truly terrible war.

(The paragraphs are numbered only for ease of reference—normally, of course, remarks would be written nearer to the text commented on.)

Remarks on Student A's Work—A good answer on what you think were the worst things in the war—each point clearly made, separate from other points.

Next time—(a) always put things in your own words, don't *copy* like in paragraph (1) and (6). (b) When there is a new word to use, like 'total' war, tell me somewhere what you think it means, may be at the end. On this task you might have said—'To sum up, "total war" is when. . .'

Exercise 12

Write remarks on these following examples of students' work.

Student B

Total War in World War II

To an extent unequalled even by the massive conflict of a quarter-century earlier, World War II was a 'total' war.

To prove this the first fact is that World War II had battles in many more places than before, in Burma and Africa and China and also a lot more bombing of towns by aircraft and more U-boats sinking ships. In 1914–18 nearly all the battles were in Europe, except for the campaign in East Africa where a most gallant force of German troops and native 'Askaris' held off greatly superior force of British and Indian troops for the duration of the war.

Many of the battles in 1914–18 war, were very bloody, much worse than World War II, e.g. The Somme, Paschendale. But World War II was a total war because everybody had to be in the army and in 1914 it was volunteers.

The worst thing in the war was the concentration camps in Germany where millions of Jews were killed with gas. There were also great bombings of German towns, i.e. Dresden but these were not as bad as the concentration camps were, because the Germans started the war, and using gas is worse even than bombing people.

Back in England, the thing most people remember is rationing, about the war. Even children's sweets were rationed which showed how this was truly a 'total war'.

Student C

Nationalism in 1914

Serbia is a small country fighting for Nationalism. In my opinion, Serbia was the course of World War I. Serbia was full of many nationalist fanatics. Serbia started trouble which made Austria declare war on Serbia. Serbia had an ally—Russia!! Austria was scared of Russia so Austria got Germany to help them out.

So France and England next joined Russia to fight Austria, Germany and Italy.

I do not think Austria is much to fault for causing World War I. They had to fight against Serbia.

Student D

Nationalism in 1914

In my opinion it was Austria most to blame. If they had not wanted to get Serbia more of it would have happened and they only want Serbia for themselves not for Serbians' good. Russia disagreed so all countries started to fight.

France, Italy and Germany were not much to blame, they only helped other countries like Serbia and Austria who had themselves to blame. Russia and France and England fought four years three months against Germany and Austria who lost.

Student A

Sutton Hoo

I am a Viking warrior in a Viking village near Sutton Hoo. The King and hos warrior's were going on a hunt and I had to guard the village. The village was all made out of wood and their were about twenty huts in the village. The village was surrounded by a wall of logs to protect it. The village was quite lively with children playing people talking. There were cows and chickens in the village. When the hunting party came back the king was lying over his horse dead, they took him in his hut. I went to one of the warrior's and he told me that they were chasing a boar and another one went in front of the kings horse and the horse bucked and the king fell off and broke his neck. When the warriors told the village a week of moaning started everybody was sad and praying and crying. After the week passed we started digging a borrow. When the hole was dug we took a ship and dragged it under rollers. When they got it in the hole they put the king's body in the ship then they put all his treasures with him. Then they started dancing and praying. They put all his treasures with him so he will be wealthy in the other world. Then they covered the hole up. Then the council made me the kind.

Student E

Sutton Hoo

One day in a village a king died and the next day the Saxons had a mourning. It lasted a whole week and then they started to dig a hole and they put a ship into the hole and then they put in his treasures into the ship. The king got killed a by battle and he got shot by an arow. The kings name was called Englebert. Then they put the king in the bout and they dug a tunnel and put a boulder in front of the tunnel. Then they shosed a new king.

Student G

Sutton Hoo

In a village near Sutton Hoo the king had just died and all the people are in mourning and know one knows how he died but they think he's been posiand they are just diging the burial hole. The king was king Edward his town was not very big with wooden hits dotted about. They have just finished diging the burial hole. Here comes the ship being dragged to the hole before they put the ship in they put all his treasure in to the ship then they put the body in to the ship and put ship in the hole. Then they start to dance up and down. After they have finished dancing they put the rock in front of the cave.

Student H

Sutton Hoo

The village was a collection of wooden huts and wooden sense which was now broken down. Their had been an attack on our saxon village. But the most disturbing thing was the kings death. King Edmund had bean killed in repelling the invaders. The howel village was in mourning for seven days. Then the people dug the burial hole. We dragged the ship up to the hole we put the ship in to the hole (without the mast or sails) and placed all the treasures of the dead king into the boat we then placed the body in and held a servise. The people sadly make a barrow and closed it up. The barrow was so high on the hill that you could see it for miles and remember his grateness.

Project Work and Synthesis

In the above examples, it may have struck you that the students might have done better work if they had been set a more clearly defined task. The students may have been carefully briefed on how to answer on 'Total War in World War II' but as it stands it is an indefinite sort of title, leaving unclear exactly what the teacher wants the student to do. As we have observed before, the first essential step to getting good student work is to set a good, clear task.

With project work, by definition, though, the students to some extent have to set their own tasks. This gives an extra dimension to the synthesis problem with project work and the analysis section has something to say about this. Project work, though, offers a useful opportunity in the field of synthesis, as well as an extra difficulty. It offers the chance to students to make genuine, major decisions about the form of presentation, as well as its ordering. In their earliest, preparatory project work, students should be set problems like: 'Would words or a map or a graph make this point best? Could we have an imaginary dialogue to get this point across? Which of these pictures illustrate the subject best—or would a picture plus a map be better?'

As well as encouraging them to think out different ways of synthesising material, and encouraging them not to assume that words is the only way, we must give them practice in criticising ways of presentation. Thus, if a student includes, say, a picture in a project, he must be asked questions like 'What is it for? Is it just decoration or is it illustrating something? Would this other picture be better for your purpose?'

Putting together your end product in a way which you can explain and justify is as important a part of the whole process of tackling a task as any other part. When students both understand and agree with that proposition they have taken the major step towards excellence in the skill of synthesis.

Exercise 10—Suggested Answers

Student B's idea of Swedish troops acting as a kind of UN force in 1642 England is eccentric, but much more serious is student A's lack of understanding of the idea of taxes ('King must stop all taxes . . . He can get money from France'). The misguided ingenuity of the idea of the government being run on money from France then leads to the confusions of the first half of the piece. It also lets student A lose sight completely of the need to elaborate some kind of deal between King and Parliament, in his welter of complicated wars.

Neither A nor B have put together particularly well-ordered, well-synthesised answers, but student A's apparent lack of grasp of the idea of taxation is what needs tackling first.

Synthesis—Generalising

Suppose a student had considered and listed these facts about the world in 1945:

(1) World War II was over.

(2) Many soldiers and concentration camp prisoners were able to go home.

(3) Many factories turned back to peace time work.

(4) People were scared by the A-bomb.

(5) Trouble was beginning between Russia and the West.

(6) Many people in Europe were refugees with nowhere to go.

(7) New wars were on the boil in Indonesia, China, Vietnam.

(8) Britain and other European countries were much poorer than in 1939.

Suppose we then said to the student, 'Make the shortest accurate general statement you can about the way things stood in 1945, basing your statement on that list'. We have asked the student to generalise. Generalising is a kind of synthesis, of 'putting together', but it involves more than putting together a good piece of prose, so it is worth thinking about separately. We can see what it involves by looking at some answers to that particular 1945 task we just set.

Student A : 'Europe in 1945 was in a mess'.

Student B : 'Wars settle nothing'.

Student C : 'The war was over but there was trouble with Russia and many refugees. Also war in China and Vietnam. The Atom bomb scared people'.

Student A's answer clearly falls short of being a good generalisation because it takes account of only part of the facts and ignores Asia. Student B goes far beyond the given facts, and comes up with the historian's bugbear— 'a wild generalisation'. Student C has not got a generalisation at all. He has done what students very often do, when asked to generalise, or 'summarise', or 'pull it all together'—he has taken it to mean 'condense', and pulled out a few of what he takes to be the salient elements in the material. He has not done the central act involved in generalising, i.e. come up with a new concept or concepts to apply to the facts.

'New concept' does not have to be as high-flown as it sounds. In this context, some quite ordinary ideas, but ideas which are not present in the original list, will serve, e.g. 'good things' and 'problems', giving, for instance, the generalisation 'In 1945, some good things were happening, but there were also many problems'. Student A offered 'mess' as his 'new concept' and it is a genuine example, if a bit crude.

To sum up—a good generalisation actually is a generalisation—it offers some general concept, thought up by the student, and applied to the given set of information. This general concept can be quite simple—like 'mess' or 'good thing' or 'problem'. It takes account of all the given information, but does not (like student B) go beyond the information.

We ought to consider two points before we get down to business on how to improve students' skill in generalising. First, a 'good' generalisation does not have to be one the teacher agrees with. When a student asks himself, 'What simple, general term or idea best expresses what I want to say about this set of facts?' there is clearly a large evaluation element in that question. Suppose a student, when asked to generalise on those given facts about 1945 said, 'The end of World War II meant the world got instantly duller, but there were hopeful signs of some excitement for the future, notably the A-bomb.' We might not like what he says, but by the three criteria we have offered, we cannot say that it is bad generalisation.

Second, the very term generalisation is often viewed by teachers, especially history teachers, with suspicion. Should we be teaching it at all? Should we not rather be teaching students *not* to generalise, but to avoid generalisation, to have a scholarly emphasis on the particular truth of particular instances?

It is probably student B's type of ill-founded and sweeping generalisation which has brought the whole process into ill-repute with history teachers. This is a pity, because generalising is not so much a desirable skill as an unavoidable one, if we are to have discourse at all with each other. 'Abraham Lincoln had many problems' is a simple generalisation. If we cannot speak and write at that level of generality, we can hardly communicate at all. However, as we shall see, promoting good generalising does not involve being easy on sloppy, wild or otherwise unscholarly utterances.

Improving the Skill of Generalising

As with the other skills, the keys to success are: start early, with the youngest students; make clear what you want; give examples; give lots of small-scale practice.

The earliest sorts of exercises might involve application exercises, where we give the students the possible generalising concepts, or 'summing up' words, and ask them if they think they apply. For instance, 'We have to write just one sentence to sum up what we have learned about the early days of the New England colonies, would it be best to say, "The colonists had many *battles,* or many *difficulties,* or had the *worst* time anyone ever had"?'

In such a very simple way we can make the points that a summary should be brief, and hinge around one or two 'new words', that it should not go beyond the fact ('*worst time* anyone ever had') nor fail to take account of all the facts (*battle*).

At the earliest stage, we should also introduce the idea of tentativeness, of 'may be', 'up to a point' and 'perhaps'. Our parallel use of tasks of evaluation, tasks on interpreting sources, and 'what might have happened' extrapolation games should all be strengthening their grasp of the concept that history is not a series of teacher-stated truths. However, we can also reinforce the concept, and teach the language of tentativeness directly, quite early and simple, as here: 'Now let's sum up about the Pilgrim Fathers' first year in America—which would it be better to say, "They had shown that colonies *would succeed* in America", or should we say that "Colonies *might perhaps succeed*"?'

The next, critical, stage is for students to make up their own generalisation unaided. At first, they could have the information to be generalised about in a handy form, like a list, made up either by you or by them, like the '1945' list at the start of this section.

A useful task for a further stage would be to give students generalisation about material at the start of a topic, and make the theme of the work on that topic the checking out of how true the original generalisation was. Thus, work on the Communist world might check out a generalisation like 'Communism only gained power in backward countries'. Learning about Czechoslovakia and East Germany, as well as Russia and China, could lead the students to make a better generalisation of their own, knowing from the start of the work that that was what they were ultimately trying to do.

As with some other skills, especially synthesis, 'Knowing that that is what they were ultimately trying to do' is the key to success with generalising—that is, awareness of it by students as a separate skill; a knowledge of precisely what criteria of excellence are being applied by the teacher; confidence from the knowledge of having done it many times before.

Exercise 13

Make up lists of eight or more items, on historical material of your choice, about which you could ask students to write a simple, one-sentence generalisation.

6

'Attitudes' and Evaluating Progress

1. Attitudes

Our emphasis throughout this book has been heavily on people learning skills, concepts, information. Teachers are also interested, rightly, in other aspects of students' learning, less measurable, more pervasive things, which are sometimes summed up under the general heading of 'attitudes'.

All teachers would agree that they should try to foster favourable attitudes to work, to school, to doing their particular subject. We could usefully pull together here the main recommendations we have made so far about this, as we worked on the different skills. We might note:

(1) The importance of genuine acceptance of a students' opinions and judgements, particularly in discussion, in evaluation work and extrapolation work.

(2) The importance of making sure students understand the teacher's plans and proceedings and the precise purpose of their work. This is a universal rule, but particularly important when introducing new styles of work.

(3) The importance of students having success, and being praised for it—especially less able students.

(4) The importance of good feedback. Students must see their written work being treated with respect, and being used as a useful basis for future progress.

(5) The importance of making some move to interest and motivate students, in every session, however, simple and unelaborate that move might be.

If a teacher is seen by students to be at least trying to observe these five principles, the chances of gaining co-operation, approval for himself and his subject, and generally 'good attitudes' will probably be greatly improved.

There is a second group of attitudes, which is more specific, but yet sufficiently general for all teachers to approve of them in principle. Under this heading we would have mainly the scholarly values, ideas like 'respect for truth', 'respect for evidence', 'willingness to suspend judgement until all evidence has been considered', and so on.

Some people consider that the study of history in itself is likely to promote these attitudes. On the face of it, this seems pretty unlikely. History can quite well be taught as a series of authoritative judgements (known to the teacher) based on well-established facts (known to the teacher). Even if a great deal of apparently free discussion takes place between students and teacher, it is quite easy for a teacher to 'win' all the time, by mere fluency, or by introducing evidence not known to the students at the outset of the discussion, or simply by the weight of his authority. This is an unlikely way to produce 'respect for evidence', but quite a common approach, still, to teaching history.

If we really want people to have those particular attitudes, we must make clear to them that these attitudes are admired by us, and reward them, with praise and, where appropriate, with good grades, when they are manifested. Hardest of all, we actually have to display them ourselves. This is really quite difficult to do, when you are surrounded by people (students) who have less knowledge of the relevant evidence than you do, and who are vastly less skilled in interpreting and evaluating and presenting it. Merely being presented with the results of scholarship cannot make anybody scholarly.

A further discouraging circumstance is that students do not notice this particular set of attitudes being exemplified or apparently greatly valued in the world outside the classroom. Even professional academies do not always feel it necessary to back up assertions with evidence when they are talking about, say, contemporary politics, or education. So, by all means, try to foster these attitudes; in fact, it would be difficult in conscience not to try—but have no illusions about the size of the task.

The third set of attitudes is the contentious set, e.g. 'attitudes' like 'a favourable attitude to the underdog', 'tolerance for people of other countries and creeds', 'hatred of war and oppression', 'appreciation of the value of their own country's role in the world'.

Around this point we can get very near setting up as a goal that students come to share our opinions, under the guise of 'forming good attitudes'. Whether it is right to do that is a moral and a private matter. It might be worth noting though, that researches are pretty discouraging on the possibility of teachers affecting student attitudes in controversial areas, and particularly pessimistic about teachers actually changing pre-existing attitudes.

Broadly, the picture seems to be this. Other influences, such as the home and the peer-group, are much more powerful than teachers in attitude formation. Teachers are quite likely to produce an effect the exact reverse of what they are seeking. This seems to become more true, the more overtly and vehemently the teacher puts his own view.

So, if you want to make them hate the Fantasians, the best policy seems to be to tell them enthusiastically what a great people the Fantasians are! (Alternatively, you could choose students whose parents are confirmed Fantasia-phobes.)

Two Things to Read on 'Attitudes'

(1) H.C. Triandis, *Attitudes and Attitude Change,* John Wiley, 1971.

(2) L.M. Watson, 'Cigarette Smoking in Children', *Edinburgh Health Bulletin,* No. 24 (of more general application than the title suggests).

2. Evaluating Students' Progress

It is important that we know whether or not we are succeeding as history teachers. Leaving aside for the moment the question of students passing or failing examinations, we can succeed or fail at two levels, the level of general aims, or of specific objectives.

'General aims' cover long-term goals like 'to make students better citizens', 'to give them a historical perspective', 'to make them historians', 'to get them to understand themselves better as people'. Figuring out whether or not a general aim has been achieved or partly achieved by, say, the end of a year is usually difficult, sometimes just about impossible.

In the case of the aim 'to make them historians', we could write a list of characteristic ways in which historians usually behave, like the kind of things they say when faced with a statement or question about the past, or with a piece of documentary evidence. We could then give students examples of such statements, or lists of evidence at the start of a year, and at the end of the year, and see if the kinds of things they said about them had altered.

With the other examples of general aims quoted, it would be harder to make up such a test, and in the case of 'To get them to understand themselves as people', one feels a bit unclear about what such a test might even look like.

Perhaps the importance of general aims has been over-written. Teachers don't seem to go about testing whether they have achieved them and people often react unfavourably to the idea of testing at all in this context. Very similar syllabi and methods are used by teachers whose avowed general aims are very different; teachers don't really seem to spend much time thinking about general aims at all. What your own general aims as a history teacher are is your business—but one interesting exercise to try would be this: what sort of test could you imagine that could check out whether or not your general aim was being achieved, with a given class, after one year?

Then there are specific objectives, which fall into three broad classes: concepts, skills, information. The first two are obvious enough—no general aim of any kind could be achieved if students were not significantly increasing their grasp of concepts, and their expertise in the cognitive skills. The third, whether or not students are learning information, is the easiest thing to find out and also easy to get confused about. Suppose we have been teaching about the post-1950 independence movements in Africa. Let us consider exactly what information we would want students to be able to give us, in say a straight recall test, a week or so after we finished the work.

We could usefully divide the information into two parts. First, illustrative information—they must clearly be able to give some examples to illustrate concepts like 'nationalist leader', 'new nation', 'ex-British territory', 'ex-French territory', 're-named territory', 'colonial war', 'federal state'. Two examples of each, perhaps, might be reasonable to ask for.

'Uhuru' means 'freedom'. 'Accra is the capital of Ghana'. 'The Algerian war started in 1954'. These are examples of information not illustrative of any particularly abstruse concept but which inevitably come up in talking and reading about the topic of post-1950 Africa. Is any one of those three items more important than the other two? Would you care if students could not remember any of them? Would you care if they could not remember them in a year's time? These are questions to which you can only give your own answer, but one thing is obvious—we should be quite clear in our own minds exactly what we want the students to learn in this area of 'secondary' information, i.e. information not illustrative of a particular important concept.

Thus, when we write our initial plans, the section on 'information objectives' should look something like the following. 'Students should be able to recall: (a) two examples of nationalist leader, new nation (and so on); (b) dates of Ghana independence, Algerian war, capitals of Ghana, Nigeria, approximate population of Africa in 1960'—or whatever you think necessary.

No use at all is to plan like this: 'information objectives—general information on Africa, climate, etc.; main outline of independence movements'. Such planning would actually imply that students have to learn may be 100,000 items of information ('general information on Africa') which is a lot for three or four sessions.

It is hard discipline, to ask ourselves exactly what pieces of information we really want people to recall, because it makes us face the unpleasant fact of the massive scale of student forgetting. We have to do it, though, if we are to evaluate sensibly the success of our teaching from the angle of information-learning. Above all, we must get clear the difference between mere information and information needed to illustrate and thereby strengthen the grasp of a concept.

The problem with concepts and skills is the reverse of the problem with information. There is no problem specifying what concepts we want 'learned', because they have been on our mind right from the stage of planning the outline scheme of work. In planning individual sessions, the section 'Specific Objectives—Concepts' is easy to fill in.

As for skills, we are also pretty clear about which ones we have in mind to emphasise in most sessions. But how do we evaluate students' advance in understanding of a concept, or improved expertise in a skill? Let us look at concepts first.

Suppose we had pre-tested someone's understanding of the term 'mercenary soldier' in two ways.

(1) a straight translation question: 'What is a mercenary?'

(2) an application question: 'Were German soldiers in World War I mercenaries?'

At the pre-test, we got these responses from the student:

(1) Mercenaries are cruel soldiers.

(2) Some might have been not all.

Now suppose we do work on Renaissance Italy, some of it directed to improving understanding of the idea of a 'mercenary soldier'. We then give exactly the same two questions to the student as a 'post-test' and get these responses:

(1) A paid soldier.

(2) No. They had to fight (conscripts) in World War I.

Now the understanding shown is still not perfect (for example, the model response to question (1) might be, 'volunteer, paid soldier, willing to change sides quite readily for better pay, loyal to commanders, not to states or nations'). However, these later answers certainly represent a visible advance towards the ideal answer. If we had time and inclination we could probably divide the 'understanding' of the term 'mercenary' into nine or ten stages and say that the student had advanced from stage two to stage five, or something of the sort, but as teachers we must settle for a positive answer to this question: 'Has the student's understanding of the concept advanced at all?' In this case we can say that it has. Usually, though, real life is not as clear-cut as that. For example, these following responses to the same two questions:

(1) *What is a mercenary?*

(a) A soldier who will do anything he is told.

(b) Soldiers especially good at fighting.

(c) Soldiers who don't mind what side wins the war.

(2) *Were World War I German soldiers mercenaries?*

(a) Yes, they had to obey orders.

(b) Yes, they were good fighters.

(c) No, they wanted Germany to win—would never fight for someone else, or France especially.

In both cases, the answers under (c) have now got the idea of the mercenaries' lack of moral involvement in the wars of the time, and we could say, mark a clear advance, although they don't make the point on payment which is central to our ideal answer. The sets of answers (b) and (a) say things about mercenaries which might sometimes be true of mercenaries or of any soldiers. They present, however, an advance on the possible confusion with the word 'merciless' which may well be the origin of the initial pre-test answer, but it looks like a very slight advance.

In these real-life responses, we can note two things: (a) we need a pretty clear understanding of the concept ourselves to detect whether an advance has taken place; (b) an answer can show a real advance, but with an emphasis that is not what we had in mind, as student (c) emphasises moral detachment rather than money.

Exercise 1

Work through these examples now. In each case a pair of pre-test responses is given, and three 'post-test' responses. What you have to do is work out which of the post-test responses represents an advance in understanding and, if you can, which represents the greatest advance, which the least. Assume that the 'post-test' responses are paired, i.e. in the post-test 1 (a) and 2 (a) are from the same student, and so on.

Example 1 (twelve-year-olds)

Unemployment

Pre-test questions

(1) What is 'unemployment'?

(2) Can you give an example of an unemployed person?

Response (pre-test)

(1) When people don't work.

(2) Old people

Post-test response (same questions)

(1) *(a)* If people cannot go to work.

(b) No work to do for the people.

(c) People idle all day at home.

(2) *(a)* Sick or aged people or children.

(b) Depression between the wars.

(c) If your factory closed.

Example 2 (fourteen-year-olds)

Depression (economic)

Pre-test questions

(1) What does the word a 'depression' mean?

(2) Suppose a lot fewer children were born, and so a lot of teachers lost their jobs—would that be a depression?

Responses (pre-test)

(1) People losing their jobs for a long time.

(2) Yes.

Post-test responses (same questions)

(1) *(a)* Mass unemployment world wide.

(b) Trade got less so people would lose their jobs.

(c) People have less money, so spend less on things, so less money all round and so on.

(2) *(a)* No, unless happening all over world.

(b) No, must be to do with money.

(c) No but yes, may be you could say 'a depression for teachers'.

Example 3 (seventeen-year-olds)

Rationalism (context of eighteenth-century Enlightenment)

Pre-test questions

(1) What is rationalist?

(2) What would be the attitude of a rationalist to the Christian Church?

Responses (pre-test)

(1) Open minded. A person who listens to all opinions.

(2) He would be tolerant, allow people to choose which sect or religion they wished to belong to.

Post-test responses (same questions)

(1) *(a)* Liberal-minded, in the context of the eighteenth-century Enlightenment.

(b) In favour of a scientific approach.

(c) Weighs up reasons before deciding for or against a particular view.

(2) *(a)* He would have opposed its cruelties in the eighteenth century.

(b) Thinks Christianity is false.

(c) Agnostic, but would value all opinions.

Example 4 (fourteen-year-olds, very able)

Absolute King (seventeenth-century context)

Pre-test questions

(1) What does it mean to say a King is 'absolute'?

(2) Is the Queen of England today 'absolute'?

Responses (pre-test)

(1) The only King in a country.

(2) Yes, but Duke of Edinburgh helps her to rule.

Post-test responses (same questions)

(1) *(a)* A King is absolute when no-one else has sovereignty.

(b) He has right alone to make and declare laws.

(c) He is the only one with soldiers in the country.

(2) *(a)* No, because Parliament has sovereignty in England now.

(b) No, Parliament and Commons make some laws.

(c) There are police and army does not all belong to Queen (except Guards) (so No!!).

For this exercise, we presumed that the way you would test the success of concept-learning would be by a test using the same type of question, or even the same actual question, as you used on the pre-test. That is the most straightforward way to do it, and probably gives the most accurate picture. But you don't want to do this all the time. You don't want to give students the impression that you are test-crazy'; also, you will not always want to wait until the end of a teaching cycle to check out the students' progress.

So a lot of the time, you will be trying to evaluate students' progress on the basis of longer pieces of speech or writing than a short test-answer. Let us look at a few examples.

Exercise 2

In this exercise, try to evaluate in the case of the responses to the tasks whether the students are demonstrating an advance in understanding of the concept in question, compared with the understanding of the concept in question shown by their pre-test responses.

Student A

Concept—Conquer (1066 context)

Pre-test—'What does it mean if somebody conquers a country?'

Pre-test response—If one side wins the battle, that is conquering.

Later application task—'After they conquered England, the Normans want to conquer Wales. Make up a plan how they might do that.'

Response— 'Fight a battle and win in Wales somewhere may be the North. Kill some of the Wales people to scare others. Build castles, get Saxons to build them, so if Wales army attacked you would be safe.

Student B

Concept—reactionary (nineteenth-century Europe context)

Pre-test— 'What is a "reactionary"?'

Pre-test response—Violent ideas. Person with ideas very strongly held.

Later application task—"Write a short piece as by a reactionary person, about the idea of Prussia having a written constitution'.

Response—The idea is a disaster. Total collapse will break out, Prussia will no longer exist as a nation. All freedom will be lost. The country might be destroyed in a few more days by France or Russia.

Student C

Concept—economic imperialism (nineteenth-century China context)

Pre-test— 'How is economic imperialism different from any other sort of imperialism?'

Pre-test response—If a country puts its colonies to economic use, not just e.g. as naval bases.

Later application and interpretation task (discussion)—Focus your discussion on this: Suppose someone said: 'The West were not Imperialists in China—they seized hardly any territory except Hong Kong, and China was independent the whole time'. Draft a reply as a group, agreeing or disagreeing, with reasons.

Response— [evaluate only student C's contributions]

Student C—Well, Hong Kong was used for trade and . . .

Student X—I think he means the rest . . .

Student Y—The rest of China. The main bit.

Student X—They sold them, sold them railways and machinery, ships. They sold them at a big profit and made them pay. . .

Student C—That's just selling, that doesn't make it Imperialists.

Student Z—Economic Imperialists.

Student C—Only if they forced them. If they sailed up and said, 'You've got to buy all this cotton or anything or we will take over the country and be a colony or blow up Pekin'.

Student Y—They did go in 1900 Boxer . . .

Student Z—They could force them in other ways. Could say make them buy or we won't let you sell your stuff . . .

Student D

Concept—capital (as 'capital city')

Pre-test— 'Say in your own words what the capital of a country is'.

Pre-test response—Main town. The one where most people go, and most live.

Later extrapolation task—'Suppose Borovia City the capital of Fantasia was destroyed in an earthquake, what problems would that make for Fantasia?'

Response—Buildings destroyed. Dead people. Disease. Many casualties. Nobody knows what to do. President or King would have to go round and make orders, but might be dead himself, so new King needed. Elections for new President or King. Elections would have to be at Borovia City, but not possible now.

Student E

Three concepts together in this example: political, economic, social

Pre-test 1— 'What would you say politics was to do with?'

Pre-test 1 response—Elections, how people vote for. Choosing Presidents.

Pre-test 2— 'What does "economic" mean?'

Pre-test 2 response—To do with money.

Pre-test 3— 'What would "social history" be about?'

Pre-test 3 response—Less important things.

Later evaluation and synthesis task— 'What do you think were the most important results of the Civil War? [America, 1861–65)

Remember that we have learned about political effects, and also social and economic effects'.

Response—I think most important was in politics. U.S.A. kept together, and had same President in both parts and so were strong enough for World War I and to win Cuban war in 1898.

This was important. The U-boats might have beaten the U.S.A., if the U.S. had been split up.

Economic effects is next. Gold was found in California in 1849, there were railroads built to California. Population grew, and industry grew up everywhere. Black people now get paid instead of being slaves so people began to accept black people, slowly, because they had their own money and economies now. Some worked in factories. The Cattle Kingdom might not have happened to be so great in 1885 if Texas had been in one country and Chicago in another in the North. Cattle would have had to cross a border now and there could have been outlaws on the border.

Dress changed a lot after the war, especially for women, but that was not the war I think. Other big social changes were changes in outlook with the meteoric rise of the robber barons. People changed in many social things.

Evaluating Progress in Skills

The special problems of evaluating progress in skills are fairly obvious. First, if you introduce a new skill to students, say extrapolation, you can probably get a visible surge of improvement in competence, from their first fumbling effort, to about their third or fourth attempt, by which time they have begun to form an idea of what is involved. After that point, though, progress is likely to be slow and therefore hard to detect. Second, in the case of some skills, like translation, it is difficult to separate the idea of progress in the skill from progress in understanding the ideas which are being translated (except in the case of exercises with maps and pictures and graphs, of course).

On the first point, what we can do is look for progress in skills over a longish period, say half a year. As to the second point, we can say this: in the case of some skills, we can say pretty clearly whether a person is getting better or not, in fact, we can virtually quantify it: evaluation work and extrapolation work depend largely for their quality on the number of factors of which a student can successfully take account.

Equally, in the case of analysis, we can say that if student A is doing better than student B in, say, analysing what is required in a project, what he is doing is working out *more* of the sub-tasks that need to be done than B is.

With synthesis it is difficult to describe why one student's synthesis is better than another one, but, happily, pretty easy to recognise when it is so, which is good enough for our present purpose of evaluating progress. (Of course, it would not do to tell a student that his synthesis of essays and so on was not good enough, in certain incommunicable but vital ways. For purposes of giving students feedback, we have to get down and say exactly what is wrong).

That leaves translation, interpretation and application. Except in the case of work with graphs, maps and so on, it is probably not of practical use to try to separate progress in the skill from progress in understanding the material involved in using the skill, in the case of translation and interpretation.

The case of application is a little different. Look at these two examples of response to an application task:

> *Task*—A country has an elected President, everyone can vote in the elections for President. This country is also divided into counties. The counties are ruled by councils, but people do not vote for the councils, they just have the ten richest men in the country. Is the country a republic?
>
> *Response A*
>
> All the people vote for President which is right, but there are no county votes which is not fair, people should vote in county as well.
>
> *Response B*
>
> No, because people in the counties don't vote, only rich men.
>
> Both responses show the same lack of understanding of the concept 'republic'. But B is a better piece of application—it says clearly whether the concept will apply or not, with reasons.

Students can fail to carry out application tasks properly in more sophisticated ways than the one quoted above, as in this case:

> *Task*—When the allies defeated Napoleon and put Louis XVIII back in France, was that a *revolution*?

Response—They really had no choice, Napoleon could not be trusted after the 100 days. They could not have a republic, as Austria would not have allowed that, or Russia indeed, therefore only the King of the House of Bourbon was left.

If Napoleon had stayed on would have been the true revolution if he had carried out to full measure the Spirit of 1789.

Obviously, this is not an answer to the question, not a piece of application at all, except for the veiled hint about 'true revolution'. So we might note the rather banal but important point that 'doing less well' at application might involve the student no doing application at all, but taking trouble to disguise the fact.

With application tasks, also, we can 'of course' use the idea of 'number of factors used' as a measure of progress. Thus, as an answer to the 'France 1815' task we just looked at, Response A (below) would be better than B.

Response A

Yes, because (a) violent change, by force, of rule, (b) big change in the government, (c) changes in everyday life for peasants, etc., (d) peace would reign—a big change. Only a small revolution though; because changes would not be major like before 1789.

Response B

It could not be one because it was people from outside the country did it. The people did not rise up to affect changes.

As to which of these students has the better understanding of the concept of revolution—that is a different question.

Remarks on Exercise 1 (page 232)

Unemployment

Response 1(c) does not seem to show an advance, but the response 2(c) has the important idea of unemployment not being voluntary. This shows the usefulness of having a two-barrelled test, and the way in which a straight 'Does *x* mean?' question can sometimes not be adequate in revealing understanding.

Similarly 2(a) clearly shows up lack of understanding where response 1(a) from the same student sounds pretty good.

Depression

Response 1(a) illustrates an important point. Sophisticated language— 'Mass unemployment world wide' can sometimes mask lack of understanding quite effectively. Response 2 (a) seems to show that this student has, in fact, only latched on to the idea that depressions have to be widespread to count as depressions. Responses 1(c) and 2(c) are clumsily expressed, but have more of the idea, e.g. the idea in 1(c) of a *cycle* of economic problems.

Rationalism

Response 1(a) again shows how in a 'post-test' a student might merely clothe exactly the same level of understanding he had at the pre-test in elegant new language. Responses 1(b) and 2(b) seem to show clearest advance.

Absolute King

Response 1(a) also shows up this same point, only now, with the addition of the term 'sovereignty', it gets confusing, because we don't know for sure what the student means by it. He might take it to mean 'power' in which case there has been a real advance, or he might mean something like 'the legal right to be King', in which case he is simply dressing up the original pre-test level of understanding. Response 2(a), though, might well indicate that he takes 'sovereignty' to mean power.

Remarks on Exercise 2

Student A—Conquer

Certainly an advance beyond the idea of 'winning battles'. Still some areas of ambiguity revealed by the apparent continued existence of a 'Wales army', but basically a reasonable advance.

Student B—Reactionary

This is a tough one. A reactionary might indeed have said all these things, but the student seems to be emphasising the violence of the opinions as much as their content. This is a good example of the sort of response that we must accept as a 'good answer', and yet feel disquiet about.

Student C—Economic Imperialism

The most promising sign is when student C says the Westerners might threaten to 'blow up Pekin'—that is the only sign he gives of moving away from the idea that economic imperialism necessarily involves holding territory.

Student D—Capital

Much rather confusing mention of kings, presidents and elections indicates, probably, a grasp of the idea of a capital as a political centre, in his second response. The idea that elections have to take place at the capital is a nice illustration of a student putting his own, very concrete, interpretation on the idea of 'a political centre'.

Student E—Political, Economic, Social

Both 'politics' and 'economic' seem to have developed well beyond the original limited nations of the pre-test. 'Social' is obviously still pretty problematic to the student, and the probable lifting from a book of the phrase 'changes in outlook. . .robber barons' is a classic illustration of one of the standard moves made by students when they know they don't understand something: 'When in doubt, put something down that sounds good, straight out of the book if possible'. We should not be hard on students for doing this, it is only the equivalent of our adult trick of talking rather faster and using jargon when we don't really understand what we are saying. If you detected this tactic, though, it is a very reliable indicator of lack of understanding in the student.

Final Exercises

(1) You can evaluate how much sense this book has made to you personally in quite a simple way. Look back at the five quotations from teachers at the beginning of the Introduction. What advice, if any, could you give those teachers now?

(2) This book has been largely concerned with day-to-day problems of planning, carrying out and evaluating teaching tasks, so more general questions like the justifying of the place of history in the curriculum, or discussion of the ideal content of a five or six-year history syllabus have not been directly addressed. However, it might be interesting to look at those two questions as a final 'exercise', as it were.

(a) Justifying the place of history in the curriculum

Some of the justifications put forward for the teaching of history suffer from one or more of the following defects:

(i) They are not justifications at all, but merely descriptions, as when we say 'History is the study of change in time', without saying why 'change in time' is worthy of study.

(ii) They make claims which ought to be supported by evidence, and are not so supported—as when we claim that study of history helps people to form a sense of their own identity or makes them generally wiser, better or more agreeable than people who do not learn history, without adducing evidence to show that this is so.

(iii) They make claims that history as a subject does certain things for people, without specifying that the history would have to be taught in a certain way to do these things—for example, in the 'attitudes' section we noted the implausibility of the common claim that history fosters independent thinking, in the context of some traditional history-teaching methods.

Can you justify the place of history in the curriculum, avoiding these three pitfalls?

(b) The content of an ideal history course, for students of 11 to 18

Could you devise and justify such a course, in the light of a concern for development of a big range of specific concepts and of a range of cognitive skills? How useful as guides are the linked ideas of concept development and skills in tackling this question?

7

Classroom Observation

Classroom observation can be used in several different but related contexts. Indeed, there is a strong argument that teaching should be much more open to scrutiny than it has previously been, particularly by teachers themselves. It is a great pity that the tradition in a field like surgery, whereby surgeons learn from each other by studying video-tapes, or watching live and even joining in as assistants, when new techniques are being developed and perfected, is not imitated more frequently in teaching. Although the surgery/teaching analogy does not always stand up to close inspection, the open sharing of new ideas, the convention of 'sitting in' with fellow practitioners, are matters that could spread to teaching with profit, provided appropriate time and resources are made available.

This chapter will describe seven contexts for classroom observation in action. These are:

(1) Initial teacher training.

(2) In-service training and professional development.

(3) Studying pupils.

(4) Curriculum development and evaluation.

(5) Job analysis.

(6) Teacher appraisal.

(7) Observation by lay people.

The eighth context, research, will be covered in Chapter 8. All the seven fields mentioned above can, of course, be the subject of research. However, much greater rigour and depth of analysis are required in research, which usually involves investigation in a systematic way, using one or more of the traditions of enquiry described in previous chapters. The emphasis in this chapter is on informal and semi-formal classroom observation for the purpose of looking at, or attempting to improve, the quality of teaching and learning. Research, particularly action research and R & D (Research and Development) projects, can also have the same aspirations, trying to improve teaching and learning through research, and these will also be addressed in the next chapter, but for the present the emphasis is on day-to-day classroom observation in informal and semi-formal settings within normal resources.

INITIAL TEACHER TRAINING

Patterns of classroom interaction can be laid down quite early, even during training, and in a study of over a 100 postgraduate student teachers which I conducted (Wragg, 1973) it emerged that some had already established fairly stable styles of teaching even when on teaching practice. Looking at one's own or someone else's teaching, therefore, can be an important part of initial training. For many teachers their initial training was virtually the only time in their career when they were observed. Good or bad habits, first of observation, second of reflection on one's own or another student's or teacher's practice, can be fashioned during initial training.

Observing Others

The tradition of observing other teachers was already well known in the nineteenth century, and in the 1830s the Scottish pioneer David Stow introduced the 'gallery lesson' into the Glasgow Normal Seminary where he taught. Trainees and their tutors watched a student teach from their seat in the gallery, hence term 'gallery lesson'. Some literally 'played to the gallery' and showed off in front of their fellows.

Nowadays there are two regular opportunities for trainees to watch teaching, the first is live observation, the second is videotape. It is a useful exercise for trainees to watch a good video of one or more teachers at work in their classroom. The opportunity to stop and start the tape, guess consequences or discuss outcomes away from the pressure of taking a class, can raise important matters of principle and practice. The development of interactive videodisc is an extension of this facility, offering an even higher quality of picture, as well as the ability to hold or 'freeze' a single frame and study a still life picture of the classroom. Most of all, because it can handle both print and pictures, there are rich possibilities for individual and small group self-supported tutorial work.

One videodisc option that is liked by student teachers is the interrupted story, when a classroom scene is played and the individual or group can then select one of three or four options and see the consequences of their choice. For example, the scene may show a pupil misbehaving. When the film stops the trainee is invited to make a choice—(a) to ignore it, (b) to punish the child, (c) to reinvolve the child in his work or (d) to discuss the misbehaviour with the pupil concerned and others. Having made a selection the trainee can then see filmed consequences of the choice. The major problem with this neat looking approach is that the film maker or director may have simply programmed personal prejudices into the story line. If someone believes that it is 'best to reinvolve pupils in their work, then when they film the consequence of this choice of action it is easy for them to portray a positive outcome. Inexperienced trainees might then assume all similar problems have the same solution. Nonetheless, the immense storage capacity of the interactive videodisc, the high quality pictures, and rapid access, using barcode technology (passing a barcode recorder over a barcode to find almost instantaneously the place on the videodisc) offer a variety of possibilities to discuss dilemmas and decisions, if sensibly handled.

With trainees early in their training programme, when they observe a teacher live in the classroom it might be best to use either a simple set of headings, or invite them to make freehand notes. A simple structure for looking at the strategies of questioning and explaining, either in their own teaching, or when watching an experienced teacher might look like the one below. Several student teachers can use the same structure and then compare their observations, either of the same lesson or of different ones. They can also interview the teacher concerned, or talk to the pupils, to see what they understood, if the teacher agrees.

QUESTION LOG

A. *Questions asked* Write down three questions asked during the observation period and the responses obtained. In each case write the actual words of the question and the sort of response obtained.

Question 1 ____________________________

Response ____________________________

____

____

Question 2 ____________________________

Response ____________________________

____

____

Question 3 ____________________________

Response ____________________________

____

____

B. *Sequences* Write down a sequence of between two and five questions that belonged together and followed each other. Write the actual words asked and brief notes about the reasons behind the sequence and the actual outcome.

Question 1 ____________________________

Outcome ____________________________

____

____

Question 2 ____________________________

Outcome ____________________________

____

____

Question 3 ______________________________

Question 4 ______________________________

Question 5 ______________________________

Your reflections on the sequence

EXPLAINING LOG

C. Explanations Write down two explanations given, either to the whole class, a small group or an individual pupil. Describe the context, the strategy used and what the result was.

Explanation 1

Explanation 2

D. Explaining to different pupils Write down an explanation given to a more able and a less able pupil during the day. In each case note the context, the strategy used and the outcome.

Explanation to more able pupil

Explanation to less able pupil

The agenda for discussing these with fellow students or teachers/tutors is quite simple. There are several ways of reflecting on what different observers have discovered about their teaching. These include the following possibilities:

(1) Teachers take it in turn to talk about some of their questions/explanations.

(2) Members of the group try to see what they can learn from each other's strategies.

(3) Look at any common features (e.g. use of vocabulary when explaining to more and less able pupils).

(4) Persuade some brave souls to video lessons when they are asking questions or explaining a new topic and discuss ways of improving what is done.

(5) Ask a member of the group to explain a personal interest to the rest of the group (a favourite painting/piece of music, how to play backgammon, the joys of fell walking, running your own finances, a scientific principle, how a car engine works, making your own pasta.) Then discuss how you would explain the same topic (a) to a 6 year old, (b) to a 13 year old, (c) to an intelligent Martian.

(6) Discuss views with others on matters such as (a) should you call only on children who put up their hand to answer, or sometimes address others, (b) what you should do when you don't know the answer (e.g. a child asks why some grains of sand float, even though most sink to the bottom of the water container), (c) what you should do when children answer incorrectly (give them another chance? ask someone else? give them a clue?).

The research evidence on the effectiveness of micro-strategies of this kind is by no means conclusive, so there is plenty of scope for discussion and exploration.

Pair Working

One effective way for both novices and experienced teachers to work together is for the to work as a pair. Each acts as teacher and observer, using the identical approach. Activity 7.1 shows how two trainees or a trainee and a supervising teacher or tutor can engage in such reciprocal pair work to improve their vigilance in class. The observer learns to look carefully to find children not engaged in the task, the person teaching, knowing what the observer is doing, becomes very vigilant.

ACTIVITY 7.1

A. *Eyes*—For ten minutes watch the teacher's use of eyes, both eye contact or lack of it, and use of eyes to swep across the class. Make notes about how the teacher uses his/her eyes.

B. *Pupils not engaged in the task*—Look for two pupils not engaged in the task, for whatever reason. Study each one for five minutes and make notes below about what each child does.

Pupil 1

Pupil 2

C. *Discussion*—Discuss what has been observed with the teacher and then swap roles.

Supervision

A common feature of initial training is the discussion of what has been observed with a supervising teacher or tutor. Student teachers react differently to their supervisor, some with affection and respect, others with contempt or even apprehension. The supervisor/student relationship is crucial, and negative stories often result either from a supervisor feeling that the student is rigid, arrogant, lazy or unwilling to take advice, or from the student complaining that post-lesson critiques concentrate on negative aspects and do not bring out the positive. Very capable students sometimes feel let down if the supervisor simply says, "That's fine" or "You're very good", as they too want to improve.

McIntyre (1977) looked at supervision in three different contexts: students taught lessons which were videotaped, and they were then invited to analyse their lesson either with a tutor, or with other students in groups of three. Students tended to prefer a tutor to be present. If students do want dialogue with a supervisor, then supervision is in itself a craft which observers who are also responsible for students' professional development need to develop, and exploring various styles of post-lesson analysis is just as important for supervisors, as trying out different styles of teaching is for teachers. Stones (1984) argues that supervision is a greatly neglected craft and one that should lie at the centre of developing teaching skills and understanding how children learn. Some possibilities include:

(1) The supervisor gives an analytical account of the lesson and asks the student to comment.

(2) The student gives an analytical account of the lesson and the supervisor comments.

(3) The supervisor and student hold an unstructured or semi-structured conversation about the lesson, with neither taking a dominant role.

(4) The supervisor collects critical events and then discusses these with the student.

(5) The supervisor makes a sound tape or video of a lesson and then plays it back with the student, stopping and starting it whenever one of the two participants wishes to talk about what is happening.

(6) The supervisor uses some agreed checklist or set of headings to complete a pro forma which is then discussed.

(7) The supervisor chooses positive and negative aspects of the lesson, as he/she sees it, and then feeds back either the positive ones first, to avoid undermining the student's confidence, or the negative ones first, to get them out of the way.

There are as many style of supervision as there are supervisors, and most use a variety of approaches. Supervisors need to be aware of two tendencies. The first is to *project themselves as a paragon ideal,* that is to imagine themselves teaching flawlessly the class they are observing, forgetting their own errors and infelicities. This can give rise to a temptation to take over to show how it should be done, or to talk entirely in terms of their own preferred strategies. The second in the tendency to *compensate for their own deficiencies,* that is to feel they must correct particularly strongly any aspect in which they are themselves weak, for example, tidiness, or the use of visual aids. Mutual trust and respect are essential ingredients for a healthy relationship between supervisor and student.

Micro-teaching

The basic format for micro-teaching was originally developed at Stanford University in the 1960s (Allen and Ryan, 1969). It is an attempt to scale down classroom life so that trainees can develop one aspect of their skill with a small number of children, rather than have to work at everything with 30 pupils to teach. There are seven main features:

(1) *Preparation*—The student prepares a short lesson, often in the light of preliminary discussion with supervisor, attempting to concentrate on some aspect of teaching and learning.

(2) *Skills*—Particular attention is devoted to one aspect of teaching proficiency, like class management, explaining or questioning.

(3) *Class size*—A small group of children, from three up to half a class, is taught.

(4) *Time unit*—A small amount of time, from five up to 20 minutes usually, is available for the student to teach the class and be videotaped.

(5) *'Teach' phase*—The student has a first attempt at teaching the group.

(6) *Feedback*—The student receives feedback (from a supervising teacher or tutor, fellow students, childrens' written responses to a questionnaire about what they have experienced, or from watching the videotape).

(7) *'Reteach' phase*—The student has a second opportunity, often with a parallel group of children from the same class, to teach the same topic, but this time in the light of feedback and reflection.

(8) *Debriefing*—After the full cycle has been completed the student has an opportunity to discuss what has been learned and reflect on future teaching strategies.

An illustration from a micro-teaching session right at the beginning of a trainee teacher's course illustrates the potential when the process goes well:

> Helen has, with enormous care, prepared a lesson on volcanoes. She teaches the first lesson by giving the class a number of pieces of information about the nature of volcanoes: "Today I want to tell you a little bit about volcanoes. Here is a model of one and you can see that this is the crater and, as you probably know, this is the lava, and this part here is called the magma chamber. Perhaps you've heard of volcanoes before. There's one in Italy called Vesuvius. . ."

When she watches the videotape she is disappointed by the class's poor response on the rare opportunities she has given them to contribute. Here supervisor suggests she might start the reteach phase with the second group of children by simply asking the class what they know about volcanoes and following up from this. Gradually, after a few hesitant responses, more children contribute, referring to television programmes, their friends' and parents' holiday and travel experiences, things they have read in books, mentioning Vesuvius, Etna, the dust from Krakatoa travelling several times around the Earth, crates on the moon, Icelandic geysers and various other notions, using terms like 'lava' and 'eruption'. Helen is delighted, but also surprised by the breadth and depth of their existing knowledge.

It is not always the case that the second lesson is 'better', and indeed it is arguable whether Helen's first lesson was necessarily 'worse' than her reteach. What is important, however, is the opportunity to learn about teaching and explore alternatives is an environment where there is time to do it properly. There are several reservations about micro-teaching, however, which need to be considered. First of all it is very labour-intensive and demanding on supervising teachers or tutors, which is why it has not been as widespread as was originally hoped by its instigators. It has also been criticised for being artificial, too unlike 'real' classrooms, for atomising teaching into separate discrete skills, when according to its critics, teaching should be seen as an organic whole, and for emphasising the performance elements of teaching, the presentation skills, rather than such matters as listening to pupils, or sitting and talking to an individual.

There is another important point about the videotaping of trainees and that is about self-confrontation generally. There is an assumption that to see oneself is *ipso facto* to improve. Nothing could be further from the truth. Though some people are perfectly able to look at themselves on video and see aspects they can make more effective, others become tense and find their self-confidence is undermined. We carry around with us a self-image which can be rudely shattered when we see ourselves on video for the first time and realise we are just as frail as the rest of humanity. It is essential, therefore, that students should see themselves on video more than once to overcome what is sometimes known as the 'cosmetic effect' ("Don't I look awful").

Indeed, it is well worthwhile trainees purchasing their own special videotape at the beginning of their course, and they will then be able to assemble a collection of scenes from their own classroom experiences, giving them a unique record of their personal and professional development. Like other forms of lesson observation and analysis in initial training, micro-teaching and the videotaping of lessons is something that, if skilfully handled, can be a valuable learning process, but done in a ham fisted manner can be counter-productive.

IN-SERVICE TRAINING AND PROFESSIONAL DEVELOPMENT

Many of the points made about initial training above apply to the further professional development of experienced teachers. They too can work in pairs, see themselves on videotape, look at lesson protocols and transcripts, and study videotapes of other teachers' lessons. Indeed, going to someone else's classroom to observe practice is often highly esteemed by teachers on the occasions, somewhat rare, unfortunately, that they have the time for such visits. Schools would do well to schedule visits to classrooms, when possible to other schools, not just their own, into their staff development policy and practice, if they can manage it.

Furthermore, the link between classroom observation for initial training and for in-service purpose can be a strong one. It is difficult for teachers to observe a student's lesson in a systematic way, looking perhaps at teacher-pupil interaction, class management strategies or lack of them, or the nature of the task being set for individual pupils, without reflecting on their own practice. Looking in a student's lesson for 'questions which invite children to formulate a hypothesis', for example, makes you wonder whether you ever ask such questions yourself, and if so, what the outcome is, or if not, why not? If student teachers did not exist it would be worth inventing them as a means of fomenting critical analysis of professional practice.

Reciprocal pair work, whereby two teachers pair up to study and observe each other, is a rich form of professional development. Most teachers prefer some degree of structure for such activities, otherwise post-lesson discussion can be bland and soothing ("Seemed fine") or unfocused. Teachers can either use an existing structure, or negotiate a bespoke task which they both agree to be worth investigating, like the following:

(1) Two infant school teachers look at how they hear children read, monitoring progress so that they can see if any changes they make lead to an improvement in children's reading ability (need to beware of simply 'teaching to the test' and manufacturing a spurious rise in reading test scores).

(2) Two secondary science teachers sit in on each other's laboratory sessions to watch small groups during experimental work, noting how harmoniously or otherwise they work together, and how effectively they learn the topic (the observer can interview some of the children after the lesson to see how well they understand what they have been doing).

(3) Three teachers of 5, 6 and 7 year olds watch each other's lessons (A watches B and C, B observes A and C, C watches A and B) in a similar subject or topic area (for example, technology, mathematics, science, writing, humanities-type projects, the use of broadcasts) to see how much continuity and coherence there appears to be in the curriculum for 5 to 7 year olds.

(4) Two physical education teachers study each other's lessons, concentrating on six target pupils, two each of high, medium and low ability in PE, to document what kind of movement each does during a lesson or competitive game (video can be valuable here, if available).

Studying Pupils

There is a tendency, in many of the published classroom observation schemes and handbooks, to concentrate on what the teacher does, especially when the emphasis is on the development or enhancement of teachers' classroom skills. However, it is equally enlightening to look at pupils, and some of the activities suggested in this book do precisely that. By studying what pupils do, observers can learn a great deal not only about the impact of teaching on the learner, but also about the child's perspective and the influence that individual and groups of children have on the lesson.

Pupil Pursuit

One of the most frequently used approaches to eliciting the child's eye view is to follow a single or sometimes a pair of children around for most or all of their school day, the 'pupil pursuit' as it is sometimes called. In primary schools this often involves sitting in the same room for most of the day, logging the child's activities and movements, but in secondary schools it can mean visiting seven or eight different locations. The principal intention is to capture the flavour of what it means to be a pupil in a particular class or group, without making the child concerned too self-conscious.

There are problems of selection, of course, and making generalisations about the experience of a whole class on the basis of the sole disruptive child or the most capable pupil would distort the true picture of events for the rest, which is why some observers choose a pair of children, or even six different target pupils, a boy and a girl from each of high, medium and low ability children. However, logging the experiences of a pupil can reveal a number of interesting aspects of classroom life. I once took a group of student teachers to a secondary school which wanted to know more about how its language policy was working out in practice. Each student was attached to a class and target pupils were followed for the day. The students kept a detailed log of what kind of language activity was happening, noting, for example, whether each child was reading, writing, listening, talking, at various stages of the lesson.

The findings were most interesting. Some children went to seven different lessons and completed seven workcards, one in each lesson. Others listened and wrote a great deal, sometimes copying from books or the blackboard, but did little practical activity, or talked to the teacher or each other. Yet others were highly active in their use of language, reading, talking, asking questions of the teacher, discussing with fellow pupils, writing in a variety of contexts for different purposes. At the end of each of the three days of observation the students wrote a freehand account entitled "Had I been a pupil in this class today . . .".

When the findings were fed back to the teachers a lively discussion ensued. Most had little idea of what had happened in previous lessons, so when the teacher said, in the seventh lesson of the day, "I want you to do this workcard", the groans at death by a thousand workcards could be explained by what had happened in previous lessons. It led to the teachers reviewing their use of workcards, and also looking at the range of activities being employed with pupils in different year groups.

Sometimes, alongside a freehand diary type record of what a pupil is doing, it is worth recording a time sample every few minutes or so of some aspect of the child's behaviour that can amplify the record. This could be a record of movement, a checking of what the child is doing at the moment of audit (reading, writing, listening, talking to a fellow pupil), or a note of what the teacher is doing and the child's part in it (or not, as the case may be). One possibility is to use the simple structure for recording time on the task and misbehaviour. Every ten minutes or so from the beginning of the observation period, a quick check can be made, and two ticks inserted in the relevant columns:

	Involvement level			*Deviancy level*		
Time	*low*	*medium*	*high*	*none*	*mild*	*serious*
9.00	/				/	
9.10			/	/		
9.20			/	/		
9.30		/		/		
9.40			/	/		
9.50	/				/	

Groups

Another focus on children is to study a particular group of pupils, perhaps working together on a project, or sitting at the same table. There are numerous questions which can be addressed in such an exercise:

(1) Are the pupils working separately or collaboratively (both are perfectly permissible)?

(2) How were groups assembled? Free choice? Teacher directed?

(3) Are they working harmoniously, or is there discord? If so, why?

(4) Does the assignment appear to be clear, or is there some confusion as to what they should be doing?

(5) Is the task appropriate to the group, or is it beneath/beyond them?

(6) Is the work shared evenly amongst members of the group, or does one child dominate and not allow others to contribute?

(7) What is the role of different pupils? Are the groups single sex or mixed? Are there differences in the way that boys and girls are working?

(8) How does the teacher monitor what the group is doing and what children are learning?

There are no omni-purpose 'correct' answers to these questions, but they do raise issues about group work in the classroom which are worthy of discussion and further reflection and action.

CURRICULUM DEVELOPMENT AND EVALUATION

The busy nature of teaching, with its numerous repeated and rehearsed strategies and the frequency of its interactions, has been pointed out several times in this book. If teachers engage in a thousand or so interpersonal transactions in a single day, then it is difficult for them to step back and scrutinise what they are doing. Someone who has been teaching for five years or more will already have engaged in over a million exchanges in the classroom, and patterns of behaviour have been laid down which are not always easy to change. Yet a new curriculum or examination syllabus may require not just new subject–matter to be introduced, but different strategies to be employed.

Consider some of the changes that have been introduced into the primary and secondary curriculum in recent years, like the encouragement of investigation in mathematics, learning to construct a 'fair test' and conduct an enquiry in the domain of physical sciences in the primary school, greater emphasis on oral and written communication in modern language teaching, pupils negotiating their curriculum in prevocational courses, basing remedial reading programmes on effective diagnosis of needs and difficulties, and many others. In each case there is an assumption that teachers may well need to reconstruct their favoured teaching patterns if they adopt a new curriculum.

Each of the developments described above may need little change from some teachers, as they may already foster enquiry or engage in extensive oral communication, but others may need to change dramatically what they do. All the programmes described above, should they be novel to a particular teacher, pre-suppose a significant shift in classroom behaviour. Instead of telling pupils, the teacher may have to set up conditions under which they can find out for themselves, or equally the obverse may apply and the teacher may need to transmit more information than previously. In the case of the negotiated curriculum, both teacher and pupil may need to act more flexibly and responsively to each other. In looking at the curriculum there are two elements that lend themselves to classroom observation, namely *implementation* and *evaluation*.

Implementation

The simple questions in the case of implementation studies are: 'Is the teacher doing what the curriculum developers intended?' and 'Is the teacher doing what she herself intended?'. In this context classroom observation can be used to match intent against action. However, it must be made clear from the outset that this should not be used as a repressive measure. Teachers should be able to use their imagination, not be expected to act as clones of some curriculum developer. The purpose of looking at implementation is to see whether there is a mismatch between intention and strategies. Someone seeking to improve pupils' competence in speaking a foreign language might be expected to encourage them to use it in the classroom. If observation showed that there were hardly any opportunities to use or listen to the target language, then this would be something that could be brought to the teacher's attention.

The first stage of looking at implementation is for the teachers concerned to discuss the new curriculum and consider what changes in practice might be required. The next stage is to draw up some agreed form of observation, so that an observer, who might well be a fellow teacher, or a deputy head responsible for curriculum, has a clear idea of what to look for. Finally, there can be a discussion of what has been found. Suppose, for example, there is a curriculum policy that children should learn to conduct their own enquiries in science lessons. The process might involve:

(1) Teachers looking at the outline of the curriculum to see what kind of topics and activities might be devised with children of different ages to foster scientific enquiry, for example, devising a fair test to find out which of a tennis ball, a table tennis ball and a ball made of clay will bounce higher, hypothesising what will happen if you pass an electric current through more than one light bulb, or working out how much energy people or machines need to carry out their work.

(2) An observation outline is drawn up, concentrating on the opportunities teachers give children to devise experiments, what the teacher does, what six target pupils do, followed by a brief interview pro forma or questionnaire to see how teacher and pupils viewed the process.

(3) A. deputy head responsible for curriculum observes lessons, assisted by other teachers or student teachers on an occasional basis.

(4) Staff discussion of what has been found.

Skilfully handled this can raise many professional issues and offer teachers feedback about the actuality of the initiative. There is always the important issue to consider, however, of how this will be received by the teachers concerned. If it is seen as pressure by the more powerful people in the school to ensure conformity to a singe party line on teaching, then there may well be negative repercussions. On the other hand, if it is seen as a joint effort to scrutinise, reflect on and then amend practice in the light of intelligent feedback, then it becomes a different matter, a source of enthusiasm, not resentment. There should always be room for dissent, for some teachers may argue that they feel uncomfortable teaching the 'new' approach. One answer might be to try it, on the grounds that no doubt doctors used to feel some anxiety about giving up leeches as a staple cure for many ills. If after a wholehearted attempt to make something work a teacher still feels uncomfortable, then the school must decide whether it wants all to teach along similar lines or can tolerate diversity.

It is important to remember that an implementation study can also consider the extent to which teachers' are meeting their *own* objectives. If someone wants to go round the class monitoring children's work, but then finds that she is marooned at her desk for most of the time, simply giving out word spellings to children who come and ask, then an implementation observation might reveal that she was not able to meet her own principal objective. Reflection might then come up with proposals that she spend some time showing children how to use a simple dictionary, so that she could then devote more time to monitoring their other work.

Evaluation

Curriculum evaluation involves a step beyond implementation, for instead of merely looking at whether teachers meet their own or anyone else's intention, the focus is on how effectively the curriculum and its realisation allow children to learn. In this context observation can highlight how effective the curriculum is, using a mixture of professional judgment and systematic testing if necessary.

Suppose a school has devoted a great deal of time to discussing information technology, on the grounds that it is an important field and there has been a significant investment in micro-computers and word processors. The following ingredients might be part of an evaluation package:

(1) Observation of lessons to see which teachers make use of the micros, what kind of activities take place, whether most children have a turn at some time, whether they seem to be positively or negatively disposed towards information technology. Use may be made of target pupils and a pupil pursuit, visiting lessons when it is known that information technology will be used.

(2) Observation of lessons where information technology is not used, to see what opportunities might be made available.

(3) Interviews with teachers and pupils to elicit their views and experiences.

(4) A simple test of proficiency related to the content and objectives of the courses using information technology, of the 'Can do' type, such as 'Can the pupil (a) use a database, (b) type a draft of a document and then try to improve it?' and other similar questions.

(5) Discussion of the outcome and consideration of future policy and practice.

Curriculum evaluation can be time consuming, but even if a school targets only one aspect a year to investigate systematically, using whatever time and resources are available, it is a worthwhile investment of energy.

JOB ANALYSIS

From time to time it is necessary to look at the actual job of teaching by analysing the teacher's day. This often revels many hours of activity related to teaching, like preparation and planning, assessment, meeting parents, attending meetings or courses, supervising the playground, attending assembly, marking registers, collecting money, setting out and clearing away. Part of any scrutiny of the teacher's day could involve watching someone at work in the classroom as well. If a school were considering spending some of its money on hiring a classroom assistant, for example, then observation of lessons and interviews with the teachers concerned might reveal aspects of the job which could be done by an assistant. Most dentists do not mix their own filling compounds, they hire a less well qualified person to do that, but not to do the highly skilled work.

This is an example of a job analysis with a specific purpose, namely to elicit which part of the classroom work of the teacher might be done by someone with skills, but not with the full set required by teachers. When the purpose of job analysis is so clear, then the observation methodology can be created to fit the aim. A freehand observation might simply involve noting down points in the lesson at which a classroom assistant would have been useful. Alternatively a time line or checklist might be used. A list of tasks suitable for a classroom assistant could be drawn up. In the case of a class of young children this might involve such items as 'Help with clothing' (e.g. dressing at the end of the day), 'social talk', 'collecting and distributing', 'clearing away', 'simple spellings', 'reading story to small group' and so on. Either a time line or a tick list could then be assembled, and the observer would record time spent on each task on graph paper, or check each item when it was noted. This information could then be useful in helping decide how to make best use of a classroom assistant and what kind of person to seek.

Time line

help with clothing———— ————

social talk ———— ——— ———— —————

collecting/distributing ——— ——— —————

Checklist

clearing away ////

simple spelling ///////////////////////////

reading story /

A job analysis may not always be conducted for a specific reason. Sometimes it is valuable in its own right to know how people spend their time, even if there is no immediate pressure to do anything about it. Observation is only one part of a job analysis, which might also contain self-reports and questionnaires or interviews. When under scrutiny people often behave differently, and diaries or logs of work done are notorious for appearing to be inflated, partly because respondents may be under pressure to exaggerate their burden, or because they simply do more when keeping an account.

On the other hand, it is important to audit from time to time what teachers are actually doing during their day, even if there are difficulties attached to the exercise, and looking at time spent in the classroom is only one part of that process. Larger scale studies of the nature of teaching may start with observation of teachers both in and out of the classroom. Interviews and observations can reveal a very wide range of tasks performed in a single day, which might include external liaison, such as corresponding with publishers, examination boards, the local authority, the police, social services, as well as internal administration involving governors, finances, ordering goods, and several other matters.

Some studies, like that by Youngman (1984), have assembled large checklists of hundreds of tasks of this kind and then asked different teachers to complete them. This then assembles a picture not only of how teachers spend their time, but which teachers do what jobs. Youngman studied senior teachers, junior teachers, probationers and trainees in secondary schools, and one of the conclusions form his study was that student teachers were not always invited to attend staff meetings or take a tutor group, yet teachers in their first year often did both these.

Analysis of different people's actual day allows many conclusions of this kind to be reached, and this can be helpful in the planning of training and retraining courses, as well as in making decisions about the sensible deployment of teachers themselves. Observation can reveal that it is not always the case that administration is done solely by the head or the deputy, for example, as other teachers are responsible for the children and the materials in their own classroom or home area, and often have to keep records of progress, use of materials, or other aspects of classroom life. It might also reveal not only how much time teachers spend on assessment, but also detailed information about the actual nature of it. This can be particularly important if it involves elaborate one-to-one testing, as it can with younger children, or the administering of practical tests and other labour-intensive forms of assessment, where time must be used wisely.

TEACHER APPRAISAL

The formal appraisal of teachers usually requires at least some consideration of what they actually do in the classroom, rather than just a broad assessment of the generalities of their work. If appraisal is seen as nothing more than a legally required ritual that has to be enacted at intervals through clenched teeth, then the classroom observation part of it will be perfunctory and apologetic. But if it is regarded as a sustained process, an essential part of professional life, not an unwelcome addition to it, then the appraisal of what happens in the classroom, especially self-appraisal, is an important element of keeping the school under review.

In order to make an impact any formal appraisal of teaching competence must be both retrospective and prospective, looking back at what has been achieved and forward to what might be done in the future. Furthermore, the commitment of the teachers concerned to improving individual and collective classroom practice must be secured, otherwise changes for the better are unlikely. An observer can sit in and watch only a lesson or two, whereas teachers themselves will teach thousands of lessons in a relatively short period of their career. If appraisal is meant to improve the quality of teaching, then real long-lasting changes in teaching styles are better than cosmetic changes staged to lease an observer.

Several questions need answering before an appraisal exercise is undertaken. These include:

(1) What is the principal purpose of the exercise?

(2) Who will observe whom and to what end?

(3) What kind of preparation will be necessary (training of observers, briefing of teachers)?

(4) Under what conditions should observations take place (how often, on what days, with which classes or groups)?

(5) What format will be used (freehand note taking, checklist, semi-structured schedule)?

(6) By whom and according to what principles will the format be devised?

(7) What form of debriefing and discussion will take place after observations?

(8) What will be done to support teachers seeking to improve what they do as a result of classroom observation and discussion?

The most common form of classroom appraisal is the *superior-subordinate* model, whereby a more senior person looks at the teaching of someone of more junior standing. Yet *peer appraisal*, which involves two people of equal rank watching each other teach, can also be a valuable exercise, if properly conceived, and various suggestions for that have been made earlier in this book. The appraisal of classroom competence will be most effective if improving teaching is a central part of the school's professional culture, not something grafted on at widely separated intervals, and peer appraisal is a good way of focusing on the importance to every teacher of mutually supportive critical reflection and a commitment to positive action.

Performance Criteria

The notion of 'performance' sits uneasily in many teachers' vocabulary, for the word is more commonly associated with circus animals, entertainment and a mechanical view of industrial and commercial enterprise. For those who see teaching as an art, or as a process requiring a variety of professional skills that are not always instantly demonstrable (it is not easy to stage, to order, a show of 'encouraging slower learners' or 'dealing with difficult adolescents'), the word 'performance' will not do. However, notions such as 'performance-related pay' have crept into teaching in recent years, as has 'performance-based' or 'competency-based' teacher education.

If the word 'performance, cannot be dry cleaned of its mechanical and financial associations, then it is perhaps better simply to think of teachers improving the quality of what they do over a period of time, and whether written criteria are helpful. If it is useful to write down what are thought to be the elements of skilful teaching, then the next possibility is that these might be written in the form of a *hierarchy of levels,* that is conceived in such a way that a teacher can see a line of development or progression. Thus, level 1 might be the sort of simple level achieved by a beginner early on a first teaching practice, whereas level 10 would be the aspiration of the very experienced master teacher.

Harvard and Dunne (1992) have described how primary trainees at Exeter University assess themselves and are assessed on a set of nine dimensions. These include 'direct instruction', 'monitoring', 'management of order', 'planning and preparation'. In each case, there are eight levels through which teachers can progress, level 1 being what is expected of beginners and level 8 being the mark of a competent practitioner. Some examples are:

Level 1

(1) Distribute provided materials: check children's responses.

(2) Attempt to operate some procedures for orderly activity.

(3) Plan basis resources for children working on a given activity.

(4) Give some account of own performance.

(5) Check clarity of explanation by appropriate questions: covey enthusiasm with appropriate verbal and non-verbal behaviour.

(6) Use planned and unplanned opportunities to hold conversations with children in order to establish their perspectives, be sensitive to problems of teacher intrusion.

(7) Continue with attempts to operate in an established formula of rules and procedures.

Level 5

(1) Provide a programme of guided practice in core areas of the curriculum to suit range of attainments in class: choose appropriately matched and sequenced practice exercises.

(2) Experiment with planned conversational teaching on particular aspects of the curriculum.

(3) Plan a short programme of work to engage a variety of identified skills and intellectual processes and demonstrate attention to transition between activities.

(4) Offer justifiable explanations of children's response to work: use explanations in practicable ways to plan the next phase of work: show understanding of the diversity of pupil's attainments.

Level 8

(1) Make explanations efficient and concise: choose examples for their power in the subject.

(2) Sustain a broad programme of diagnostic teaching.

(3) Achieve a situation in which order is endemic to the work system.

(4) Plan for efficiency in use of time and resources with clear reference to the careful management of the teacher's time.

There are several problems with a hierarchical view of competence, despite its obvious appeal as a clearly drawn ladder of development. One is that the highest levels can be such that even gifted teachers may pale, and all of us feel guilty that we do not attain them. Another is that the nature of the levels, despite the apparent precision, can still be vague and diffuse, using words like 'adequate' or 'considerable' that are open to widely differing interpretations. A third difficulty occurs when some powerful person draws up a hierarchy which people are then obliged to meet if they wish to receive a favourable appraisal or qualify for higher pay. Nonetheless, such a mapping exercise can help clarify what people might aspire to, and the Exeter model is offered as an example, not as a paragon ideal to be copied. It is often more effective if a group of teachers work out a set of classroom appraisal precepts to which they feel committed personally and professionally, than if one is merely imposed on them.

Incompetent Teachers

Formal appraisal is sometimes linked with, sometimes divorced from, disciplinary action against teachers judged to be incompetent. In some countries the annual or biennial appraisal of classroom competence is a time when those judged to be unsatisfactory can be warned or even dismissed. In other countries, there is a deliberate distancing between formal appraisal and rewards or retribution. Whichever approach to appraisal is adopted, some judgments about incompetence are bound to be made or confirmed whenever thousands of teachers are observed at work in their classrooms, even if the general conclusion is that the vast majority are competent.

There are few studies of incompetent teachers, partly because it is a sensitive matter, and partly because it is difficult to arrive at a teacher's class saying, "I'm doing a study of incompetent teachers and the head has given me your name. . .". In one of the few published report on the topic, Bridges (1986) looked at 141 school districts in California and concluded that incompetence was of many kinds and occurred for several reasons. Few teachers judged to be poor at their work fell down on only one criterion. Incompetence, like competence, is not unidimensional, it may include failing to keep order, not knowing or being able to impart subject–matter effectively, inability to accept advice about improvement, treat the children properly, or achieve a reasonable standard of work from them. Often several of these may be noted in the same teacher.

Bridges found that incompetence could be extremely consuming of both time and money, with high legal costs for dismissals, a great deal of time, especially from senior people, extensive documentation and considerable frustration when little seemed to be done. Heads of schools often preferred to accommodate, rather than to dismiss, because of all the legal and administrative difficulties, so they rearranged timetables to minimise the damage to one class, or assigned teachers to non-teaching duties. Some tried to secure the 'induced exit', which involved bombarding incompetent teachers with every complaint received from parents or fellow teachers until they left.

One of the most difficult problems occurred with teachers who were generally incompetent, but who were able to stage a satisfactory lesson when they were observed. If observation is part of the procedure for coping with incompetence, then there need to be several observations, not just one or two, otherwise those who can wheel out a single bright idea when visited may appear to be satisfactory when they are not. In any case there is more to dealing with incompetence than making a single visit. Most teachers who are not doing as well as they should may well have other personal problems to do with their health, relationships or their life outside school. Concentrating solely on what happens inside the classroom may ignore the underlying causes of incompetence.

Dismissal may be the only solution in the end, if all else fails, but along the way there is a long process of informal and formal warnings, counselling, spelling out what it is the teacher is not doing well and areas where improvements can be made, drawing up a specific and written set of targets, giving opportunities to attend courses or work at classroom competence in other ways. Classroom observation by a skilled person can be a useful part of this process, and there are many examples of teachers who fell on hard times but were helped back by someone who saw them teach and made suggestions, as well as some, sadly, who appeared immune to all offers of help.

OBSERVATION BY LAY PEOPLE

Fro time to time the issue is raised as to whether there is a place in the classroom for people who have a legitimate interest in a school, perhaps as parents, governors, or supporters or sponsors, but who are no themselves professionally trained as teachers. The question that is asked is either a general one, like: 'Should lay people ever observe lessons?', or a very specific one, such as: 'Should school governors take part in teacher appraisal by observing lessons?'

My own view is very simple, so it is worth stating explicitly. Lay people such as parents and governors, or others who are trying to support the school and its community, have a perfect right to see what is happening in the classroom, but should not be involved in such matters as the appraisal of teaching competence. Whatever intuitive insights they may apply when looking at teaching should simply not feature in appraisal. That is a professional matter. However, many schools encourage legitimate visitors to the classroom, provided they can accommodate them and still get on with their teaching, and there are several ways in which outsiders who do not normally have access to classrooms can observe teaching. These include:

(1) Having an open day when visitors may enter any classroom and watch what is going on (proper arrangements need to be made to avoid overcrowding).

(2) Laying out the hall in the evening so that half of it is set out like a classroom and the other half contains chairs for the audience. A Maths, English or modern language lesson can then be staged, with the teacher and a class trying to simulate what they would normally do, and the audience able to ask questions afterwards.

(3) Showing a video of one or more classrooms and explaining to the audience the nature of the activities.

(4) Inviting parents into the classroom in the evening and then putting on a lesson of the kind their children have had during the day, say a science lesson or a project, so that they can see and discuss what their children do in class.

A few years ago, I was involved in a home and school project in which schools explored such ways of giving parents the feel of what happened in lessons. Some teachers were apprehensive about being seen at work, but interviews with parents showed they were both impressed by what they had seen and grateful for the opportunity to penetrate what had previously seemed a complete mystery. There is obviously a danger that what is seen in such circumstances is a distortion of real classroom life, that teachers or pupils may show off, be on their guard, or do something unusual merely to impress. That may be a hazard worth coping with if the alternative, of not seeing what goes on at all, is thought to be worse. In the situations described above it is probably wisest to let parents or other visitors observe the process in a natural way, rather than burden them with structured schedule or other paraphernalia, but short notes of guidance, explaining what the teacher is trying to achieve and how it fits in with other work, can be helpful.

8

Research into Classrooms

Some industrial and commercial concerns, particularly in a field like the pharmaceutical or defence industry, invest a significant percentage of their profits in research and development work in order to survive and compete. Parts of the American pharmaceutical industry invest 20 per cent of their profits in research, yet in education less than one thousandth of the multi-billion dollar investment is spent on research (Biddle, 1989). Indeed, most of the research in education nowadays is done by individuals, many of whom are studying for some kind of qualification, often higher degrees on a part-time basis, rather than by large-scale externally funded project teams. Of the relatively small sum spent on educational research, a great deal goes on such matters as pupil assessment. Very little cash is donated to studies of teachers at work in their own classrooms.

There is also widespread cynicism about the purpose and impact of educational research, even within the teaching profession. Yet classroom observation research can make a significant contribution to the improvement of teaching competence, especially if teachers and schools, as a matter of policy, research their own practice and act on their findings. Rosenshine and Furst (1973) proposed a *descriptive-correlational-experimental loop* model, which would involve first of all description of what happens in classrooms, then a systematic study of the correlation between process and outcome, and finally experiments to see if the correlational findings were an artefact.

For example, a descriptive study of classroom processes based on live observation of lessons might describe the way that teachers address questions to children. A correlational study might find a positive link between the teacher calling on pupils by name and measures of pupil learning. However, a correlation does not by itself establish a cause. The province of Burgenland in Eastern Austria has sometimes had the highest birthrate in the country. It also happens to be the province with the largest population of storks, but the coincidence of these two factors does not mean that the one causes the other.

In order to establish cause there need to be controlled experiments, argue Rosenshine and Furst, so the investigator of teachers' questions might finally set up experiments in which teachers sometimes call on pupils by name to answer questions, and on other occasions only nominate those whose hands are raised. The outcome would then, in theory at any rate, indicate whether calling on named pupils led to more effective teaching and learning.

The problem with this view is first of all that experiments in teaching can often be artificial and difficult to conduct. Whereas in research in the physical sciences it is easy to keep some elements under the direct and precise control of the investigator and specify what temperature or pressure will be maintained, the same certainties cannot be built into classroom research. If an investigator wished teachers to give pupils information according to a prearranged text, for example, any neat design would immediately be wrecked once a pupil made a spontaneous observation or asked the teacher a question. At that point either natural forces would take over and subvert the experiment, or the teacher would ignore the pupils and thereby render the 'experiment' meaningless in terms of real classroom life. Most studies of classrooms, therefore, look at teaching in its natural state. In practice true experiments are rare, and *quasi-experimental design*, which looks like an experiment but is not, usually because the groups of pupils involved are not or cannot be matched, is much more common. It is much more likely that observation studies will not involve any kind of experiment at all, so someone studying the teaching of reading by different methods will compare teachers who already prefer one approach or another, rather than set up an experiment which may appear artificial.

A second problem is that most research into classroom processes tends to reveal only small relationships between process and outcome. A great deal of the research which has compared two methods of teaching has revealed no *general* difference between the two, because different teachers are able to make various methods work effectively if they believe in them, or fail miserably if they do not. Other research has shown only slight differences amounting to one or two percentage points. Gage (1978) felt confident enough, however, even on the basis of small differences identified in the research on teaching styles and pupil learning, to propose a set of 'Teacher should' statements like 'Teachers should keep to a minimum such activities as giving directions and organising the class for instruction', or 'During reading-group instruction, teachers should give a maximal amount of brief feedback and provide fast-paced activities of the "drill" type'.

In his book *Hard Gains in the Soft Sciences,* Gage (1985) counters the criticisms about small differences or low levels of significance by quoting fields such as medicine and public health where big changes in policy can be made on the basis of a degree of statistical 'superiority' that would receive scant attention in education. He quotes examples of trials of beta blockers and low cholesterol diets to reduce the incidence of heart attacks. The two sets of trial treatments showed only 2.5 and 1.7 per cent differences respectively between the mortality rates of the experimental and control groups, but the United States government terminated the research and implemented the findings immediately, on the grounds that even small percentages meant that thousands of lives could be saved and it was not worth waiting any longer if some unnecessary deaths would occur in the meantime. Yet if an educational researcher discovered a 2.5 or 1.7 per cent superiority of one method over another in the teaching of algebra, it is highly unlikely that much notice would be taken.

RESEARCH QUESTIONS

Despite the difficulties of conducting rigorous research into classroom processes it is nonetheless well worth making the attempt. In the case of larger scale projects, research into classrooms needs to be seen as adding a thin layer to what was previously known, rather than finding a miracle cure for some particular ill, or embarking on a quest for the philosopher's stone that would turn all to gold. Smaller projects, particularly those done by teachers and heads in their own school, can make a valuable impact on local practice. If there were a modest but enthusiastic research ethos in every school, not only would the quality of teaching and learning stand a good chance of improving significantly, but an important message would be transmitted from teachers to pupils, namely: 'We expect you to have an enquiring mind because we ourselves do'.

In the field of classroom processes numerous research questions present themselves. These include the following, which is by no means an exhaustive list:

(1) What do teachers and pupils do in the classroom, how do they spend their time?

(2) What kind of interaction takes place, who talks to whom about what?

(3) How do teachers manage their classes, what are the classroom rules, how are resources, time, space, pupil behaviour, their own teaching strategies managed?

(4) What do pupils learn, what tasks do they engage in and with what degree of involvement and success?

(5) What is a school day or a lesson like from a pupil's point of view, are any individuals or groups getting a relatively poor deal out of schooling?

(6) What happens to particularly able pupils or those with learning difficulties?

(7) How are different subjects/topics taught to different age groups?

(8) What happens in the classroom when there is a change of policy, a new curriculum, work scheme, textbook course, or new forms of assessment?

(9) How are classroom decisions made, by the teacher, by pupils, by both in negotiation?

(10) What happens when pupils disrupt lessons or behave in an anti-social manner?

(11) How can I improve my own teaching?

(12) Is there continuity and coherence in the curriculum, or does it appear disjointed and incoherent from the child's point of view?

(13) Do teachers in the same school or department have similar or different practices, beliefs, expectations, rewards and punishments, conventions, and are these understood by the pupils?

(14) Do teachers and children perceive the same events in different or similar ways?

(15) What happens when a child does not understand something?

(16) How do teachers explain new topics to pupils?

(17) How is pupils' work monitored and assessed in the classroom?

(18) What happens when children work in groups, what sort of assignments are undertaken, who decides what, are the groups collaborative?

(19) What is the place of subject knowledge, what knowledge, skills, attitudes and behaviour seem to be acquired, what happens if the teacher does not know the detail of a particular piece of subject–matter?

(20) How do teachers make their classroom decisions?

Some of these research questions are more straightforward than others, and often the questions which most interest teachers or administrators are not necessarily those that attract research projects, hence the importance of teachers' research into their own practice. 'How can I improve my own practice?' or 'Do some individuals and groups get a relatively poor deal out of schooling?' are legitimate questions, but are not immediately translatable into research terms. First there has to be greater clarity about the meaning of words like 'improve' or 'poor', for these would be differently understood and interpreted by different people.

On a day-to-day basis it is perfectly possible to make personal and professional judgments about such questions, and we could not function if we did not do so, as the hundreds of events in which teachers and pupils are engaged every day cannot wait for a fully fledged research project to report. However, when time is taken to mount a proper enquiry, then it is worth taking the trouble to define the purpose, focus and intention of it, before embarking on a series of lesson observations. There are numerous other questions about classroom processes that can be asked, and many of the ones stated above can be the focus of a quick and dirty piece of *ad hoc* enquiry, using occasional classroom observation, or a lifetime's study.

TRAINING OBSERVERS

If the findings of observers are to be credible then they must receive training, or at least have the opportunity to discuss their purposes, procedures and intentions to the point where there is general agreement on what they will be doing. If a research project is using mainly qualitative methodology, then the researchers need to agree what questions are to be addressed, how they will collect data, whether they will make notes or operate to some other agreed procedures, and how their findings will be analysed and reported. It is particularly important that the main focus of the investigation is known, as books full of notes on lessons, or sound and video recordings, can soon proliferate to the point where they defy analysis.

Once this is clear then training can involve analysis and discussion of lesson transcripts, observation of videos and visits to actual lessons, with observers talking through what they see until there is some agreement about the way in which events will be scrutinised and the form in which records will be assembled. One way of doing this is known as *triangulation*, a process analogous to that used by surveyors, who draw a triangle on a map and then take measurements at each of the three corners that can then be related to each other.

Triangulation in classroom research involves checking the perceptions of more than one person to see if one's own interpretations have any support. This might involve talking to fellow observers, teachers, pupils, where this is agreed, and other forms of record, like documents and accounts of meetings. Thus, if a teacher rewarded a child for getting full marks in a test and said that this had been made school policy recently and all children knew about it and were in favour of it, the observer could study other events, interview participants, and look at policy documents and minutes of meetings.

Denzin (1985) distinguishes four different kinds of triangulation: (1) *data triangulation* involving different time, space or people, (2) *investigator triangulation* where various observers cross-check each other, (3) *theory triangulation* which brings different theories to bear on the observations, and (4) *methodological triangulation* whereby more than one methodology of enquiry is employed. In all of these approaches both the similarities and differences between the perceptions of various participants and observers or methods of enquiry are of interest.

When a category system or checklist is employed then the procedure is similar, except that it is necessary to make a formal quantified check of how much agreement there is between observers. This can be done in many ways, depending on how complex the system is. Training can begin with observers learning the category system and then applying it to a transcript of a lesson and discussing their assignment of events to categories. For example, if they are using a category system to code teachers' questions, they would need to decide whether a question like "Is a duck a mammal?" would count as a simple closed information recall question, since "No" is the only correct textbook answer, or as something of a slightly higher order, if the teacher's tone and manner appear to be inviting the child to explain why, and give a "No, because . . ." answer.

There are usually two formal measures of agreement between observers when more than one person is involved. These are (a) *inter-observer agreement,* the amount of agreement between two or more observers, and (b) *intra-observer agreement,* or the extent to which observers agree with themselves on another occasion. Usually, the same videotape is used before and after the observation part of the project, so that observers can compare their first coding of it with their second coding some time later. The type of comparison depends on the nature of the quantitative data being collected. If rating scales were being used, then a correlation between the first and second set of ratings might be appropriate.

If a category system is being employed, then the simplest check would be the percentage of agreement on each person's tallies of the same events. To do this you simply count up all the occasions when observers agree and all the ones when they disagree. Thus, they might agree on 82 per cent of their codings and disagree on 18 per cent. This figure would then be reported in the research account so that the reader knows how reliable the data are. If there is less than about 70 per cent agreement, then some caution would have to be exercised in interpreting the results. If the category system had numerous categories that never occurred (like 'teacher flies round room' or 'pupil pole vaults through window'), then it would be easy to obtain high agreement figures because of the many empty cells, but most category systems are not as comically unrealistic as this.

Two observers might obtain the following results, based on the analysis of the same videotaped lessons before and after the project, and then calculating the extent to which they agree with each other and themselves:

Inter-observer agreement	*Percentage agreement*
Beginning of project (Observer A with Observer B)	82
End of project (Observer A with Observer B)	78
Intra-observer agreement	
Observer A (beginning of project) with self (end of project)	84
Observer B (beginning of project) with self (end of project)	71

This would tell the reader that there was fairly high agreement between the two observers at the beginning of the project, a little less at the end, and that Observer A showed greater stability in coding over time (84 per cent agreement) than Observer B (71 per cent).

Some researchers use a *chi square* to compare frequencies actually observed with what might have been expected. This is a commonly employed statistical technique which looks at the extent to which a certain distribution of events could have happened by chance. It is described in most introductory statistical texts. Flanders (1970) used Darwin's chi square, a variation of the normal chi square, which has been modified to recognise that communication events are not independent of each other (for example, a pupil's answer is more likely to follow a teaçher's question that occur randomly). The main point about training, however, is to secure agreement about principles and practice, clarity about purpose and actions, and to give time for different observers to discuss any disagreements or sources of confusion.

RESEARCH INSTRUMENTS

A description of the various approaches to classroom observation has been given in earlier chapters, but sometimes more than one approach is used in research. Observers may wish to amplify or corroborate their observations with interviews, questionnaires, videos or tests of various kinds.

Interviews

Commonly used to elicit the views of participants, they can be either *structured* (yes/no, either/or, multiple choice type items, etc.) *semi-structured* (written questions asked to each interviewee, but with probes and open ended questions to encourage a certain amount of natural conversation) or *unstructured* (free-ranging conversation). Semi-structured interview schedules are often preferred by classroom researchers, as they raise key questions, but also allow the observer and teacher to have some natural conversation about events. A semi-structured interview schedule used to amplify critical events might look like this:

Can you tell me what happened when . . .? (cue critical event)

What do you think led up to. . .? (critical event)

What is your own reaction to. . .? (critical event)

How do you think X and Y (any pupils involved) feel about what happened?

The interviewer is then able to insert probes and prompts as conversation develops. Powney and Watts (1987) have written a useful book on interviewing.

Questionnaires

Questionnaires are over-used in research generally, and since the classroom observer is present with the teacher concerned, it is often better to use a structured interview schedule on the spot, rather than leave a questionnaire behind. However, questionnaires can be useful in surveying large numbers of teachers about their classroom practice, an approach used by Bennett (1976) in his study of teaching styles. Bennett devised a questionnaire that asked teachers to report whether they gave regular spelling tests, used group work, allowed children to choose their own seat, preferred teaching single subjects or cross-curricular topics, and was then able to compare profiles and draw up a series of clusters of teachers with similar preferred styles. Questionnaires allow teachers the time to give a considered reply to questions, and also permit the researcher to select a sample of teachers with differing or perhaps similar accounts of preferred practice, and then observe them at work in their own classroom. The major disadvantage is that mailed questionnaires, especially if teachers are busy, can have a notoriously low return rate, below 10 per cent being quite common. Oppenheim (1992) has written a comprehensive text on the construction of questionnaires and attitude measures.

Tests

The number of tests on the market is now so enormous that huge textbooks and catalogues have to be compiled even to display a relatively small selection of them. Classroom researchers might use tests of attitude, personality, subject knowledge, or other focus such as self-concept. Possibilities include studying the relationship between teacher attributes and classroom behaviour ("Do introvert and extrovert teachers behave differently?" 'What relationship is there between stated attitude towards innovation and actual implementation of it?'). A common use of testing is to see what pupils have learned, or how their attitudes have changed, often known as *process-product research.* Eggleston, Galton and Jones (1975) used tests of both attitude and learning in their observation study of science lessons to see how children reacted to different styles of teaching, and found that poor achievement and attitude was associated with lessons which were largely theoretical in approach and which involved little or no practical work.

There are many other research techniques that can be employed, such as the repertory grid developed by Kelly (1955), which allows qualitative researchers to elicit children's or teacher's constructs by presenting them with three names of fellow pupils or teachers, and then asking them to describe ways in which two of them are different from the third. This permits the investigator to assemble a picture of each person's individual construction of the world and then compare it with what happens in the classroom. This approach was used by Nash (1973) who found that pupils had a clear idea of their own and others' relative achievement in reading and mathematics, even though their teachers thought that they did not. Cohen (1976) has described numerous tests and other instruments for use in classroom research, and Keeves (1988) has brought together a collection of articles on different research instruments that would be useful to investigators. The best advice to classroom researchers, however, is to start with the questions, not the instruments. Choice of tools should come after the relevant questions have been formulated and purposes and intentions clarified.

LANGUAGE IN THE CLASSROOM

They study of language in the classroom is so labour-intensive that it is much less common than other forms of classroom interaction research. It is, however, a focus of scrutiny much favoured by qualitative researchers, sometimes as a topic for investigation in its own right, sometimes as a source for making inferences about the significance, intention and meaning which lie beneath events. Malinowski (1922), the anthropologist whose pioneering studies of Trobriand Islanders have been influential on participant observers in other domains, advocated assembling a 'synoptic record', a collection of statements from informants, which could form a basis for making inferences about the structure and purposes of behaviour.

It is one thing to have a collection of transcripts, lesson protocols or interview statements, but quite another to know how best to analyse these. Some of the researchers into classroom language have been people with a background not in education, but rather in linguistics. Sinclair and Coulthard (1975), who worked in a university English department, found classroom discourse a fascinating subject to study in its own right: 'We . . . wanted a situation where all participants were genuinely trying to communicate and where potentially ambiguous utterances were likely to have one accepted meaning'.

They found just that kind of situation in the classrooms they studied. Their analysis was divided into several ranks, beginning with *lessons*, then *transactions*, within which were *exchanges*, which in turn enclosed moves, which eventually zoomed in on specific acts. They found that teachers frequently had to structure not only the relevant knowledge, but also the form in which it was to be purveyed, so there were often meta-statements, that is statements about the process itself, like "Let's see who understands what I've just been explaining". The 'moves' included opening something up ("Suppose . . ."), focusing ("Look at this picture and see if. . .") and following up ("That's right").

Detailed linguistic analysis of transcripts often results in insights that can easily be missed in the rapid exchanges of classroom interaction, like the identification by Barnes (Barnes, Britton and Rosen, 1967) of questions that were genuinely open and those that were 'pseudo-open', that is, appeared on the surface to be inviting a wide range of possible responses, but in reality sought just the one preferred by the teacher. In these circumstances pupils frequently realise the kind of guessing game involved and scan the teacher's facial and linguistic responses to help them grope towards the approved reply.

Some analysts of transcripts prefer to read them through carefully and pick out key concepts or notions using highlighter pen, or extract relevant quotations on to large sheets of paper under different headings. Thus, a researcher studying teachers' reactions to pupils' answers might pull out examples of 'reinforcement' ("Good", "Well done"), 'criticism' (No, you fool", "You've not been listening to what I've been saying"), 'enhancement' ("Yes, quite right, and what's more. . .", "Now John's just told us that we're going to need warm clothes, and the reason for that is. . ."), or 'switching' ("No Susan. . . Melanie, you have a try").

Analysis by computer is often used to cope with large numbers of transcripts, and a good deal of software is now available for qualitative analysis of speech. There is nothing magic about these packages. The researcher simply invent or uses an existing coding system and then attaches the relevant coding to each segment of text. A set of terms like 'diagnosis', 'response', 'reprimand', 'opening' or 'closure' may be used. It is possible for segments to overlap, and most programmes have other flexible features, allowing the researcher to search for and recall all segments that have been similarly coded. Whole lessons, as well as individual teachers and pupils can also be given codes, allowing the investigator to compare instances involving the same people, for example. Computer programmes are not a replacement for intelligent analysis, but rather a useful tool for those doing a lot of it.

The classroom is a place where pupils learn and practise a wide variety of forms of expression, some of which are highly stylised exchanges and rarely occur outside education, like the rapid drilling and closed questioning which only happens during schooling and the interrogation of suspects by the police. Other exchanges, however, are valuable rehearsals for life itself, as Edwards and Westgate (1987), advocating the importance of language research in their valuable book on classroom talk, point out:

> Most of our everyday life depends on skills in talking and making sense of the talk of others, as we work or trade or simply pass the time of day. These skills go far beyond the uttering of sounds related to objects, actions or ideas. In our speech we select and organise our utterances according to our sense of what is correct and appropriate in a particular setting. This is partly a matter of grammar, partly of social etiquette, partly of culture, and essentially of assuming that others will be perceiving the same situation as we do.

ACTION RESEARCH

One of the most attractive forms of investigation is Research and Development (R & D) or *action research* as it is often known. Here the investigator not only observes lessons, but takes action on the basis of what is witnessed. When it works well, there is a strong feeling that something is being done and that research is more than just documents lying on a library shelf. Action research, because it involves *intervention,* is not especially easy to conduct in a rigorous manner. Investigators may, in the end, be researching themselves and the effectiveness of their intervention programme, and that can be highly problematic.

There are two principal kinds of action research, and classroom observation can have a part to play in both. The first type is largely *rational-reactive*. The investigator looks at what is happening in the classroom, usually with a specific focus on something known to be a problem or in need of improvement, and then draws up a programme to react to what has been discovered. The second type is more *intuitive-proactive*, which means that the researchers or prime movers know, or think they know, what needs to be done, and so implement an intervention programme first and then visit classrooms to see how well it is progressing.

As an example of action research that is reactive, let us suppose that a school in a tough neighbourhood is concerned about the number of pupils involved in rowdy behaviour who are frequently being excluded from the school or contained in some way that is not thought to be satisfactory. The following set of procedures might be followed:

Stage One

Observe lessons to see what kind of disruptive behaviour was occurring. Use a mixture of systematic observation with a schedule of events like 'illicit movement', 'aggression towards fellow pupil', 'altercation with teacher' or 'damage to property', and the noting of critical events.

Stage Two

Analyse classroom observation data and discover that the problems mainly occurred with pupils aged 13 to 15, that most poor behaviour appeared to result from boredom, lack of or inconsistent application of classroom rules, inappropriate tasks which appeared not to motivate or engage pupils, and that most misbehaviour involved about four or five pupils in each class.

Stage Three

Discussion of findings with teachers and, if available, external or internal adviser. Draw up action/intervention programme involving different approach to difficult classes with shorter projects and more practical work, in which the objectives were clearly spelled out, so that pupils could see what they would achieve in a certain time. Teachers discuss with pupils, and if necessary parents, classroom rules that would be enforced, and also recognition of good behaviour. Agreement about consistent ways of handling certain kinds of poor behaviour, and who would take responsibility for what, for example, the role of senior teachers and the deputy head and head of the school.

Stage Four

Further classroom observation and interviews to see (a) the extent to which teachers are implementing the agreed programme, and (b) what misbehaviour occurs, using the same mixture of structured observation and the noting of critical events as was employed before the new programme started.

Stage Five

Evaluate the findings and modify or fine tune the programme as necessary.

A proactive approach is usually based on someone's bright idea for improvement, often on intuitive grounds. It would follow most of the stages described above, except that the initial data collection would be different if the progenitors of the idea felt that they already knew what was needed. Curriculum development work is often of this kind, where teachers feel that they know intuitively, from teaching their classes, what needs to be done, so they simply use their imagination to devise a new programme to replace the old one. The research part, therefore, might be largely classroom observation after the innovation to see what happened. In practice the distinction between reactive and proactive action research is often more diffuse than is portrayed here.

The difficulties with action research projects of any kind are first that they are often conducted by the innovator themselves (and the research literature is heavy with accounts of intervention programmes that are deemed to have 'worked' for their pioneers, but not for the sceptics who tried to replicate them), and with experimental groups that beat control groups. Only rarely does the control group ever 'win' in these circumstances. It is frequently the sheer drive, energy and enthusiasm of the instigators of the programme that are being evaluated, rather than their methods. One way round this compounding of subjectivity is to try and involve an external evaluator or more objective in-house person who can approach the classroom observation and interview part of the project competently but with some emotional detachment. Lack of proper resources for action research means that the people and time needed to implement it rigorously are not always available. Yet when done well action research can be one of the most rewarding and effective means of improving teaching, and investment in it is thoroughly worthwhile.

RESEARCH DESIGN

The classic research design of an experimental and control group matched in every respect, apart from the experimental component, is not always possible in classroom research. Even two classes thought to be parallel may be sufficiently different in important respects to ruin the experiment. For example, if out of two groups of children who were supposed to be matched for ability and social background, one group happened to contain two particularly disruptive pupils, then any study of a programme to reduce disruptive behaviour would be affected by the influence of the two very badly behaved children. If they happened to be in the control group, the experimental group might be deemed to be a great success, but if they were in the experimental group, then the experiment itself could easily be labelled a failure. Most studies of teaching take place in a naturalistic setting, and the investigator frequently has no control over which pupil is in which class. Even when groups are carefully matched on some criteria, they can be unmatched on others.

Campbell and Stanley (1963) described a series of designs, from the one shot case study to complex models with groups of different kinds. Three designs for classroom observation are shown below. In each case O = observation and/or testing, X = experiment.

Model A

Group 1 (Experimental)	O	X	O
Group 2 (Control)	O		O

This is the classic experimental and control group design, observed before and after the experiment. In theory only the experimental 'X' is different, so if the groups are initially matched any changes (test scores, pupil or teacher behaviour, etc.) in the second observation are explained by the effects of the experiment. In practice it is not quite so clear cut, as matching is often less than perfect and experiments appear to work because of the enthusiasm of the experimenters, the greater attention paid to the subjects, and other effects, often referred to as the *Hawthorne Effect* after the research into improving worker performance in the Hawthorne factory of the Western Electrical Company, in which output improved under each of the experimental conditions tried by investigators largely because of the positive response by workers to being shown interest.

Model B

Group 1	O1	O2	O3	O4	O5	O6	O7	O8
Group		O1		O2		O3		O4

This is one of many possible designs for a time series of observations, and different groups may be observed on different occasions to monitor changes over a period of time. Some observations can occur at the same time for the two groups, or on different occasion. Group 1 above is observed eight times, but Group 2 on only four occasions to coincide with the 2nd, 4th, 6th and 8th observations of Group 1. This would enable observers to see whether changes over time were, for example, related to the presence of an observer. Perhaps Group 1 would be better behaved because it felt itself to be more under scrutiny. It might also reveal whether it was necessary to go as often as eight times, when four visits might suffice, in terms of collecting sufficient data. If experiments were introduced between certain observation visits, then this two group design might reveal whether the effects were immediate or delayed.

Model C

Group 1 (Experimental 1)	O	X	O
Group 2 (Control 1)	O		O
Group 3 (Experimental 2)		X	O
Group 4 (Control 2)			O

This four group design is too elaborate and complex for most observers, but it attempts to discover whether the experiment itself has an effect, or merely the presence of researchers. For example, let us suppose that a researcher is studying the interactions between teachers and pupils of different abilities, and that the experimental 'X' is a teacher workshop on the teaching of more able and less able children in mixed ability classes. If groups 1 and 3 are different from groups 2 and 4 on the second set of observations, then the changes may be the result of the workshop, but if groups 1 and 2 are different from groups

3 and 4, then changes may be the result of the teachers changing their behaviour because they have found out after the first visit by observers that interactions with children of high and low ability are being scrutinised, so they may give such pupils more attention on the second set of observations.

In practice, since relatively little classroom observation research is based on experiments, most research designs are plans of campaign. The investigators decide what forms of observation they will use, what interviews, testing, attitude measures, or forms of analysis they will use, with whom and how often. Two valuable steps can be taken by all researchers, whether engaged on national project, or in small scale research. The first is to draw up a time scale, describing at what point it is intended that each stage of the research should be reached. This can always be modified in the light of experience and actual progress, or lack of it, but at least it is there as a statement of intent.

The second step is to conduct a pilot study using exactly the same procedures as will be used in the main study. This is important even if standardised or commonly used procedures are to be employed. It is easy even for experienced researchers to be over confident about how many lessons they will observe, or how many teachers they will interview. Even observing and interviewing one or two teachers will reveal how feasible the procedures are, how long the process will take and what will be involved in the analysis of the data.

STATISTICS

It is not possible here to cover the vast array of statistical techniques that have been used in classroom research. In any case, it is important that researchers start with questions, rather than techniques. If an observer wants to know whether the contacts between the teacher and various pupils are significantly different in some way, or if teaching method A leads to more effective learning than teaching method B, then there are probably several statistic approaches, if the data are in quantified from, that might be appropriate. Most of the standard books on statistics for education or the social sciences, like the widely used texts by Guilford and Fruchter (1978) and Kerlinger (1973), cover the common procedures, and in any case, those in doubt should take advice.

Many classroom researchers, especially teachers doing projects for higher degrees or further qualifications, are put off using statistics because of the mystique surrounding them. Some courses on statistics, especially those given by experts unable to empathise with the lay person, are so baffling that participants with mental blockages can find these have got worse rather than better. Yet most of the common techniques use little more than multiplication, division, addition and subtraction, or the odd square or square root. The actual mathematics is within the grasp of the average 14 year old, but it is often the pages of formulae with unfamiliar Greek characters like χ or σ, as well as meaningless looking subscripts, that put lay people off. The most helpful textbooks are the ones with worked examples.

One problem with classroom observation data is that some unusual distributions can be obtained. Many statistical techniques assume that there is a normal distribution, that is to say that most scores will be around the group's average, or middle of the range of possible scores, with fewer and fewer as one reaches the extremes. Thus, on a typical standardised test, most pupils will score in the 40 to 60 per cent range, and very few will get under 5 or over 95. Classroom observation data can be different. Analysis of teacher talk will find that most teachers speak a great deal, either to the class or to individuals, during a lesson. Rarely does a teacher say nothing. Indeed, having laryngitis necessitates developing a whole new set of teaching strategies for most people, so dependent are we on our voice.

By contrast, a classroom researcher using a schedule with categories like 'teacher uses an analogy', 'pupil strikes teacher', or 'head teacher enters class', may find that these events are much more rare, and in many lessons do not occur at all. Although some forms of classroom event are normally distributed, many are not, and the investigator may need to consider what are known as *non-parametric* or *distribution free statistics*, that is techniques that can deal with rank orders or frequencies, instead of the usual numerical scores. Also since single or rare events, like the entry of the head or an incident of violent behaviour by a pupil, can have an impact and effect that are far more significant than single instances of commonplace events, the researcher might in any case be better off using a qualitative approach, rather than the procedures that are more common when there are numerous occurrences.

This is not a statistics textbook, so it is not possible to go into proper detail. Some statistical techniques are simply ways of telling the investigator how likely it is that the results obtained would have occurred by chance, hence the convention of talking about the level of significance in terms of the probability of something occurring by chance being 0.05, 0.01 or 0.001. Since a probability of 1.00 means absolute certainty on 100 per cent of occasions, these three figures simply mean that an event could have occurred by chance in 5 per cent, 1 per cent and 0.1 per cent of cases respectively, in other words, with a 1 to 20, 1 in 100, or 1 in 1,000 likelihood. Sometimes the asterisk convention is also used when reporting results, with one, two or three asterisks respectively, so that a treble asterisk would mean the likelihood of this result occurring by chance was 1 in 1,000. A correlation coefficient (*Pearson's r*) of 0.76, which the relevant statistical tables showed was likely to occur less than once every thousand times, would thus be reported as $r = 0.76^{***}$. With computers nowadays it is possible to have the probability calculated to several decimal places, but the three figures above are still used as general indicators.

Many researchers not experienced in statistics often do not know which statistical techniques to look up in the relevant book, and many books contain only a limited repertoire of techniques, ignoring, for example, Bayesian statistics, which considers the probability of an event taking place in the light of other related events. Below are some common needs and a mention of some approaches that, used in proper circumstances, might be appropriate. It must be stressed that anyone uncertain should check with a statistician, rather than misuse a procedure.

Relationships between Measures

Most commonly, when a relationship is sought between two measures such as amount of misbehaviour and number of pupils applying themselves to the task, a *correlation coefficient* will be used. This ranges from +1 for perfect agreement (the more of one, the more of the other) to -1 for completely inverse relationships (the more of one, the *less* of the other), with zero meaning no relationship. Thee are many forms of correlation, depending on the nature of the data, *Pearson's r* being the most common for two sets of continuous measures, like test scores. Two sets of rank orders, or the comparison between a score and a yes/no measure, would involve different forms, such as *Spearman's rho* and *point biserial correlations*.

Comparing Groups

This depends on the type of measure involved. If a frequency count has been taken, then a *chi square* might be appropriate. If the occurrence of reprimands in the lessons of teachers in four different age groups were to be compared, then a 'goodness of fit' chi square would look at the distribution actually obtained and compare it with what might have been expected.

When the scores of two groups on something like a rating scale are compared, then if the distribution is roughly normal a *t test* would be appropriate. Suppose the investigator, having rated teachers on a scale from 1 to 10 on some dimension, wanted to see if there was a significant difference between the scores of the male and female teachers, then an *uncorrelated t test* might be used. A *correlated t test* is employed when two sets of scores for the *same* group are compared.

For three or more groups, or for measures that are repeated several times, *analysis of variance* may be used. If scores obtained from watching maths, science and English teachers are subjected to analysis of variance, then the resulting F ratio will reveal whether the differences between all three groups are statistically significant or not. In order to test the significance between any pair of these (say maths and science, or English and maths), a 'gap test' such as *Tukey* or *Scheffé* will be needed. If the distribution of scores is not normal then non-parametric forms of analysis will be needed, like the *Mann-Whitney U* for two groups, and the *Kruskal-Wallis* analysis of variance for three or more groups.

Measuring Change

One of the biggest problems in educational research is the measurement of change when groups do not start off equal. Raw unadjusted league tables of schools' test results are an example of the problem of inferring effectiveness from final rather than initial cores. If initial scores are known, then it is possible to calculate what is sometimes known as 'value added'. If two unmatched groups showed the following scores before and after a teaching programme little of note could be deduced about teaching quality:

	Average class test scores	
	Before	*After*
Group A	35	55
Group B	60	70

We could deduce that the teacher of class B was better than the one who taught class A because the final test score is higher. We might equally conclude that Teacher A must have been better, because class A went up by 20 per cent, and class B by only 10 per cent. That, however, would mean that the teacher of the class that began with a score of zero would almost always look 'better' on the post-test than one whose children began with a score of 100, unless all scores remained the same. Various statistics can be used to try to even out the effects of initial differences, such as *analysis of covariance* and *regression analysis*. The usual procedure is to take a measure which is thought to affect initial differences, like social class, and use that as part of the procedure in an attempt to 'even up' the groups, but the use of this approach is almost always controversial.

Predicting

Regression, particularly *multiple regression analysis*, is often used to make a prediction. One variant of it is *stepwise multiple regression*, which involves taking the predictor which shows the highest correlation with the outcome measure and then combining it step by step with others to improve the correlation. An example would be if the observer wanted to know how best to predict scores on a pupil 'attitude to science' test. There might be a correlation of +0.5 between the attitude scores and a rating measure of the teacher's enthusiasm in the classroom. The next best predictor might be a measure of the amount of practical work done, and by combining these two measures, the correlation might go up to +0.7. A third measure, say 'teacher's own knowledge of science', when added to the first two might push the correlation up to +0.8. Stepwise multiple regression rarely produces such neat ordering and high values in real life classroom research, but can still have a place where prediction is of interest.

Reducing Complexity

Sometimes researchers find that their data looks complex and needs reducing in complexity so that sense can be made of what has been found. With large data sets, therefore, *factor analysis* and *cluster analysis* can be used. Factor analysis is a way of putting together sets of measures that correlate with each other and reducing these to fewer factors. Scores gathered by classroom observation using the Flanders FIAC system might show that short teacher questions, brief pupil answers and praise all correlated quite highly and came together in the same factor. This might then be given a name like 'programmed learning' to reflect the stimulus-response-reinforcement nature of the interactions.

Cluster analysis is another way of putting together scores in more parsimonious form, but this time individual teacher's profiles can be grouped together, in a similar way to creating a taxonomy of plants that are in the same family because they share similar characteristics. There are many forms of cluster analysis that group people's profiles, and Bennett (1976) applied cluster analysis to the questionnaire responses about teaching strategies from a large group of teachers, creating 12 groups whose styles of teaching seemed different from each other.

This brief description of some statistical procedures is by no means complete, and indeed a great deal has been omitted. There are many articles on different aspects of statistics in education in the comprehensive research handbook by Keeves (1988), and novices are urged once more to proceed with caution.

Aggregating Findings

There are several ways to put together findings from several different pieces of classroom observation research. The technique of *meta analysis* described and developed by Glass (1978) is a process for aggregating the findings from several studies to see whether they can offer consistent findings. There are two parts to meta analysis, the first being the actual process for putting together data from projects which may have used different statistical procedures, like chi squares, correlations, t tests or F ratios from analysis of variance, and therefore need converting for aggregation. The second part is the devising of an overall effect size, and this can be calculated for all the studies under review, or there can be separate effect sizes for, say, larger and smaller studies (to see whether size of sample makes a difference) older and newer research, or studies judged to be rigorous according to certain criteria, and those deemed to be less so.

Different investigators analysing the same or a similar set of studies can, however, reach different conclusions, depending on what criteria they use for aggregation. Winne (1979) analysed experimental studies of questioning where teachers asked certain types of questions, and came to the conclusion that there was no causal link between asking higher order questions and pupil learning, whereas Redfield and Rousseau (1981), who did a meta analysis of most of the same studies, decided that there was a positive association between higher order cognitive questioning and children's learning.

SMALL SCALE RESEARCH

Although the most well known research projects tend to be the ones that were conducted on a national or international scale and resulted in published books, articles and conference papers, there are numerous small scale pieces of research that can be important to those who conduct them. Thousands of trainee or experienced teachers and administrators, or organisers of projects will undertake an investigation as part of their training or professional work. Thus, a trainee teacher might study a teacher at work for a dissertation or term paper, a teacher or head may observe lessons as part of a thesis for an MPhil or PhD. Carefully done, not only is this kind of exercise worthwhile, but it can fulfil the role which research has done since the beginning of human life, by adding to our stock of knowledge.

Some of the most interesting and significant educational research has been carried out in one school. There are, of course, limitations, but provided that the writer does not make claims that stretch beyond the legitimate confines of the one shot case study, much of value can be learned. *Hightown Grammar* by Lacey (1970) and the account of 'Lumley Secondary Modern' in *Social Relations in a Secondary School* by Hargreaves (1967) were both insightful accounts of individual schools which became significant books in the case study literature.

When Her Majesty's Inspectorate (DES, 1978) visited several hundred secondary schools to see how they taught classes of mixed ability, they commented on the comparative reluctance of teachers of mathematics and modern languages to teach classes containing children with a wide variety of achievement. However, this broad brush account lacked the warmth that an in-depth study of real life experience can bring, and it needed the significant case study by Ball (1981) of Beachside Comprehensive to document more precisely the attitudes and actual classroom practice of teachers in a single school that was changing from a broad banding policy to one of mixed ability classes. This revealed in considerable detail, through accounts of lesson observations and interviews, that it was the mathematics and modern languages staff who were reluctant to make the change, and how the English teachers saw themselves as pioneers.

Individual researchers, especially those working alone on a part-time basis for a degree or wanting to study practice in their own school, face a number of difficulties. Not the least of these is the matter of subjectivity. First time investigators encounter the inevitable criticism that they are not just inexperienced, but likely to view their own school or a single classroom through a distorted lens, having only their own perceptions, experiences and prejudices on which to draw.

A number of procedures can be adopted, however, that will at least minimise this compounded subjectivity, even if they do not eliminate it entirely. It is worth trying to avoid setting up a project in which the investigator is simply seeking to justify his/her practices. Self-evaluation is possible, but only if undertaken with an open mind rather than defensively. This is particularly important for heads or other senior people who carry some responsibility for what goes on in a school, and may be threatened by, rather than relaxed about, their own investigation.

Trying to find a second person who may be interested on an occasional basis is also worthwhile, or even someone willing to share the burden of the research more equally, as many teachers have worked as a pair to study their own school or each other's classroom. This is useful for checking one's own interpretation of events, seeing how much agreement there is with another person when using a structured observation schedule, selecting exemplary quotations from interviews or illustrative extracts from lessons, or the double scoring of children's work or the tests they have completed. Most first and higher degree regulations allow for more than one person to collaborate, provided that the final account makes clear who did what. The individual contributions must not only be clearly identifiable, but each must be worthy of the award in its own right.

Valuable work can, therefore, be done on a modest scale of enquiry, and individual investigators should conduct their study as rigorously as possible in the circumstances. They should also try to write and publish an account of what they find in an appropriate journal so that it reaches a wider audience. Amongst many feasible topics which individuals, pairs or small groups working in modest circumstances can undertake are the following:

(1) A study of a single or pair of classrooms over a period of time to document some kind of change, like a new curriculum, a change of teacher, or the effects of a new policy.

(2) Observation of all the teachers in the same primary team or secondary subject department, with focus on a particular aspect, such as the teaching of a common theme, like 'electricity' or 'algebra', or on a more general topic such as classroom rules, expectations about pupil work, or the kinds of questions asked.

(3) A series of pupil pursuits, as described in Chapter 7, to document the daily experiences of a group of target pupils, preferably avoiding diffusion and concentrating on some pre-determined element, such as how they interact with different teachers, what reading and writing they do in a day, how they behave, what they appear to be learning, or how coherent or disordered their day is.

(4) A study of one or more groups of children, perhaps those that sit at the same table in a primary school, observing how they interact with each other, the extent to which they collaborate with or hinder one another, the roles played by individual members, how the teacher interacts with them.

(5) A modest classroom experiment. One or more teachers can try out two different methods of explaining a new topic, see the effects of summaries given (a) entirely by

the pupils, (b) entirely by the teachers, (c) shared by both, or try different approaches to dealing with pupils who misbehave.

Small scale research can be vitally important to the people who do it, and need not be insignificant to others. Embarking on an enquiry into classroom practice can teach the investigator valuable transferable skills, such as observing and recording, interviewing, data processing and report writing. Though thousands of individual investigators only carry out one enquiry in their lives, and then often for a specific purpose, like obtaining a degree or fulfilling a requirement in a training programme, there are numerous others who, having had the courage to investigate and acquired the relevant skills, do go on to conduct further research on a modest scale. The 'enquiring school' or 'teacher researcher' are concepts worth supporting.